Highbridge

The Clock Tower, Highbridge.

**The main road through Highbridge (A38) passed by this landmark clock
and over the narrow 'high' bridge, that was a feature of the Town for many years.**

A Somerset Market Town

and its People

HIGHBRIDGE HISTORY PROJECT

An Aerial View of Highbridge – circa 1946
Centre - **Town Clock**
Top right to centre left - **S&D Railway line to Burnham**
Top Centre - **Recreation Field**
Foreground - **River Brue and A38 from Bridgwater**

This book was published in August 2004 by the Highbridge History Project

on the occasion of the 150 year Anniversary of

the Somerset Central Railway's arrival in Highbridge

ISBN   0-9548266-0-4

Whilst every care has been taken to ensure the accuracy of the information contained in this book,
the publishers disclaim any responsibility for any mistakes which may have been inadvertently included.

CONTENTS

ACKNOWLEDGEMENTS

We acknowledge with gratitude all those willing contributors who have made the publishing of this book possible, residents of Highbridge both past and present, who provided information or gave their time to help this book take shape. Many contributed text and photographs, without their assistance we would not have been able to evaluate the vast amount of information that we received. We thank them all most sincerely.

We are extremely grateful to all those people who permitted us to use photographs and other mementoes of their own and of their families past. Also, we were fortunate to find people who were able to identify faces from the past in old photographs and put names to them.

The 'Highbridge History Project' Team that published this book comprised: - Gerald Buncombe, Fay and Ken Burston, Alan Cook, Mary Draper, Fred Faulks, Jack Foster, the late Jack Major, Rex Major, Maureen McLaren, Eileen Picton, Pearl Rawles, Doreen and Ray Reddish.

Members of the earlier 'History in the Making' Team comprised: -Fay and Ken Burston, Leslie Dale, Mary Draper, Jan and Greg Dyer, Fred Faulks, Jack Foster, Charles and the late 'Madge' Langdon, Maureen McLaren, Collin Moore, David Newton, Jo Osmond, Eileen Picton, Roy Preston, Pearl Rawles, and with assistance from others.

During the Teams' research into the History of Highbridge it was necessary to obtained the help and advice from many local people, their knowledge when locating many of the historic records of the town was invaluable. We thank also, all who have provided material on specific subjects, for lending photographs and providing information; where it is applicable their names accompany the item. Photographs that do not carry accreditations are mainly the property of the Highbridge History Project.

Finally, there are those who have, in a variety of ways, given of their time to help us and to these we express our extreme gratitude: -

Richard Culverhouse, Mrs. Pat Foster, Derek Hand, Mr. & Mrs J. Hatcher, Godfrey Hebdon, Ken Hindle, Mark Johnson, John Lamb, Eddie Upton, Mrs Jean Whitehouse, Somerset Records Office, Head Teachers at St. John V.C.School, Beechfield School and King Alfred School and the late Peter Wilson whose slides and photographs have been invaluable. Plus many more who provided valuable information on innumerable subjects.

FOREWORD

At the beginning of the 21st century, it may be difficult to picture Highbridge as it was at the start of the 20th century.

Highbridge became a busy industrial town between the 1840's and 1960's; this was due to the arrival of the railway. In Victorian times there were aspirations that Highbridge would have a great future.

During this period the town grew and became not only a railway town, but also a typical Somerset Market Town. It was a vibrant, bustling community supplying the needs of the surrounding area. An open-air market in the Town Square provided a place where local produce could be offered for sale and this, together, with the thriving commercial centre with its shops and businesses, attracted the inhabitants of the surrounding villages. Large cattle and cheese markets helped make the town into a real market town with people regularly going about their business.

By the mid-sixties, as you will note, the bubble had burst and the inertia in the town had disappeared. At the start of the 21st century the outlook is brighter, there are Business and Industrial Parks that offer employment and the town itself is undergoing a regeneration programme.

It was in 1999, under the auspices of the Local Community Education, a group was set up to look into the history of the town. This group called itself the Highbridge Express, the name of an old local newspaper. The research team comprised volunteers and retired persons; they started to dig into past records and gradually accumulated sufficient information about the town to organise and present an exhibition. This proved to be a success and encouraged the team to press on in order to complete the project by staging a larger exhibition in March 2002. The funding for the project ceased at the end of March 2002 but the team decided to continue; to raise their own funding and publish a book that would present the history of Highbridge to future generations.

This is a potted history of the town and we trust our readers will enjoy learning something about this Somerset Market Town. With the resources available we were unable to verify all the information supplied; it came from many sources and we could not, therefore, vouch for the authenticity or veracity of every detail. We apologise for anything we may have forgotten or missed out.

CHRONOLOGICAL ORDER

1324	Outlet of the river Brue at Highbridge
1327	Landmark Bridge at Highbridge
1485	First Clyse Constructed
1500	Church seating for Well Cathedral – arrived at Highbridge Wharf
1606	Great Flood
	Huish House (Old Burnhan Road) Possibly 17th Century
1700's	Highbridge Hotel (Grade II listed Building
1737	Richard Locke born at Pillsmouth
1774	Richard Locke produces one of the country's earliest provisions for old age
1795	John Billingsleys Agricultural Survey (Moor Drainage)
1797	Plots of east and west Wharf Highbridge now Market Street
1800	Until 1800 Religious meetings held in private houses
1802-6	Course of River Brue diverted from the River Axe
1803	New Cut – River Brue by passing town centre constructed
1806	Death of Richard Locke ,
1819	First Church in Highbridge – Baptist
1844	Bristol & Exeter railway station opened
1851	Cattle Market Established
1854	Somerset Central Railway Station opened for regular traffic
1856	Foundation stone of St John's Church laid
1858	Somerset Central Railway line opened from Highbridge to Burnham–on–Sea
1859	St John's Church and Vicarage opened
1860	Granted an Ecclesiastical Parish,
1860	Highbridge wharf (Burnham Tidal Harbour & Railway Co. formed)
1862	Somerset Central Railway & Carriage works opened
1863	Church of England school opened (next to church)
1865	Wesleyan Chapel opened
1869	Opening of Hope Baptist Church
1873	Earliest ship at the wharf wooden ketch"Julia"
1874	S.D.J. Railway Highbridge to Evercreech became a branch line
1875	John Tyler's (Ironmonger's)Founded
1876	Stuckeys Bank opened (Nat West)
1878	Gas Lighting, Street & In house established
1878	Angling Association founded
1884	Frank Foley born
1885	Original Town Hall built by Market House Co
1885	Police Station opened (Bank Street behind Town Hall)
1885	Town cemetery designated
1886	Water Works (Huntspill Road) established
1890	Highbridge Bacon Factory established (Huntspill Road)
1890	Chubbs Cheese factors established next to the "George Hotel"
1892	Wilts & Dorset bank opened (Lloyds Bank)
1894	Separate Administrative Parish
1894	Newspaper "Highbridge Echo" established
1897	Original Town Clock erected

1905	Telephone Exchange (Newtown Road)
1906	Mains water supply established
1910	1st Scout Troop in area
1912	National Provincial Bank (Huntspill Road) opened
1913	Post Office (Market Street) opened
1913	Infants School built (Beechfield School)
1914	Original Social Club Opened
1920	Cinema built (called the Picture House) in Church Street
1920	Highbridge "Express" Newspaper established
1921	War Memorial dedicated (Church Street)
1921	Buncombes' Steamrollers Depot established (Huntspill Road)
1922	Highbridge "Independent" Newspaper established
1922	Barclays' Bank opened (Cornhill)
1925	Highbridge Branch-British Legion (Mens' Section) formed
1929	Highbridge Branch-British Legion (Womens' Section) formed
1929	Swimming Club (River Brue) dissolved
1930	S & D Main Railway Works closed (300 men)
1932	St John Ambulance Unit formed
1933	Shipping interests of S & D wound up
1933	Recreation Field officially opened
1933	Highbridge & Burnham-on-Sea Councils Amalgamated
1933	Highbridge "Independent" incorporated into "Bridgwater Mercury"
1935	Bristol Omnibus bus station built by Bristol Bridge
1935	Highbridge Young Farmers formed
1936	Highbridge Chrysanthemum Society formed
1936	Parlatex (Walrow) established (Mallets and Roller Rubbers)
1936/8	Highbridge Cheese Market- Largest in the country
1939	Pigeon Club formed
1940	Highbridge Cheese Market closed (due to rationing 2nd World War)
1941/5	United States Army Fuel Depot on S & D land (Works)
1941	Highbridge Town F.C. registered with Somerset A.F.C.
1945	Carnival started in Highbridge
1946	Morlands Ltd. Established in Market Street
1947	Highbridge "Independent" incorporated in Burnham Gazette
1948	Last timber ship the "Jola" to use Highbridge Wharf
1948	Highbridge "Festival of Arts"(Music Festival) started
1948	Morlands Ltd moved to Burnham Road (New Estate)
1949	Woodberry Bros & Haines established (Springfield Road)
1950	Last vessel to use Highbridge Wharf tug "Rexford" scrapped
1951	Regular traffic Highbridge to Burnham-on-Sea S & D Railway closed
1954	Centenary train Glastonbury to Highbridge & Burnham-on-Sea
1955	Railway Wagon repair works (S& D) destroyed by fire
1956	Willsher & Quick Ltd established (now at Walrow Industrial Estate)
1957	King Alfred School opened
1958	Visit by Queen Elizabeth II (Radio Station)
1960	Last Highbridge Carnival
1960	Telephone Exchange (Newtown Road) closed
1960	Southwell Gardens opened
1961	Southwell House opened

1960's	Cinema closed (became Regal Club)
1962	Highbridge & Burnham-on-Sea Excursion trains on S & D closed
1963	Highbridge & Burnham - Goods trains S & D closed
1963	Highbridge Bacon Factory closed
1963	Willsher & Quick moved to Walrow Industrial Estate
1963	West of England Creamery (Huntspill Road) closed
1964	Original Town Clock destroyed by lorry crash
1964	S & D Railway Line from Highbridge Station to Highbridge Wharf closed
1964	Wharf closed for private shipping
1976	General Higgins House opened
1976	Southwell Crescent built
1977	Jubilee Gardens opened to mark Queen Elizabeth II Silver Jubilee
1977	St John Ambulance H.Q. moved from Railway Hotel to under Town Hall
1977	King Alfred school sports centre opened
1977	"Parlatex" Factory closed
1979	Doctors surgery opened "Alpha House"
1980	"Normans" Supermarket (Church Street) opened
1981	Flood and Storm damage
1981	Morland Factory closed
1981	New Social Club Building opened
1983	Western Region Railway original station building removed
1984	Town Hall demolished
1985	New Headquarters for St John ambulance opened
1990	Tyler Way opened
1990	Newtown Road became Cul-de-Sac
1990	Isleport Business Park opened
1992	Pepperall Community Resource Centre opened
1992	New Community Hall (Market Street) opened
1993	Doctors surgery moved to Pepperall Road
1993	Barclays Bank closed
1995	"Wade House" (Church Street) opened
1998	Post Office moved from 9 Church Street to (In Store) in" Normans" supermarket
1999	Lloyds Bank closed
1999	Speedway Stadium (Bristol Road) opened
2001	Highbridge Chrysanthemum Society dissolved
2001	Referendum for Highbridge to create own Council defeated
2001	Foot and mouth disease- Temporary closure of Cattle Market
2002	Farmers Market started Community Hall
2002	Old River bed (behind Market Street) cleared to original stonework
2002	"Normans" Supermarket closed
2002	Cattle Market re-opened after foot and mouth disease
2002	"Woodberry Bros. & Haines" moved from Springfield Road to Walrow Ind. Est.
2002	"White Hart" Hotel Closed (Church Street)
2003	"White Hart" Hotel & "Arian Products" Demolished (Church Street)
2003	Post Office moved from Normans Supermarket Site back to 9, Church Street.
2003	Pigeon Club disbanded
2004	Community Nursery opened adjacent to Beechfield Infants School
2004	Housing Development on site former S. & D. Railway Station
2004	Household Waste Recycling Centre opened at Walrow

Chapter 1

THE TOWN

Highbridge is a market town astride the A38, 7 miles north of Bridgwater and 2 miles from the Bristol Channel coast. It is a town that has experienced many changes over the past two hundred years or so, but the arrival of the railway in the mid 19th century led to its development as a railway terminus and a thriving market town.

Prior to the development there was very little written about this cluster of houses and shops on the main road between Bristol and Exeter. Before the 19th century it appears that the 'birth' of Highbridge had not been documented in any way. When the Domesday Book was prepared in 1086 it produced evidence that a large part of Somerset was the land of Walter De Douai. Huish(Hiwis) and Alstone(Alsistune) were holdings of a lay 'tenant-in-chief'; Huntespill(Hunespil) was an administrative hundred. Highbridge was not mentioned; it did not have a centuries old church where parish records may have been kept. However, there is a reference to the 'hundred' of Huish(Hiwis) a Saxon word meaning 'farmstead' or 'family settlement' and an Enclosure Map from the 18th century shows a small settlement of 12 – 15 holdings near a bridge over a river (Brue). Further, a Roman name of "Pons Altus" has been found and this, apparently, means near a High Bridge.

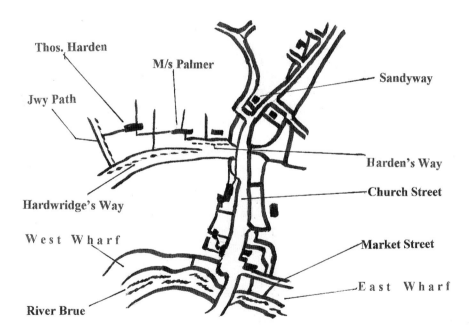

Information obtained from a 1797 Local Enclosure Map

It has often been assumed that Highbridge got its name from the former hump-backed bridge that carried the old coaching road over the river or is it possible that the true origin may be a corruption of 'Hythe' bridge as hythe implies the presence of a wharf. The Enclosure Map, referred to, shows that there was a wharf each side of the bridge near the settlement. So you have a choice: - Highbridge, because there was one, or a corruption of 'Hythe' Bridge.

Documents preserved at Wells Cathedral show that as long ago as 1324 the name Highbridge was in use and an ancient manuscript of 1327 makes reference to "Juxta Altum Pontem" which means near the high bridge. Although Highbridge does not have a recorded history; it is known that the Romans were in the area in the first and second centuries A.D. Evidence of salt production has been found, plus pottery and Romano-British coarseware. In the 19th century workmen digging new drainage channels found Roman potsherds and broken fragments of brick and several mouldings for casting coins.

The town and its bridge have, over the years found themselves on a highway of history. Old maps of Somerset show the only available road from the Midlands to the South West was the one out of Bristol, passing by Wrington, along by Axbridge and over the humped- backed bridge at Highbridge to Bridgwater, Taunton and Exeter. Down the road must have passed the packhorses, which carried the merchandise, then wagons, stagecoaches, kings, queens, including the infamous Judge Jefferies, great statesmen and the preacher John Wesley. They all must have passed through Highbridge.

It was told that although the bridge was of vast importance to the public it "is not kept in repair at the expense of the County but by sundry Lords of neighbouring manors" who appointed the expenditors and were reimbursed by a rate divided in three equal shares. One of which was discharged by the landowner of the Manor of Huntspill. The remaining shares were sub-divided between the lords of West Mark, East Mark, Wedmore, Churchland and Mudgeley. An undated newspaper cutting states: - "In Highbridge there is an old and very inconvenient bridge over which the main road traffic roars daily. Evidently at one time there was a fair sized waterway beneath it. Now it is full of mud, with a struggling stream in the centre, through which some sort of drain flows. The bridge is hump-backed and obstructive. It seems curious that it still survives on this important highway".

This 19th Century mile stone can be seen in the wall next to No 10 Church Street

In the early 19th century High Bridge and Huish comprised of a number of holdings. The River Brue still following its original course. But in 1806, the digging of the large Clyce, had an effect on the area, it changed the parish boundaries. This parish border originally followed the centre of the river, but now the 'river' had moved. This meant that the "Highbridge Hotel and the area around it was no longer in Huntspill but in Highbridge.

The collection of dwellings that comprised the town would have come under the authority of Glastonbury and Wells, being part of several different Parishes until 1860. It was then that the 'area' was granted an Ecclesiastical Parish status in its own right; no longer being part of West Huntspill or Burnham parishes. It remained as such until 1894 when it became an Administrative Parish.

Earlier in the 19th century the birth of Highbridge started with the arrival of the Bristol and Exeter Railway around 1844. This later became the Great Western Railway and it produced an increase in trade; consequently many new houses, shops and inns were erected. It became a place of considerable commercial importance.

On August 17th 1854 there was much rejoicing when the first train steamed into Highbridge on the Central Somerset Line from Glastonbury. Leaving a short while later from the gaily- decorated station on its return journey to Glastonbury where there was a big procession through the grounds of the Abbey. There was obviously much criticism about the line, "going from nowhere to nowhere over a turf moor, with but one town on the whole line and that with less than 4000 people". As one eminent writer of the time put it: " The level headed traders of Highbridge and the dignified residents of Burnham shook the mothballs from their Sunday go-to meeting-suits, trimmed their beards and side-whiskers. They dusted their top hats and welcomed the arrival of the first train, as if it were going to open to them the untold riches at the end of the Yukon Trail". There were, in fact, visions of an era of fabulous prosperity in which Highbridge would become the Birkenhead of the west with Burnham the New Brighton.

This was a "boom time" in Highbridge it was growing apace. The river was made navigable for ships up to 750 tons, trade was good; a bank arrived and a public house "The Coopers Arms". A Company was formed in 1878 for lighting the town with gas and in 1886 a waterworks was erected. There were also timber yards and sawmills of considerable size in the town. A National School for four hundred children was erected in 1863, followed by the Town Hall in 1885 and later the Adult School in 1891. Brick and tile making were also a major industry.

It was in 1894 when it was rapidly developing as an industrial town, that the County Council made it a separate parish. As such it still remained under the jurisdiction of the Axbridge Rural District Council until 1897, when it absorbed part of Huntspill and became the Highbridge Urban District Council. It was getting somewhere at last. Unfortunately, this identity did not last long, for in 1933 under the Somerset Review order, the Urban Districts of both Highbridge and Burnham were amalgamated for administrative purposes. Once again Highbridge had lost out.

This merger was bitterly fought out; Highbridge strongly resented having its identity linked with Burnham. Although the demise of the industrial life of Highbridge was a gradual process, there were many aspects conspiring against the town. The coming of World War Two slowed the decline, but it was only a brief respite.

For centuries the main highway from Bristol to the South West had to pass through Highbridge. However in recent years the build up of traffic was choking the life out of the town and in 1973 a motorway, the M5, was opened just east of the town. This has helped to relieve the congestion and make life more acceptable.

Recently (2001) there was a referendum to determine if the two towns wished to remain together or revert to their original Councils. Regrettably, for many, the voting indicated that the majority wished to maintain the status quo. So the towns, happy or not, are resigned to facing the future together.

The people of Highbridge at the start of the 21st century are taking action and the Highbridge Regeneration Group is attempting, as the title implies, to regenerate and reconstruct the heart of the town. It is felt that within the next 10/15 years Highbridge will, like the phoenix, rise again and is planning for its future.

This is a view prior to 1984; this area, between the Town Square and Bank Street (formerly Quiet Street) included the Town Hall and a number of shops, with private residences.

This is a view in 2002 showing the Town Green and New Community Hall.

After all the buildings shown above had been demolished the new building was erected. It was in response to a Public Appeal Fund for cash to be raised in order to replace the Town Hall that had, for many years, been the publics' meeting place for all special occasions.

(*Photo supplied by Collin Moore*)

TOWN SQUARE

The Town Square was once the focal point of the town's activities, a gathering place and central area where the community would come together to celebrate special occasions, or meet to take part in a social function. People new to the area will no longer see any sign of the large open space that was once looked upon with pride by the local populace.

Where was the square was situated? In Market Street adjacent to where the new Community Hall now is. The entrance to the original Town Hall (which is covered later) was on the right of the building and looked out over this large open space, with buildings to the left and Market Street passing to the right, towards the "Cooper's Arms" and Walrow Bridge. "Alpha House" now covers part of the area that was once the Town Square.

An Aerial view of the Town Hall and Square

Looking to the left from the Town Hall entrance was the "Constitution Club", a small building between the Hall and the "Railway Hotel". This had a long frontage onto the square. At the end of the hotel the square widened further to include, at its rear, buildings which housed the "Bridgwater & Highbridge Cab & Postings Co."

On the opposite side of the square there was a line of open fronted stables and the "Railway Vaults", a drinking house that was approximately opposite the chemists shop in Market Street. This completed the square; it was of a considerable size.

The "Central Somerset Railway Inn", later known as the "Railway Hotel", was a large building dominating the square. In the early days, up to the 1930's, its main business was overnight stays, for not only 'holiday' visitors to the town, but also agents arriving and departing by rail, having come to the town to attend the market. Buyers for national company's attended the well-known cheese market that was held on a regular basis; next to the "Cooper's Arms". The hotel had two large function rooms for weddings and other such functions, parties, etc., a skittle alley and a large ground floor bar area. It was described as a 'Family and Commercial Hotel.

Town Square outside Cab and Posting Company

Between the 1920's and the late 1930's there also existed a "Cab & Posting Co"; it would supply horse drawn carriages, to meet trains arriving at the railway station or for other special occasions. Horses were trained to harness at the rear of the buildings, and this is where the horses, used by the company, were stabled around a paddock. Horse drawn carriages for funerals and weddings would be supplied and in later years charabancs and brakes could be charted for pleasure parties. On the far side of the square, was the "Railway Vaults".

Many celebrations and other activities have taken place on the square. An open-air market, unlike those of today, would be set out to sell mainly vegetables and fruit, also poultry and dairy produce, brought in by farmers.

Parades for all occasions either started or finished in the square. The early days would have seen the hunt assemble on the square, prior to heading out into the local countryside. Even in the 1950's and 1960's car rallies would use the area as their starting and finishing point. Moving into the late 1950's and 1960's the square was being used less and less. Community celebrations did not have the same pulling power as in the early days, but the square was still available and probably still held its place as the core of the town.

In the mid 1970's a decision was made to remove the square and the building, but not the Town Hall (this was demolished in the mid 1980's) and build "Alpha House", the ground floor becoming the doctor's surgery. The surgery later moved to Pepperall Road and was replaced by the library. Unfortunately "Alpha House" was built where the 'Railway Hotel' had stood and thus it eliminated the Town Square.

A view of Market Street, the Town Square and the Town Hall during 1958.
You will see that the Square covered a large area,with the Railway Hotel on the right.

This the view in 2004, shows the New Community Hall and Alpha House,
the Town Square being replaced by a recently laid garden feature.

TOWN HALL

The Highbridge Market House Co. Ltd. paid for the original Town Hall erected in 1885 alongside the Town Square. It had a seating capacity of 600. The hall was entered from the Town Square, steps leading to the upper floor, part of which was used for a number of years as Council Offices for the Highbridge Urban District. It is understood that the Somerset County Council held its first meeting in here in 1894. The main hall on this floor had a stage and a small kitchen.

A rear exit and stairs went down into Bank Street where on its corner, for many years was the local Police Station, which opened for business in 1887, this comprised the usual offices plus a cell for those who had caused a misdemeanour. When the station closed is not known but the police house in Church Street opposite the War Memorial replaced it. The Works Department of Highbridge Urban District Council was in Bank Street until the amalgamation of the Highbridge and Burnham Council took place in 1933.

Within the Town Hall area was an open quadrangle, selling poultry and dairy produce (eggs, butter etc.) these were held in conjunction with the larger open market held on the square. Unfortunately the market ceased in the early 20th Century when the shopping habits changed. The St. John Ambulance Division, which was registered in 1932, met in the Council Chambers of the Town Hall and their ambulance used a garage beneath the building. Unfortunately this facility disappeared when the Town Hall was demolished in 1984. During World War II a voluntary night ambulance, which supplemented the County Service also kept in the building.

Highbridge Town Hall and the Town Square, for approximately one hundred years, was the centre for all local and national celebrations. If it was important to Highbridge – parades, social or political gathering, they happened on the square or in the hall. Businesses held their annual dinners, clubs held their dances and socials, carnivals their concerts, awards ceremonies and dances and the Chrysanthemum Society its annual show. The Town Hall was home to Boxing Club contests, Badminton Club matches, a weekly baby and toddler group, plus countless private parties and was the original venue for the Highbridge Festival of Arts. As time went by the hall was used less and less, it lacked facilities for the disabled, the catering area needed modernisation and finally it emerged that the roof required replacement.

Many heated meetings were held in the Hall during 1982/83 with angry residents and council officers voicing their opposition to the District Council's decision to demolish the old Victorian Hall. It was all to no avail because; in 1984 the Sedgemoor District Council demolished the building. There followed, over the next two years many public meetings; these were called to discuss what action the people of Highbridge could take to build a new 'heart' and, over the ten years, 1984 to 1994 the town moved from "Town Hall to Community Hall."

Between 1984 and 1986 a public meeting held at the King Alfred School formed a Steering Committee; this comprised local residents and traders. The Executive Chairman owned a Post Office and was a Town Councillor, the Secretary was a resident who had recently graduated, (also being a Town Councillor), a Bank Manager looked after finance and a local solicitor tacked the legalities (free-gratis). There was also an architect and District Councillors in this determined highly active and first class group. Because they did not have a hall in which to meet the group met in a variety of places, a Hairdresser in Market Street was one such venue when the committee needed to sit themselves amongst the driers and salon furniture.

(Photo Supplied by Fraser Campbell)

Toddlers Group Christmas Party in the Town Hall - 1957

There followed a constant battle to keep the building site clear of litter; every opportunity was also taken to organise Fetes, Jumble Sales, Boot, Garage and House Clearance Sales, the site also being used, on occasions, to publicise their efforts to raise funds and keep the subject firmly in the publics' mind. Fetes were held on the Towns' Recreation Ground and no matter the weather, should it be wet, dry or windy the band of willing and hardy workers turned out to meet the challenge. During this time there were several boosts to the funds; a sum of £25,000 was discovered by the Secretary, following information received, and after a bit of research, it was found that the New Community Hall (as it was known) fitted the criteria to release the bounty, a stroke of luck. Another boost was the Secretary becoming Mayor of the two towns and the Mayor's Supper was held at Salvo's, this was well subscribed and resulted in more money becoming available for the hall funds.

On 8th June 1986 a Public Meeting at King Alfred School adopted a Constitution for the Highbridge Centre Community Association.

In January 1988 building commenced and Committee Meetings were held at Ilex House, the home of the chairman, it had become an extended committee. Most of the original members were still there, architects, clerk of works and District Councillors, all attended the meetings, and Somerset Community Council Officers who also helped toward the completion of the ground floor later supplemented these. A Grand Autumn Fayre in 1994 marked the Official Opening by Sedgemoor District Councillor Mrs L Cartwright.

The Community Hall as seen today, 2004, has a main hall, frequently used for dances, exhibitions and similar functions, plus a newly completed modern kitchen downstairs; there are two stairways to a first floor suite of meeting rooms (one with kitchen facilities), and of course the usual toilets on both floors. Highbridge now has its Hall back again and, when the title became 'The Highbridge Community Hall Trust' it gained a Government Community Initiative Grant, an achievement for which the people of Highbridge can be justly proud.

TOWN CLOCK

A landmark seen by many motorists travelling through Highbridge in the 1950's, on their journey south, would have been the Victorian style clock erected in the centre of the road at the junction of Church Street and Market Street. (The Cornhill).

On March 17th 1897 a Committee was formed to decide on what should be done to commemorate Queen Victoria's Diamond Jubilee. The decision was to purchase a clock that should be positioned at the Cornhill, it was to be designed by "Rainforths" of Bridgwater. The clock was completed by June 22nd, Jubilee day of that year 1897.

The Clock and the Corn Hill in the 1920's

Little was changed on the clock, except for the lighting in the early days, it was oil, then gas and finally electric. For many years the clock was maintained and regulated by Mr. Robertson who was a watchmaker and repairer who had shop premises nearby at 6a Church Street. The clock dominated the towns' main streets for sixty-seven years, until on the 8th March 1964, when it was hit and destroyed by a lorry.

The 'New' clock was erected in a 'safer' position (1965)

It was replaced by a newly designed clock that was positioned between two bollards about a metre from where the original clock stood and nearer the centre of Market Street to provide more room for vehicles passing along Church Street. The clock was electric, had three faces and cost a total of £1200; on top of clock was the Urban District Councils Coat of Arms. When the clock was erected in 1965 a local paper stated, "There was some considerable interest and no little excitement". It was stated that on various occasions the three faces of the clock each showed a different time and it became known locally as "Three Faced Liar". The master clock had been installed in John Tyler (Highbridge) Ltd.

In 1972 the clock was re-sited on derelict ground approximately above the original Clyce lock gates. Later in June 1977 it was to become the centrepiece of "Jubilee Gardens" created to celebrate Queen Elizabeth II Silver Jubilee.

(Photo Supplied by John Channon)

A view of the original Town Clock –circa 1905

Highbridge Town Clock

The 'Town Clock' has had a very chequered career and in its original form suffered a number of knocks. A lorry demolished it in 1964, but it has now come to our attention that it suffered a 'knock' prior to this, in 1963.

The story goes that a local 'lad' asleep in his bedroom, not too far from the Cornhill, was awoken by a noise, "tyres squealing" from the vicinity of the clock. Upon investigating, he found that car (Mark 1 Cortina) carrying two Chinese gentlemen had hit the clock with a sideways blow and they could not get out. They were trapped, the car suddenly burst into flames, he immediately fetch a fire extinguisher from the shop where he lived and aimed it under the bonnet from where the fire appeared to be coming. Another person arrived with some bolt cutters and chopped through the battery cables, this stopped the fire, which had obviously been electrical.

The Chinese gentlemen in the meantime were still trapped in the car. Eventually an ambulance, which had been summoned by our storyteller's parents, arrived and took away the occupants of the car who were not, apparently, badly injured. The initial damage to the clock was caused by this incident, the final indignity came some time later when a lorry which had travelled down Church Street, hit the Clock and knocked it towards Tyler's shop.

The consequences of this are that parts of the clock went missing and are now scattered around the area. Two of the Clock faces are in the possession of our narrator and he has an idea where the third is. A person in Mark has the 'trap' door from the base of the clock, through which a Mr. Robertson used to wind it.

ARCHAEOLOGICAL EVALUATIONS

During research into the area it was learned that an archaeological evaluation (a dig) had taken place in the north of the town during 2003. A number of sites had previously been recorded in the area the latest evaluations were in the King Alfred's School and Beechfield School, both in Highbridge.

The evaluation reports are obviously very detailed in their content and it was not possible to re-produce all the information, but the following is given purely to confirm that there was early occupation in this area. The Somerset County Council Sites and Monuments Record (SMR) have entries relating to a number of evaluation sites. Coarse Romano-British pottery was found by Mr. S.E. Nash (ca 1957) and there were signs of Roman occupation i.e. coarseware sherds, pottery and dressed lias blocks found over a large area. All were mainly adjacent to the Worston and Burnham Roads.

At King Alfred's School, (Burnham Road) a number of trenches were dug, Roman pottery and other materials were found. Briquetage plus Samien and coarseware.(Briquetage comprises fragments of fire clay containers used in the manufacture of salt, an important commodity in the early centuries for the preservation of fish and meat; it was an industry which was carried out in the area of alluvial soil levels. There being many sites in the Highbridge and Huntspill areas).

In the Beechfield School (Coronation Road) area, Roman pottery and briquetage was again found, plus unglazed 14th century sherds. A medieval spoon was found at an earlier date. From the report it was noted that Roman activity may possibly have been associated with a harbour or docking facilities on the inlet of the River Brue, which could possibly have been deeper and wider in that period than it is at present.

The manufacture of salt, south of Highbridge, to avoid the rising levels of alluvial flooding, moved further inland. Samuel Nash had plotted a substantial tidal creek south of and pre-dating the present course of the River Brue, this is sometimes called the 'Proto Brue'. During the Romano-British period the coastline may have been several hundred metres to the west of today's, suggesting that in the first and second centuries, King Alfred's School site and surrounding areas were much further inland and less likely subject to flooding.

Environmental work in 1998 on the coastline recorded several peat layers with associated radio -carbon dates of between 3780 B.C. - 3370 B.C. for the upper band and 5440 B.C. – 5000B.C. for the lower band.

The information relating to the archaeological evaluations has been included with the kind permission of Charles and Nancy Hollinrake, Consultant Archaeologists; from their reports No 300 & 307 re-produced for the Somerset Property Services.

When work started on the M5 motorway, Bristol University assigned a team under Dr. Peter Fowler to keep a watching brief on the excavations, this was thought sensible in case historical remains were unearthed. The late Mrs Marjorie Langdon (Madge) led the local team of archaeologists and the foundations of an early Roman Settlement were unearthed. Madge and her husband Charles were two of the founder members of the Highbridge History Project team.

(Permission to use this material was granted by the Somerset Property Services and Charles and Nancy Hollinrake)

THE RIVER BRUE (& Clyce)

The River Brue rises from a source in Kings Wood Warren, part of the Bruton Forest in South East Somerset and wends its way North West through the County to eventually flow into the River Parrett near Highbridge. Along the route it absorbs from the Somerset Levels thousands of gallons of water that runs off the low-lying moorland, the River Axe ably assists it along the way.

An area at the bottom of the Brue Valley is known as Brent Marsh and during the 4th and 5th centuries the sea levels stabilised when flooding by the sea brought the final deposits to the area; by that date deposits had already finished their growth. It was these incursions by the sea that buried any evidence of early man, although flint tools, arrowheads etc. have been found. There is in the Somerset County Museum, a preserved section of the "Sweet Track", this was a man made track set through the marshes just above water level. It is thought to date from 2300 B.C. and is probably one of the earliest signs that man inhabited the Somerset Levels.

Further evidence of human occupation during the Bronze Age and Iron Age have been found and recent observations have shown that the raised areas were occupied by Romano-British up to about the fourth century. The Saxons reached the River Parrett in the seventh century. (See Chapter 1-Archaeological Evaluation)

Two natural rivers – The Axe and the Parrett enclose this area of the levels and were the main waterways with access to the sea. First efforts to control flooding were around 1200 A.D. on the River Parrett, sea walls and sluices, a clyce (locally known as 'clyse' or 'clyce') were constructed to let fresh water out but prevent seawater coming in. The control gradually changed the marshes and levels from saline sea marsh to fresh water lagoons and bogs. All this was recorded around 1200 A.D. and was a prelude to agricultural reclamation; similar work may have taken place at an earlier time, but is not recorded.

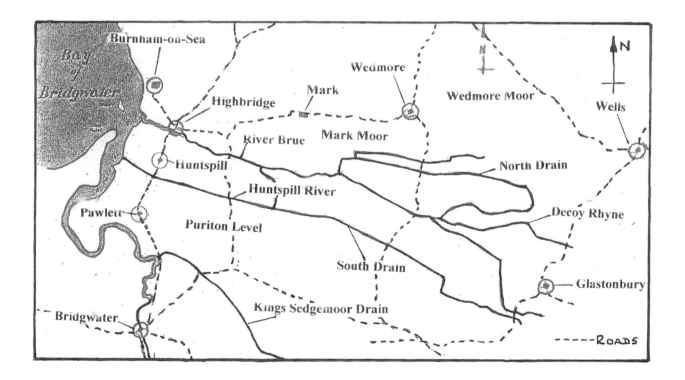

Mr.Samuel Nash's observations and other factors led some to the conclusion that the early course of the River Brue may have run from the Mark area, along what is now Church Street and to link up with the "Siger" River which ran into the sea north of Burnham.

During the thirteenth century the levels were considered marsh and should be avoided, it is probable that the Monks of Glastonbury looked upon the inhabitants of the marshes as a tribe, equivalent to Aboriginal Indians. These people would have survived by wildfowling and trapping marsh animals. The community of monks was probably the first to see the potential for clearance, enclosure and drainage. They were the landlords of the area with the ability to plan and design schemes, also richer than all except the greatest of noblemen. In 1316 A.D. a great engineering feat was carried out, this was the construction of the Pilrow Cut and the changing of Ferlyng Mere so that it became the huge Mere Pool of the Middle Ages. The sea route from Glastonbury, via Meare, to join the River Axe opened up a means of getting to the sea; the work was completed in 1316 A.D. The rivers Brue, Hartlake and Sheppey were diverted to Mere Pool that was considerably enlarged in the reign of Henry VIII, the pool being five miles in circumference and one and a half miles long. Land around the levels had once been well drained and fertile but the levels themselves were frequently wet, exposed to fogs, mist and drizzling rain.

Financial incentives to carry out reclamation had been destroyed following the Black Death of 1348 to 1349. The work for the whole system was completed about 1500 A.D. The dissolution of the monasteries in 1536 – 9, during Henry VIII reign destroyed the central ownership and control, which had been responsible for the medieval draining projects.

The present outlet of the River Brue at Highbridge was known to exist around 1324 A.D. but it may not have been connected to the Brue Valley. The once important river way from Glastonbury to Bristol used in the 1500's, and of which parts still remain. Is now a ditch that may be followed from the North Drain pumping station on the River Brue, along field boundaries to join a wider section on the Wedmore/Mark/Burnham Road. At the "White Horse" pub in Mark it turns north and peters out in a maze of minor ditches. If you can imagine such a scene! – this empty countryside once echoed to the sound of people poling or towing barges on the river.

It was around this time that Highbridge may have been referred to as "Huish" or as in earlier times "Huish Juxta Altum Pontem" i.e. "Next to a High Bridge". The manor of "Huish" covered Highbridge, Watchfield, Pillsmouth and Sandyway.

The first Clyce to be constructed at Highbridge was dated about 1485 A.D. it is now buried under "Jubilee Gardens", this indicates the position of the old riverbed. Little is known about the area for about three hundred years, the land around belonged to the Dean and Chapter of Wells Cathedral. In their archives are notes stating that a boat was built in 1681 A.D. for use on the river, this was purchased for the sum of £6.

During the eighteenth century there was probably some trade on the river, being mainly coal and agriculture. Work on the levels accelerated around 1770 and in 1777 the Brue Drainage Act was proposed. Late in the century (1799 A.D.) the sea wall was breached at Huntspill and the vale was filled with seawater, which lingered for five months moving into the nineteenth century. An Enclosure Map shows two simple wharfs in Highbridge – East Wharf (Market Street) and West Wharf (west side of the old bridge). Archives at the Somerset Records Office for 1797 A.D. list these as Plots 226 – 234 and Plots 235 & 235A respectively. In 1801 the Brue Drainage Act was passed and between 1802 – 6 the course of the River Brue was diverted from its then path on the east and north of Wedmore running into the River Axe, to a new course south of Wedmore and into the sea. The 1801 Brue Drainage Act called for the river to be straightened and a new Clyce was dug, this new deep cut is the present course of the River Brue. The Brue was made wider and straighter near its mouth and another Clyce was built further downstream.

The River Brue and Clyce (circa) 1912

John Billingsley recorded around 1795 A.D. that roughly 17,000 acres of land had been drained and enclosed but there remained in the Brue Valley 9,000 acres un-drained. Billingsley's agricultural survey suggested a drainage plan and in 1801 A.D. the Clyce at Highbridge formed part of the plan when a lower sill was constructed. A new Rhyne, later to be widened into the North Drain and the South Drain were cut with outfalls into the River Brue, although the resultant flow was not sufficient, it still had beneficial effects. Before that 1000's of sheep were recorded as having rotted in the parish of Mark each year. Controlled flooding was then introduced to raise the land to prevent silting.

The Clyce at Highbridge is referred to in "The Drainage of the Somerset Levels" by Michael Williams,it refers to an estimate by a James Parry:-

Estimate for a new bridge and sluice near Highbridge dated 6th October 1801 to be paid in 7 instalments of £500 00s 00d = £3450 00s 00d.

		£. s. d.
Estimate for dwelling house –	Brickwork and plain tile	£60.00.00
	Carpentry staircase and flooring	2.15.00
	External doors – Deal	10.10.00
	4 Frames ledgered	36.00.00
	Windows	6.16.00
	Tiles floor	12.16.00
	Plastering 380 yards	15.16.00
	Paving 420 ft.	12.05.00
	Foundations	10.10.00
		£167.08.00

From an engineers report at Hartlake Bridge (On the Street to Wells Road) in December 1802, water from Whitelake River was not moving fast enough, it was proposed that they had to lower the level by 4 ft instead of 11 inches in 2 1/2 miles, to speed the flow into the River Brue. This will now give the 4ft. 11 ins in 1 7/8 miles giving a ratio of discharge of water between Hartlake Bridge and the termination of the new cut to the proportion of 33 to 26 instead of 33 to 10. This should prevent further injury from flooding in the area.A surveyors report from the 1809 states that the lock gates in the Clyce were not operating properly, due to not having been hung correctly. A meeting held at the Highbridge Inn in 1812 agreed that. "It is ordered that a proper quantity of stones be ordered and placed in the holes where necessary. A proper wall built at the northwest end of the wharf with steps for the easy landing of coal, timber and other goods. The walls of the Clyce and the new bridge, are to be pointed with proper mortar; doors of the sluice to be corked and tarred. With a proper gate to be put up at the entrance of the said road against the turnpike. Signed Joseph Stephens landlord of the Highbridge Inn 1812."

A Lock Keepers Annual Salary in 1812 was £26.00s.08d(equal to 50p per week)

Floods again reached Glastonbury around 1816. West Sedgemoor was now looking something like its present appearance with rhynes, 5ft. deep by 4ft. wide at the base and 8ft. wide at the top, bounded with willows as boundary markers, acting as cattle barriers, as well as drains. By 1815 A.D. the coastal belt had the highest rents in Somerset (70/- an acre) as the number of cattle in the area increased. A trade in shipping cattle to Wales and Ireland began around this time, resulting in there being important trading at Highbridge. The area soon became a centre for the making of cheese and its sale, both locally and for export. During the nineteenth century, Highbridge grew from almost nothing into a thriving town, there was brick and tile making in and around the town, plus bacon curing, a creamery and the wharf was busy – timber, coal, grain, etc. came in, with cattle, bricks, cheese and tiles going out.

Better communication was planned with the opening in 1832 of the Glastonbury Canal; this however, had a short life because it was bought up by the Bristol and Exeter Railway Company under its Act of 1848. In 1852 the Somerset Central Railway started laying lines along the course of the canal and two years later the track opened and ran under lease from the Bristol and Exeter. Some sections of the old canal were retained to aid the drainage of the levels and are still in use

At a meeting in the "Railway Hotel" (1870) it was agreed that it was necessary to do repairs to the Clyce but due to the scarcity of water (drought) the work could not be completed. The removal of mud was absolutely necessary and the sum of £15.00.00 was set aside.

A surveyors report said: - "The accumulation of mud both inside and outside Highbridge Clyce has for some time penned the water. The large ships continually lying on the north bank below the canal outlet were turning the course of the stream considerably to the south. Works ordered by the Committee in 1870 have now been completed, it is recommended that the banks be sloped more to reduce the sliding into the river".

Clyce keeper William Vowles complained in 1871 that vessels moor near the West side and endanger the safety of the doors, it was proposed a chain be fixed to prevent the boats mooring.

In 1873, Highbridge had a report made by a N.A.W. Estridge, a civil engineer. He reported that the poorer houses just had conduits to the river for drainage and that in the east part of the town Huish Rhyne was used as a sewer and was therefore very polluted. The richer inhabitants had siphon closets and cesspits. So he recommended that a drainage system should be built urgently, he estimated the cost at £3,000. This was a matter for the Axbridge Guardians in their capacity as sanitary authority. But according to the local papers Highbridge was to suffer from flooding and bad drainage plus impossibly bad roads for many years to come.

The S.S. Coralie

This scene with the S.S.Coralie will not be familiar to many of the present day generation of Highbridge, she is making her way along the old River Brue channel towards the Cornhill Bridge. The view is behind Market Street. Note the lock gates connected to the bridge, The original photograph, taken in June 1889, was loaned to a Mrs Dudderidge of Market Street, who incidentally was the little girl on the boat; the others are Messrs Luke, Bounds and G. Wood. The day before this photograph was presented to Mrs Dudderidge the new road replacing the bridge was opened for service for the first time. This was thought to be around 1910.

In 1877 the Somerset Drainage Act had overall control of the rivers, Axe, Brue, Parrett and Tone, this control remained until 1951 when the Somerset River Board took over, this also including pollution. The Somerset River Board and Somerset River Authority merged and became Wessex Water in 1974.

The foregoing has been compiled with the aid of information taken from the following:- "The Somerset Levels", by Robin & Romany Williams, "Burnham & Highbridge" by V.J. Wrigley, "Somerset Harbours" by Farr. And Somerset Record Office.

Little has changed over the past 40 years, the River has continued to silt up and is navigable only for small craft up to the boat yard. During 2003 the Regeneration Group for Highbridge, included in its discussions, the idea that a marina could be constructed in the area of the boat yard but to-date it appears that this probability has also been shelved.

In 1803 when the New Clyce (Cut or Drain) was built all the places named had their rates increased, it was assessed that the residents would benefit from the improved drainage of the low lying areas.

ARTICLES OF AGREEMENT

Made the twenty-third day of April in the year of our Lord one thousand eight hundred and three.

Between James Parry of Bridgewater in the County of Somerset - Mason and Bridge builder of the one part and Sir Abraham Elton of Clevedon Court Baronet Richard Thomas Combe of Earnshill and Henry Tripp of Orchard Wyndham Esquires all in the County of Somerset – Commissioners appointed in and by an Act of Parliament made and passed in the forty first year of his present Majestys Reign entitled "An Act of Draining" preserving from water and improving certain low lands and grounds lying within the several parishes or chapelries of North Wooton, Pilton, West Pennard, Baltonsborough, Barton St. David, Butleigh, Street, Glaston St. John, Gleeston St. Benedict, Walton, Ashcott, Shapwick, Moorlinch, Catcott, Chilton, Edington, Cossington, Woolavington, Huntspill, East Brent, South Brent, Mark,

This is a transcript of the document on the right from which it will be noted that many places on the Somerset Levels were affected by this agreement.

The accompanying document relates to the building of the new Cut or Drain near the High bridge in the Parish of Huntshill.

Whereas in and by certain Articles of Agreement bearing date the twenty seventh day of November one thousand eight hundred and one and made between the said James Parry of the one part – and the said commissioners of the other part – He the said James Parry for the considerations therein expressed did agree with the said Commissioners to erect build and compleat a certain sluice or outlet on the new Cut or Drain then and now making and executing by the said Commissioners near the High bridge within the Parish of Huntshill aforesaid and also a certain bridge over the said Cut or Drain on the Turnpike Road near High bridge aforesaid together with a dwelling house therein also mentioned at the price or sum of three thousand three hundred pounds and the said James Parry hath since finished and compleat the said sluice but the said Bridge is not begun upon. And whereas the said Commissioners having found it expedient to make certain alterations in the form and construction of the said Bridge and to make and erect doors under or in the same and the said James Parry————- etc.

(Permission to use the foregoing was granted by the Somerset Archive and Record Service, Somerset Record Office, Obridge Road, Taunton)

Drainage of Brue Valley

The following is dedicated to the memory of Mr J.M.Hitchen M.I.C.E. M.I.M.E Deputy Chief Engineer to the Somerset River Catchment Board from January 1941 to 31st December 1947.

In 1941 a Top Secret Scheme was discussed, the purpose of which was to drain the Brue Valley in order to provide 9,000,000 million gallons of fresh water per day for a new munitions factory. Many secret meetings took place and eventually work commenced on a vast scale to transform the Somerset Levels, resulting in a scene that altered the Somerset landscape forever. A chance meeting between one of our researchers and the daughter of the man, who was appointed to be responsible for the design, has resulted in this story being told.

Mr J.M.Hitchen, was the man who dedicated himself to the project. A task that would have been difficult under present day working conditions, but in wartime it was an enormous undertaking and because of its importance, a very strict timetable had to be kept.

We are greatly indebted to Mr Hitchen's daughter Mrs E.M.Lawson for her generosity in donating, to us, the material her family has safely stored and cherished over many years. Press cuttings, photographs and copies of publications were kept. We therefore greatly appreciate the help Mrs Lawson gave to us so that we could record this important time in the history of the Somerset Levels.

A Story They Could Not Tell

For hundreds of years the land close to Highbridge has been flooded during winter months, the land remained fallow instead of being used to produce food. However, during the 1940's something was done about this failure when 100,000 acres of land was saved for food production. The remarkable feat of engineering was shrouded by wartime security, thus little was known until the end of hostilities.

The feat involved the drainage of 55,000 acres of land at a cost of £600,000; it lay in the hollow between the Mendips and the Quantocks. It is bisected by the low ridge of the Polden Hills, into areas of grass and moorland; two rivers run through it, the Brue and the Parrett, both flowing into the Bristol Channel.

The estuary of the River Parrett boasts the second highest tidal variation in the world (some 35ft) and the water is full of silt. Over a period of centuries the silt has cut off the lowland and the moors of Somerset from the sea by depositing a belt of silt at the estuary some 8ft higher than the moorland itself.

It was on these moors that Alfred outwitted the Danes (and burnt the cakes) and where the ill-fated Monmouth fought his battle, for centuries floods were a regular occurrence. The Abbots of Glastonbury owned Brent Marsh, as it was called in the Middle Ages, and the floods once swept into Glastonbury itself. Between the Mendips and the Polden Hills is a "dish-like" area where 20,000 acres were liable to flood regularly each winter and, after heavy rainfall when the Brue filled up, the side drains could not discharge, the land was then flooded until the river level dropped. Further, water levels were continually upset by peat digging in the Glastonbury area and this was an area of the moors used mostly by small dairy farmers for grazing. But because the tide and consequent flooding came so swiftly, cattle feeding in dry pastures in the morning could be in three feet of water by evening. Plans to effect a permanent cure to all this were made long before the war by the Somerset River Catchments Board, but the agricultural depression came along and plans had to be shelved.

It transpired that early in World War Two, the then Ministry of Works called in the Somerset River Catchments Board and gave their Chief Engineer Mr. E.L. Kelting a severe shock by announcing that a munitions factory was to be built in the area. The factory would manufacture R.D.X. * a new explosive and would require 9,000,000 gallons of fresh water per day.

R.D.X. was the explosive used in the bombs dropped on the Ruhr Valley dams by the "Dam Busters" in their raids.

To supply such a large quantity of water in winter would have been difficult at any time, but all -the-year-round, was asking rather a lot; farming in the Brue Valley would have been ruined. The wide ditches, (rhines) which constitute the field boundaries, would have dried up and much of the whole area would have reverted to commonland. There would have been no water to promote plant growth and nothing for cattle to drink. In 1941 the Farmers Weekly carried an article stating that the largest drainage undertaking in Britain since the Dutchman cut the rivers of the Fenland in the 17th century, was about to be engineered. The scheme would involve the drainage of some 45,000 acres, of this 4,000 acres flooded annually.

Secret meetings took place and eventually the Ministry of Works reduced its demands from 9,000,000 to 3,500,000 gallons per day, a more feasible proposition. This was a golden opportunity to drain the moors, there would not be a shortage of money or would there be difficulty in getting labour or implements. All previously pigeonholed plans on draining the moors were dusted off and re-examined. One such plan had proposed the cutting of a new river to give extra outlet from the Brue Valley to the Parrett estuary. If this New River were to be utilised as a reservoir, holding its capacity in summer and discharging the surplus through sluices to the river during the winter months, the factory would obtain all the water it required. This was the plan adopted and with a large cheque from the Government the Somerset River Catchments Board and its Chief Engineer were able to start. Due to incidental and wartime needs of the munitions factory, the farmers of the moors would soon have an efficient drainage and flood prevention scheme. The levels had needed such a scheme since Neolithic peoples had lived on piles in the lake villages of Meare; three queens in a barge had rowed the dying King Arthur to the Isle of Avalon (Glastonbury) the mythical paradise of the Celts.

The work had to be done in a hurry; in fact it was to be completed in three years from January 1940. Often draglines, scrapers and bulldozers were at work in pastures before the farmers had any idea of what was going on. Matters were not improved by the complete secrecy that had to be maintained as to the main purpose of the work. The military looked enviously at the fleet of earth-moving equipment and made unsuccessful attempts to requisition some of it.The New River would be 5 miles long and 200ft wide, and would run in practically a dead straight line, entering the Parrett estuary southwest of Highbridge. It was intended that the river would be 24 ft deep, but at this depth a layer of soft blue clay was found. Tractors, scrapers and once a 30ton dragline sank in the stuff. A comprise depth of 16ft was agreed with the sides sloping at one-in-four. Because it was not possible to go deeper, the idea of running water from drainage channels into the river by gravity had to be abandoned. At Gold Corner, which is at the inward end of the river, and at the division between the lower land of the moors and the higher levels towards the estuary, a pumping station was built. When water collected in the main cuts leading to the pumps is below the level of the Huntspill River, (in June 1947 it was about 8ft below the river level) and it can be pumped. When the higher winter level is reached, it is possible for it to flow in by gravity.

The pumping station was reported to be the most imposing of all those constructed in Britain during the wartime, houses four screw-type pumps driven by diesel engines. They have a combined capacity of 620 cubic feet per second or about 1,000 tons a minute. When full, the Huntspill River contains some 232,000,000 gallons, after which any surplus water is allowed to pass into the River Parrett through the outfall sluice.

A feature of the building was the window area, giving excellent lighting inside, a very desirable requirement where costly machinery needs close attention during its operation. Glazed lights in the flat reinforced concrete roof supplement this and a section of the roof comprises a cooling water tank for the engines. German and Italian Prisoners of War were the main labour force, outnumbering the English workers.

Gold Corner Pumping Station

New Bridges

Six new bridges were necessary, five to carry the main roads, the sixth to take the Bristol to Exeter main line railway. Because of the nature of the subsoil, bridge building was not easy, all are carried on piles and in most cases these are over 60ft long, the longest being 84ft long.

At the outlet into the estuary, tidal sluices were necessary so that the river could discharge on low tides and be held back during high tides. Once, during the construction, disaster nearly struck; to keep the water out whilst the sluices were built, a U-shaped bank was built out into the estuary as protection. One dark November night a gale whipped up the high tide to nearly two feet above the predicted level and the foreman, Mr. Dixon on his nightly rounds found to his consternation that the water was flowing over the top for a stretch of approximately ten feet. He grabbed a spade and set to work building up the bank, his spade broke, but he groped about in the dark and found another, no lights were possible due to blackout restrictions. After working for an hour and a half the tide started to turn and he had won, he had saved the bank, had it given then, all the work would have been ruined and they would have been set back weeks.

When the sluices were opened a small hole was cut in the protecting bank and the water very quickly washed away the remainder of the wall. Unfortunately the bottom of the river between sluice and estuary proved none too sound and began to erode. Luckily, it was spotted quickly and Mr. Hitchen commandeered all the lorries he could and sent them chasing around Somerset collecting concrete roadblocks. About 1,500 of these, together with concrete static water tanks and a steel barge were hastily sunk in the outlet from the sluices and these now provide a firm bottom.

The spoil removed from 'cutting' the river was levelled on the bank and after due "weathering" and shrewd treatment with artificials was re-seeded and today these banks provide first class grazing. There is no question that much of the land in the Brue Valley has been vastly improved by this modern and comprehensive drainage scheme. The fact that 1,000 tons of water that once flooded the land of the valley and is now pumped into the Huntspill River every minute is testimony to that. Also the water table in the Rhines can now be controlled and a complete "drying up" can be avoided. It was considered at that time, the internal channels and ditches were still not good enough to get the water to the main drains leading to the pumps. Apparently there was not a legal limit in England, to which peat diggers may work and this had a considerable effect on the water in the internal ditches. None the less, 40,000 acres of Somerset farmland had benefited from the country's wartime needs in the matter of explosives, the State paying the greater proportion of the cost.

Two of the new bridges featured foundation work of special interest, they were completed in 1942, the one being at Dunball; the other at Huntspill. They were constructed to allow the new river channels to pass under the main railway lines. The building of railway bridges in the area presented many problems and, at that time, it was a case of humouring nature. Especially in alternately coaxing and commanding the co-operation of that highly persistent and intractable element, water.

The new channel at Dunball was a diversion of the old King Sedgemoor Drain, which was constructed in 1795 to take the waters of the River Cary, but the Huntspill was an entirely new river. The construction of which had already involved the excavation of 5 million cubic yards.

Dunball Bridge was constructed entirely from reinforced concrete, having two 20ft spans. There already existed a railway bridge and station platform, these prevented a track diversion. A very fine quicksand of considerable depth was encountered some five feet above the New River bed; this caused serious difficulty in the excavation work. This problem was eventually overcome by the use of a de-watering system of "well-points". A special diesel pump capable of extracting 60,000 gallons per hour was used to deal with this volume of water in the "well-points". When a considerable volume of water had been extracted, the sand became sufficiently firm to be easily removed by ordinary excavation methods. The Huntspill Bridge has five spans-one 50ft main steel span and two 16ft spans of reinforced concrete. It is carried on reinforced concrete piles, driven through the soft clay and peat beds to rock lying at a depth of 80 ft below railway track level; the driving of the 65ft piles, each weighing about 7.5tons, was facilitated by making a diversion of the tracks for a distance of five hundred yards, during the construction of the bridge.

Although a major engineering feat was carried out some 60 years ago, the Somerset Levels are still affected by floods. Whether this is caused by 'global warming' or by some other environmental reason has yet to agreed but the inhabitants of the area suffer every time there is heavy and prolonged spells of rain. Perhaps another drainage scheme is the answer, who knows?

The Huntspill River with the Gold Corner Pumping Station, the new sluices into the River Parrett to control the tidal flow and the sluices on the Brue River all help to reduce the risk of flooding on the scale experienced pre-1940's. The drainage schemes put in hand in the 1940's help prevent much of this flooding, but a lot still needs to be done. However, they were able to say that work started by the Abbot of Glastonbury seven hundred years ago has moved a little more towards completion.

(Permission to use the foregoing material was granted by Mrs E Lawson)

Chapter 2

EDUCATION

THE CHURCH SCHOOL

Today it is accepted that everyone goes to school, this was not always the case. The Church provided forms of teaching to children and their parents; one penny a week covered the cost of a child providing the parents were churchgoers.

In 1841 The Schools Sites Act allowed for the conveyance of land so that a school could be built, with the help of the landed gentry, Colonel and Mrs. Henry Acland Fownes Luttrell a trust deed to the Minister and Wardens of St John The Evangelist Church together with the National Society was presented and a school was built. Mrs. Eva Luttrell had laid the foundation stone and on 6th May 1863 education began for everyone at: -

The Highbridge National School

The school building mirrored church and vicarage having large rooms with windows reaching up to the vaulted ceilings One main room was split into sections by means of large windowed screens, these could be pulled across the floor, possibly in metal grooves, to accommodate the different ages ranging from 5 to 14. The Church was heavily involved as a governing body, the Vicar being the Chairman. Many went to school for the first time, walking along gas-lit roadways. Queen Victoria was on the throne and demanded high moral standards. Ladies wore long dresses to conceal their legs; even table legs were required to be covered with thick chenille. Lifting lace curtains to peer out was also frowned upon; some children could expect a sharp smack to the legs at such times.

Original National School next to St. John Church
(Now a private residence)

An increase in the population meant the school had to expand and two further rooms were added; temporary accommodation was used, such as the Baptist Chapel, where great fun was had sliding down the banisters in between lessons. By 1883 the school had to be enlarged, or be handed over to a School Board. This did not meet with a very ready response and many acrimonious meetings were held, but once again, Highbridge decided to carry on the good work that Mrs. Luttrell had begun. Feeling they would be dishonest to her and their trust if they gave up their schools, they put their shoulders to the wheel and added a large wing to the original building. During 1880-1890 Mr James Wood was Master of the school.

In 1891, when the Reverend A.O. Tisdall the fifth Incumbent (1890 – 1895) was vicar, another appeal had to be made for the re-building and re-fitting of the "back premises" at the cost of £30. The so-called "Free Education Act" of that year, had to be explained to the parents, who until then had been paying 1d per week, per child, although "the Managers allowed the parents to pay only half-fees for infants". The Government was offering a sum of 10/- a head in place of the "School pence". It was pointed out that "in a place like this there were many who availed themselves of the excellent education our schools offered and would yet not care to get their children educated by the state". It was suggested they might still care to pay their pence voluntarily!! But the Vicar stated that "If parents will not help our schools with a willing and cheerful heart, by all means let them keep their pence, but urge them to put the pence they save in the Penny Bank, in which we now have 49 depositors. What we fear is that "Free Education" will only mean an "Extra Pint or two or three (drink?) .As the case may be."

The Highbridge National School Records——3 to 14 year olds.

February 1893—Reginald Morrish behaved rudely to some of the children on the way home after the children had been given a lantern entertainment. He was caned for it the next day. His parents threatened to take legal proceedings if he should be punished again for offences committed on his way to or from school as they claim that the school had no right to do so.

December 1893___Absentees were regularly reported to the Attendance Officer, persistent ones were fined. Her Majesty's Officer and Clergy made regular examination

March 1894——-A sad accident occurred soon after school was dismissed last Friday. Several of the boys were crossing the railway line near the Gas House; they avoided the 'down' train, but an 'up' train passing at the same instant caught Albert James and killed him. It knocked down Frank Cresswell, injuring his arm, broke his collarbone and otherwise bruised him, so that it will be some time before he will be able to return to school. Both lads were in Standard Four.

April 1894—All teachers ill—School closed until after Easter.

November —-1898 Messrs Lever Bros (Sunlight Soap) have sent a parcel of sheets and cardboard tops as prizes for the children under ten years of age, to be competed for in a writing competition as a homework exercise one day during the present month. This is welcomed as an incentive to do well in writing and the children are busy practising.

MISS KNIGHT'S CLASS 1929

Back row
Phylis Cook, Gladys Duke, Vera Hand, Joyce Andrews, Leslie Warren, Leslie Cook, __?, Henry Cox, Walter Coggins, Stanley Lewis.

Second row
Marjorie Parsons, Ada Fackrell, Dorothy Norris, Virginia Popham, Raymond Lawrence, Reginald Hooper, Raymond Parsons, Reginald Dobson, __?, Desmond Addicott.

Third row
Hetty Wilkins, Irene Hand, Peggy Theobald, Betty Slocombe, Joseph Popham, Herbert Howell, Archie Fay, John Faulks, Raymond Young.

Fourth row
Kathleen Fear, Freda Biss, Margaret Fay, Grace Strong, Cecil Nutt, Maureen Johns, Nancy Hodge, Archie Richards.

The Log Book records a variety of reasons for absences, amongst them; truancy, mumps, measles, whooping cough, scarlet fever and bad weather. Many children walk to school over long distances.

Between 1904 – 1918 a new cloak room and offices was built, the drains put in order and an appeal was made to help the Managers face the financial responsibility laid upon them, by the great Education Act of 1902. "People do not realize that they will be heavily rated for a Council School, if the Managers cannot comply with the requirement of the Education Authority. Surely church people are not going to allow their school to go"

In 1944 under a Government Act the school became known as Highbridge V.C.School (Voluntary Controlled) this entailed funding from Government with Church representatives on the Board of Governors.

In July 1947 the local newspapers reported that there had been a suspicion locally that exam papers may have been tampered with and it caused such a concern that questions were raised in the House of Commons. EDUCATION MINISTER PROMISES INVESTIGATION.

Apparently not satisfied with the Somerset County Education Committee's decision to shelve the Highbridge examination papers probe, two M.P's have now raised the question in the House of Commons, with the result that Mr. G Tomlinson, Minister of Education, has promised that every step will be taken to solve the mystery. The Minister's attention had been drawn to the statements appearing in Somerset newspapers to the effect that the culprit was not likely to be traced and did he feel that every step should be taken to find out the person responsible-if necessary with the aid of the police. Mr.Tomlinson: I have taken steps, and I have already promised to take the inquiry further.

PETITION WITHDRAWN: Mr. W. H. Hatcher, a manager of the school who had been primarily responsible for the investigations said he would proceed no further with the petition he had been organising for presentation to the Home Secretary demanding a further inquiry.

The Highbridge V.C. School Junior Country Dance Team won the Challenge Shield at the Mid-Somerset Music Festival in 1950 securing an Honours Certificate and 92% marks.

The Team comprised: Michael Faulks, Maureen Jefferies, Malcolm Yard, Pearl Baker, Neil Barrett, Jenny Green, David Faulks, Brenda Dredge, Jasmine Cottey, John Davey, Valerie Bishop.

Their Leader was Miss M. A. Jones

In the early days the school had a system whereby children were allotted to 'houses', these were: -

Knight, Luttrell, and Wood all people associated with the original school. Later

(Photo supplied by Pearl Coulton-nee Baker)

houses became: - Grenville, Hawkins, Raleigh and Drake, all famous sea captains.

In 1952 the then Headmaster Mr. Mason devised an 'OUT DOORS' that was different to the usual Field Trip experienced by today's scholars. A copy of their journal is reproduced for our readers and for those who took part to re-visit those far off days.

Highbridge V.C. School.

A school journey. Why? Because there are things to be learned on a school journey that cannot be learned in any other way. So for a while our school books are to be shelved, our school left behind and for a short space our new school is to be the great "Out doors." Our previous school journeys have been to Windsor and London but this year it has been decided to explore as much as we can in a few days our own lovely county, Somerset. I feel sure that every boy and girl that takes part in this journey will add greatly to his or her store of knowledge and experience, and it only remains for me to wish all of you a jolly good and interesting three days.

A.J. Mason

(School journey details supplied by David Derham)

THE SCHOOL JOURNEY PARTY

BAKER JEAN	Inner Cottage, Edithmead.
BENTON NORMA	"Benena" Worston Road.
BROOKES EILEEN	Glenholm, Walrow.
COTTEY JASMINE	9, Poplar Estate.
COOMBES JUNE	Japonica Farm, Mark.
CHICK WENDY	73, Church Street.
CHICK VALERIE	1, Victoria Place.
CLEMENTS ANITA	18, Corn Moor E.Huntspill.
COX DAVID	E. Huntspill
DINHAM JOAN	52, Clyce Road.
DREDGE BRENDA	78, Burnham Road.
DAVIES NADINE	13, Grange Avenue.
DOROTHY SHEILA	4, Morland Road.
DAVIES TREVOR	72, Church Street.
DERHAM DAVID	15, Worston Road.
FISHER ANNE	East View, Bason Bridge.
GORE LINDA	161, Burnham Road.
HAGGETT JACQUELINE	9, Newmans Corner.
HAM GERALD	20, Market Street.
HEAL GWEN	Station House.
INGLEDON PHILIP	Pitmoor House.
JEFFRIES MAUREEN	16, Church Street.
LOVIBOND PEARL	55, The Clyce.
LAWRENCE PAULINE	6, Coronation Estate, Burnha
MARSH DAWN	28, Corn Moor.
MORGAN STELLA	2, Cuthbert Street.
MEAR JENNIFER	1, Worston Road.
NORRIS BRENDA	Court Villa.
POPHAM JANET	The Gables, Worston Road.
POPHAM ANN	39, Grange Avenue.
PUDDY ROY	26, Worston Road.
PUDDY GEORGE	5, Kingsway.
STOKES MOLLY	176, Burnham Road.
SWIFT SYLVIA	13, Church Street.
SEABOURNE MARLENE	41, Grange Avenue.
SMITH GLORIA	3, Market Terrace.
TURNER FRED	15, Walrow Terrace.
WATTS ANGELA	3, Cuthbert Street.

SPORTS DAY

Using the Recreation Field at the rear of Grange Avenue, these youngsters do their best to win.

The three girls are, Pearl Baker, Maureen Slater and Carol Storey.

(Photo supplied by Pearl Coulton-nee Baker)

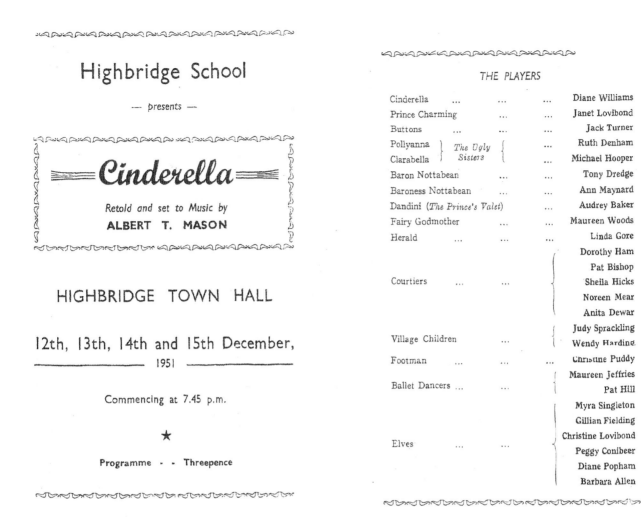

Highbridge School

— presents —

Cinderella

Retold and set to Music by
ALBERT T. MASON

HIGHBRIDGE TOWN HALL

12th, 13th, 14th and 15th December,
———— 1951 ————

Commencing at 7.45 p.m.

★

Programme · · Threepence

THE PLAYERS

Cinderella			Diane Williams
Prince Charming		... ...	Janet Lovibond
Buttons			Jack Turner
Pollyanna } *The Ugly* {		...	Ruth Denham
Clarabella } *Sisters* {		...	Michael Hooper
Baron Nottabean	... ...		Tony Dredge
Baroness Nottabean	... ...		Ann Maynard
Dandini (*The Prince's Valet*)		...	Audrey Baker
Fairy Godmother	... ...		Maureen Woods
Herald			Linda Gore
Courtiers			Dorothy Ham, Pat Bishop, Sheila Hicks, Noreen Mear, Anita Dewar
Village Children ...			Judy Sprackling, Wendy Harding
Footman			Christine Puddy
Ballet Dancers			Maureen Jeffries, Pat Hill
Elves			Myra Singleton, Gillian Fielding, Christine Lovibond, Peggy Conibeer, Diane Popham, Barbara Allen

(Programme supplied by WendyWynn (nee Harding)

Programme of a Pantomime presented by St John's V.C. School pupils

Mr A.Mason, Headmaster of the school retired in 1962 and Mr Raymond Dunbavan was appointed as Headmaster. Plans were afoot for the building of a new school, but before these reached fruition, Mr Dunbavan died very suddenly in January 1968. A new headmaster Mr Brian Riley was subsequently appointed and commenced duties in September 1968.

The school continued to function until May 1st 1973 when it transferred to new buildings in Burnham Road. It was a Co-education school with in excess of 210 children aged between 8 and 10 years of age; the original school was sold and was converted into two private houses.

During the 1980's the school made many Field Trips to a number places of interest such as, Brent Knoll, Highbridge Market, Cricket St Thomas and the Rural Life Museum at Glastonbury, the school also took time out to watch the National Cycle Race as it sped through Highbridge. There were 204 pupils in 1982. A trip to Wembly Stadium.London to see the Schoolboy Football International was arranged in 1984. The school assembled near the A38 in 1985 to welcome and cheer Ian Botham on his way along Church Street on his John O Groats to Lands End Charity Walk and in June a Class won a free trip by helicopter to South Wales. A school camp was held at Kilve in the Quantocks Hills in 1986. A choir of 50 sang in Wells Cathedral the same year. There was a trip to the R N.A.Station at Yeovilton during 1988. In this year the transfer age from Beechfield changed from 8 to 7 and the school arranged to take first year juniors from 1990 making approximately 225 pupils, this rose to 230 in 1991.

(Photo supplied by JoanneWoodberry nee Foster)

A good year for the school at the Highbridge Festival of Arts was 1989 when 88 children won awards; including 12 distinctions, 6 merits and 9 certificates, an improvement on previous years.

The first computer was installed in September 1990. The school choir entertained the members of the Stroke Club at Christmas and also presented its own pantomime. Over the years many alterations have been made to the structure of the school, addition classrooms have been added and in the late 1990's the building was modified to include a Computer Suite and on the 21st November 2002 the pupils moved into their £100,000 I.T.Centre.

Mr. David Penny, the current Head teacher (2004) kindly permitted the examination of the School Log Books.

The following account was produced in 2002 by the then Head teacher Mr. Paul Rushforth and his Assistant Mr. Christopher Burman: -

St John's Church of England Junior School was founded in 1863 – as the National School of Highbridge. It was originally built to take children from 5 – 14 but as the population grew, and other schools were built locally, it became a primary school. At the time it opened up until the mid 1970's Head teachers were required by law to keep a logbook. The log was a record of salaries, inspections and other events in the life of the school. These logbooks (of which there are eight) now provide us with a history of the school and the people associated with it.

We often hear people say that standards are not what they used to be in education. We can certainly be glad they are not what they were! Despite the cane being wielded on an almost daily basis during the early part of this century, some children seemed to get into mischief. In 1925 children crept into the Headmaster's study and wrote "rude comments" on his walls. One teacher accused the boys (for it would be boys, of course) of being in danger of "turning into socialists!" The Head teacher records that "I stopped her at that point." Days off were frequent. If there was heavy snow, or if there were crops to be harvested, the population of the school would drop dramatically. Whooping cough was the scourge of the school in the early days as was influenza. The infamous 'flu' epidemic of 1918 caused such a high rate of absenteeism that the school was closed down by the authorities for five weeks. Head lice and children who only changed their clothes on a monthly basis were also common. Not that it was only illness, work and bad weather that kept pupils away. In April 1902, it was written that "Yesterday afternoon there was a circus in town and this somewhat lowered the attendance."

Conditions, of course, for adults and children alike were not as we might expect today. In February 1917 the Head teacher reported that all the rooms were very cold. The log states "Children (were) allowed to go to the fires to warm themselves several times during each session." The extremely harsh winter of 1963 also resulted in the toilets freezing up for several weeks, along with all the other water pipes. Needless to say the children were sent home for an extended holiday. One can only imagine the difficulties parents may have had if the toilets at home froze over too!

All the money that the school paid out was collected from the Vicarage – as the Church of England primarily funded the school. The Head teacher records every month how he would attend the Vicarage and the Vicar's servant would pay out the wages to the Head teacher, who would pay the staff, purchase coal, etc. As one might imagine, this occasionally led to disputes between the Vicar and the Head teacher. One Head teacher was "banned from coming onto the site" by the Vicar. Another Vicar demanded, with five minutes notice that the whole school come to church and take part in a service he had decided to hold. He was, as the Head teacher records, "to be disappointed." The incumbent Vicar of 1903 even closed the schoolrooms on the basis that "They were required for a tea on Wednesday."

The school has been subject to regular inspections throughout its 139-year history. The results of these inspections are also written in the logbooks. There are some truly withering comments made by inspectors:

In 1932 an inspector wrote, "Arithmetic, though it receives more time than is usual or advisable, is weak." "Considering the size and importance of this school' it is hoped that a strong effort will be made by all concerned to increase its efficiency."

In 1964 the school was so untidy that the Headmaster issued a bulletin to all staff and had them sign the copy in the logbook. Some of the comments have come down to us as every day practice.

"See the children off the premises *before you go home"*

"The teacher on duty is responsible for the organising the litter squad"

He sums up by saying; somewhat bluntly "I was so ashamed of the very poor conditions of the school on Friday I spent over half an hour tidying up. *This is not my job"*

I suspect that most Head teachers find that it is exactly their job.

Memories of days at St Johns' School

I can never remember our School being called St. John's. It was Highbridge School, or on more formal occasions Highbridge V C School. I remember Mr Bick, who was my teacher at 11+ level. There were 53 pupils in our class at one time. Mr Bick having to bring the 'brighter' pupils to the front, thus having to abandon those unfortunates who were somewhat slower. I do remember some not being able to read at the 11+ exams and being so terribly worried for them. What a terrible time and my heart went out to Mr Bick.

I do remember the motto 'Mens Sana in Corpore Sana'. Why did that stick I wonder?

Dianne Williams

I remember that one Market Day a Bull escaped from the Cattle Market. He ran down the High Street and crashed into the level crossing gates, killing himself. I must have been only about three or four at the time.We lived at no.19 Poplar Estate with only a small garden that we shared with some chickens.

My younger sister Pearl was a real menace and kept removing the chicken's feathers as they walked around.1947-48

Michael Dubin

St Johns'V.C. School - 2000

HIGHBRIDGE INFANTS SCHOOL
NOW BEECHFIELD INFANTS SCHOOL

The Education bill of 1906 was intended to secure full public control of all rate-aided schools and to appoint teachers without reference to religious belief. This would have destroyed the purpose for which the church schools had been built; it encountered strong opposition from Anglicans throughout the country. In Highbridge, it raised a storm of protest and at a public meeting a resolution was passed that was forwarded to the Bishop of the Diocese the Rt. Hon. A.J, Balfour, M.P. and to the Marquis of Lansdowne, for presentation to the "House of Lords" On September 9th 1913 there was great excitement when Mr. H.Shepherd opened the Infant School for the younger children at 5.pm. It had been built to accommodate 160 children in four classrooms, with the maximum amount of access to sunlight through the windows. Classrooms were made to open up into corridors and then onto verandas, so that teaching could be done in the open air. It was heated by hot water, each classroom also having an open fire with inlets for circulating warm air.

It had been built near the Church School to allow the siblings to transport them safely to school, whilst the nearness of the Church may have been a reminder of what was owed to the Church and her labours in the matter of Education.

Beechfield Infants School previously Highbridge Infants School.

This view is in 1989 prior to major building work in 1990.

The first Headmistress was Miss Ellen S. Baiden her assistants were Miss Edith Brooks and Miss Eliza Bowering.

Miss Bowering was still teaching young pupils in 1934; it therefore appears that she was happy with her task having been at the school since 1913.

Extracts from School Log Book

February 6th 1928: from H.M. Inspectors Report:

This school possesses all the characteristics of a good infants school. The children are very bright and active, willing and eager to talk. They clearly enjoy coming to school. It is a happy place.

November 12th 1934——— The 'Milk Scheme' was started here today. Mr T. Marsh of Walrow, Highbridge supplied 91 bottles. The children drank it with relish, through straws.

MISS BOWERING'S CLASS 1934

Left to Right:

Back row:　　Chris Evans,　Gordon May,　Gerald Howell,　Gordon Chick,　John Moore,
　　　　　　　　Tommy Turner,　Gordon Norris,　Wally Pursey..

Middle row:　Audrey Pope,　Gwen Cook,　Laureen Gullis,　Joan Dudderidge,　Phylis Wells,
　　　　　　　　Ceretia Foster,　Irene Nichols,　Evelyn Smith,　Grace Sutton.

Front row:　　Annette Woodward,　Norman Quick,　Geraldine Mears,　Stella Wheeler,
　　　　　　　　Maurice Hale,　Iris Young,　Pat Baker.

(Photo supplied by Rex Major)

HIGHBRIDGE INFANTS 1938

Left to Right:

Back row:　　Howard Hand,　Clifford Heal,　Roy Madley,　Bobby Pocock,　Rex Major,
　　　　　　　　Stanley Cornish,　Melvin Hodge,　Keith Elsmore,　Tony Stokes.

Middle row:　Francis Rogers,　Margaret Brown,　Agatha Meader,　Margaret Brunt,
　　　　　　　　Sheila Gray,　Dorothy Weeden,　Rhoda Chilcott.

Front row:　　Esme Hicks,　Margaret Savage,　Audrey Duddridge,　Joyce Moore,
　　　　　　　　Alan Pepperal,　Bill Fisher,　Tom Cornish,　Daphne Popham.

From School Log

September 11th 1939 —— Gas mask drill throughout the school.
A.R.P. During closure, strips of white paper, 1 inch wide were gummed on the school windows, so-'X'
as prevention against splintering glass. Buckets of water and earth were placed outside the building. At
this time all children carried their gas masks to and from school.

In 1945 school numbers were at 260 and attendances at 91% over the previous year; staff comprised the
Headmaster and deputy, plus eight teachers. A new kitchen at the premises ensured meals were cooked
and served at school; seven dinner ladies kept order.

After St John V.C. Junior School had opened on Burnham Road, alongside the Infants School in 1973
there appeared to be a problem of identity for the two schools, it was decided to change the name of the
Highbridge Infants School to Beechfield Infants School.

With numbers at the school continuing to increase a major building programme was undertaken in the
mid 1970's to expand the school with additional teaching areas, these were added to the original
building. Then in 1990 major building took place resulting in 2 new Classrooms, Main Hall, and
Dining Area and a Staff Room.

**Beechfield School in 1977 with
Mrs J. Dunbavan** *centre*
**and Mrs B Thompson
(Head Teacher)** *far right*

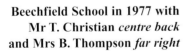

**Beechfield School in 1977 with
Mr T. Christian** *centre back*
and Mrs B. Thompson *far right*

Beechfield School in 2003
Autumn Term Reception Class
Mrs Worrall is far right

Beechfield School in 2003 and a
Reception Class with
Mrs Davison far right

Mrs. S. Aslett, the current Head Teacher (2004) and her staff, kindly provided the information and photographs.

Highbridge Childcare Day Nursery

A Community Nursery, which was built adjacent to Beechfield Infants School, opened in April 2004. The centre is the first of its kind in Somerset it is a nursery and family centre with a facility for health visiting; incorporating a toy library and play area.

More Memories of School Days in the Highbridge

I started school between three and three and a half. I remember, the teacher being very kind to me, when my Father died, he was only thirty-one. Mr Wood was the Caretaker at St' John's School.

In the afternoon we slept on raffia type mats. Miss Bowering had a large wicker basket where she kept everyone's lunches, all duly labelled with our names.

I often wondered if her family were the large 'Bowering'Mill' firm in Bridgwater who were only ten miles away. Miss Kelland was another teacher I remember, that may have been linked to a large agricultural concern in Bridgwater. When I was nine Miss Kelland had worked her way up to Headmistress, this was in 1938. Miss Knight was also a teacher I remember. When she wasn't teaching Miss Knight helped her sister Hilda run, 'The Copper Kettle' a little café in Church Street. Outside there was a large replica of a Copper Kettle hanging above the café.

I remember lots of happy times at school and can picture, Miss Bowering with her hair plaited and woven into 'bun-like' circles over her ears. Her cheeks always seemed rosy and when she looked at you with her beautiful smile, she put her head on one side, full of compassion. Miss Sellick was also very kind and a very pretty young woman, I enjoyed being taught by her.

Irene Nichols

I started at St. John's School in 1944 at four and a half years old. I can clearly remember my first day; being shocked at the children who cried, and the one who wet himself! I wasn't worried at all. My Mum would take me on her bicycle (at the beginning on a seat behind the saddle), as we lived on the Highbridge Road, near Half Way House. Once outside the school a chow dog ran into the road and Mum and I ended up on the road too! (Unharmed luckily). Mum always feared Chow dogs particularly after that, because she said he was going to attack her. Maybe he just hated bikes!

My clearest memory at school is that of Miss Sellick's class, probably the 2nd class. Miss Sellick asked me to go to another teacher with a verbal message, but I didn't understand what she'd said and I was too scared to ask her to repeat it. I went out nevertheless, but had to return to ask her to repeat the message. I was slapped across the face and called a stupid child! Later my Mother went to the school, and so unlike her gave, Miss Sellick, 'a piece of her mind'.

My Dad was born and grew up in Worston Lane, next to the Railway Line. The only time this caused problems was when the trains didn't run due to a strike, too quiet! No one could sleep. He was a choirboy in St' John's Church and St' John's school was the only school he attended. He wanted me to go there as my two brothers, seven and nine, went to St' Joseph's. I remember quite often if someone lost even a penny, we were kept after school to search for it. I would often have a really bad headache at these times, and suffered migraines as an adult. Also time to say, some of the children were very poor, and never seemed to have time for washing. I remember two boys in particular, that I had to help, being a 'sensible' girl. Both had dirty faces and lice and consequently so did I. Mum had to wash my long hair every night with black soap, the only remedy for lice in those days. These boys must have been cold at times because I never remember them having the luxury of socks, only boots.

One boy I remember was Neal, and I guess he was my first boyfriend! I remember sitting next to him in the playground. Once after school I went with him to his house. Mum arrived and couldn't find me. Eventually she caught up with me near the Cinema, or the 'Flea Pit' as we called it. I was only going to play with him, so I told her.

One girl I remember was called Maureen. She had very dark eyes, (as did Miss Sellick), and lovely dark curls that I envied. Unfortunately she used to pinch me if I didn't let her copy my work! Maureen was never a name I favoured after that.

One other girl I recall had a glass eye, how she managed always fascinated me. Sometimes she came without the glass eye; maybe it was irritating, I really don't know.

I remember being very happy at school, until Miss Sellick slapped me. I was always a bit scared of her. I guess she was just stressed that day. I remember she was a good teacher, bringing wild flowers into school. We learnt the parts of the flower by looking at Celandines. She also read to us a lot; the old books she brought into school fascinated me. So, slapped face apart those early years with Miss Sellick probably were the foundation of my love of flowers, nature and books!!

I recall I won a prize at a handwriting contest. The Headmistress wanted me to stay.

I left St. John's and went to St. Joseph's in Burnham, as my Mum thought the Nun's 'calmness', would suit me better. At St. Joseph's Mother St Anthony would ask me to write programmes for the Reverend Mother's visits.

Annette Moore(nee Hooper)

The teachers we remember were, in the Infant School, Miss Brice Headmistress, Miss Penny teaching first years and Miss Sellick the second year's.

In the Juniors Mr Albert Mason was the Headmaster, Mr Grimshaw and Miss Jones were teachers. Miss Thompson taught in the final year. Mr Witney was the geography teacher.

The girls who were taught sewing bought bus tickets to Burnham to learn under Phyllis James at the Technical College, she lived at Brightstowe Road at the time. Her husband was Graham James who taught woodwork to boys over the age of eleven. Miss Lavicore shared her skills of cooking and ironing here. I remember making jam tarts and Cornish pasties and ironing. I was looking at all the jars in the store cupboard one day, when Miss Lavicore came in. I quickly popped this little red preserved vegetable in my mouth before she saw me. This was my first experience with chillies.

We had 'Houses' where we all competed to win the most points which we got in all areas of schoolwork, each had it's own colour.

A weekly chore was Mr Mason checking the exercise books. The cane followed bad work.

Mrs Maidley   I believe was employed to collect the dinner money. I remember it was two shillings and sixpence, (half a crown) every Friday. The Dinner Ladies, were, Mrs Hand, Miss Cross and Mrs Dredge, amongst others. Mrs Haggett did the boilers and cleaning and had a daughter Valerie as well as sons, Keith and Eric.

As the school was crowded we had extra accommodation at the Baptist Church. We marched across from school. There were collapsible desks, which stacked at the back. Work was kept in shoeboxes. Chris and Brian Hawkins were sent out to get these by Mr Mason.

By 1951 the sweet ration (2oz) had finished and everyone cleared out, 'The Bon Bon' the local sweet shop The 'Jade Garden ' was then a wooden shack run by Mrs Dunbar who supplied coloured drinks for one penny, and tins of Horlicks tablets for 9d.

We earned pocket money by picking blackberries for local shops and hunting for 'Corona' bottles to redeem the few pence deposit charged on each one. Waste paper was taken to Cooper's Yard where we received a few pennies or a goldfish. Cowslips were gathered and taken to Knight's greengrocer to be sold.

Living in a shop opposite the school had its problems. Whenever young Sylvia Swift was stood on a chair or sent outside her mother could see her. She managed to find a four-inch recess in the wall, where, if she breathed in, she could hide. In those days anyone with hiccups had to stand outside until they stopped. Unfortunately one time each time she returned to the class, so did the hiccups, which had the class in uproar.

Sylvia Meaden(nee Swift)
Chris Meaden

I remember my first day at school because a boy dropped his bottle of milk and cried. I remember, being very cold, girls didn't wear trousers then. Long socks with garters, these inevitably, kept falling down. Miss Brice was Head Mistress and Miss Pasmore, I supposed was the School Secretary. Miss Grimshaw, Miss Sellick and Miss Frost, were the teachers.

Every year a van used to visit the school with fresh strawberries.

One of my worst memories was, having to lie down on rough mats every afternoon, inside in bad weather, or in the playground when the weather was fair, when we were in the Babies Class. It was such a bore. Punishment was standing in the corner with your back to the class and sometimes the teacher threw the blackboard duster at you and even the chalk. Sports equipment consisted of Hoops and Bean Bags.

There was a club called 'The Busy Bees'. We used to save 'Ship Halfpennies', which I think went to charity. Mr Silver, was the Music Teacher, he played the violin. We always performed our School Pantomime at the Town Hall, Michael Hooper often played the Dame, and he was brilliant! It was a lot of fun. Holidays were spent at Street. When I went to St. John's, I got sent to the Headmaster for the cane. My offence being, I ran after the whistle went at playtime.

Myra Spice (nee Singleton) 1947

At Infant's School, as age five or six, I fell in the playground, right at the edge of the veranda, where the rain gully was, (and probably still is). Unfortunately for me, my head struck the concrete edge of the veranda walkway and I split my forehead open. It really needed stitches and other checks, but the teacher Miss Grimshaw, put a plaster on it and made me lie on the coconut mats we used for P. E., under her teacher's table to be away from the other children. I stayed there all afternoon. Afterwards I had a nasty scar just above the hairline as a result. However, today 57 years on that scar is now several inches below the hairline! Still much in evidence.

In my third year at St. John's, while 'cramming' for the 11+ exam under Stan Bick (who was actually our second year teacher, perhaps Millie Thompson was ill) I remember being told that if you get the question, "If a pound weight of lead and a pound weight of feathers were to be dropped from the top of a leaning tower, which would hit the ground first?" the answer we must give, is that they will hit at the same time. Assuming we passed and went to Grammar School, we would then learn about 'Mass'. But as we had not learnt about such intricacies our answer would have been guesswork!

I remember at St. John's we used to sit in iron desks, which were designed in pairs, so that two pupils had to sit closely side by side. We always sat in the same places as we kept our possessions in the desks, which had 'lift up tops'. The person who sat next to me was Janice; she used to pinch my bum or bare legs, (we used to wear shorts in those days). I was always too much of a gentleman to complain or pinch her back, so I suffered in silence! Of course all boys of that age (8 - 11) hated girls anyway.

Miss Thompson (third year juniors) lived in Walrow.

Miss Grimshaw (I think 1st year infants) lived in Oxford Street Burnham.

Miss Brice (Headmistress of Infants) lived just opposite the Highbridge War Memorial.

Graham Haytor taught Science at the upper Junior School (year 4 onwards). He taught us Cycling Proficiency and marked out roads and junctions on the school playground to practice on. We all received certificates. At playtime at St. John's, we used to slide down the slopping parts of the playground wall. Over the years, the heels of our shoes wore a groove in the wall's capping stones and you can still see those grooves in them to this day. I dread to think what it did for our shoes!

David Derham

I was in the School Choir; we were entered in a lot of competitions, and won a few cups. I think Mrs James took us for that. I was also in the School Hockey Team and remember going to Burnham to practice on the beach.

The Girls also went to B. O. S. Tec. For cookery (Miss Lavacore). She was getting on a bit and also taught my Mother, (I still can't cook) we used to pocket the 3d for the bus fare and walk to B. O. S. and were always in trouble for being late for class.

I broke my leg when I was about 10/11 years old and thought I'd get out of going to school, but my mother, (Bless her Heart) borrowed an old pushchair and took me to school every day (How embarrassing). I believe the School consisted of four classrooms and the Main Hall, with playground around three sides.

Thinking about dates, when the King died, we were all taken into the Hall for assembly and were told he had died. Was that really 50 years ago? I remember living at no.19 Poplar Estate with lots of friends and neighbours around. My cousin Terry Arnold lived with us. Our neighbour Mrs Faulks had a new fireplace and Mum (Kitty) and I went in to see it. I remember it was 'mushroom' and I wondered what it would look like. I was surprised to see a beige tiled fireplace with not a mushroom in sight! I can still see that grate more than fifty years on.

Pearl Rawles (nee Dubin) 1947-48

I remember Mr Silver, our Music teacher. His trousers always seemed to go way past his waist held up by braces. His hair was brownish with a lovely moustache. He wore glasses; thick glasses and he made us all laugh playing his violin and doing tricks with it.

Mr Witney taught us Geography. He was in the R. A. F. and the lessons sometimes drifted into exiting tales about his exploits around the world in his aeroplane.Stan Bick was handsome I remember. I had done something wrong one day and Miss Thompson held my hand and gave me a hard slap to the arm. Miss Lavicore was our cookery mistress. She always wore a smart pinstriped suit and tie. Her hair was white. We learnt home-making skills such as cleanliness, ironing and cooking. I had an award for ironing a tablecloth without one crease in it. We seemed to make a lot of Yorkshire puddings and jam tarts. Part of the time we helped Miss Lavicore with her washing, learning to do it by hand.

Loom weaving to make scarves was something I did with Maureen Jeffries and Annette Hooper. We used pale blue and dark blue, the school colours.

Once a year, a lady across the road from the school, rented out her front room, so that the School Dentist could examine everyone. This was the most unpopular day of the year!

Pearl Coulton (nee Baker)

I started school when I was five, it was 1930 and I was in Miss Bowering's class. All the children who could read had to stand up. There were just two of us, we both had to read a piece out. I was so glad my Granny had taught me at home. Each day we had to lie on coconut mats at rest time, they hurt my hands and back.

In the playground we marked out Hopscotch to play and had fun with hoops and spinning tops.

War started when I was nearly nine. The field we used nearby was dug over. Everyone had a plot and grew something, flowers, vegetables and lettuce. One year we had too many there were lettuces everywhere. The boys dug up the potatoes.

I learnt to swim in the Marine Lake on the beach. After walking to Burnham, the lesson would commence by us diving into the lake. Unfortunately once I dived into a silted up area and was lost to view for a while. I remember being dragged out eventually and being banged on the back. When I sat up I had silt running out of my nose and eyes. Keep fit exercises daily kept us all in trim.

One of my favourite memories, was sitting listening to wonderful stories on the radio, like King Solomon's Mines and the history of Samuel Pepyes, they are still favourites.

When 'Rock and Roll' and 'Bopping' started Mrs James made us jive in the hall, perhaps she was a bit of a rebel! Market Day in Highbridge was so busy we had to walk on the road, when going to the sports field or the Baptist Church for lessons.

The cinema was also a favourite, I remember Mrs Flo Paget directing us down to the nine pennies quite loudly. She was a large woman with a severe haircut who you didn't argue with but we called her Auntie Flo. There were some double seats at the back, 'love seats' any hanky panky and you would feel the tap of Flo's torch on your shoulder. This was also used to control the noisier children at the front who she couldn't quite reach. In the August holidays our treat was to roller skate to Mark to buy fresh delicious doughnuts and eat them by the stream.

Where the Haines factory was there was a farm previously. Gangs were very common. To be in one usually involved initiation. This was climbing over the wall and stealing an apple, which I wouldn't do, much as I wanted to be in 'The Gang'. I went home and my dear Mother cooked a batch of

homemade toffee, that filled a 'cone of paper. Sweet rationing was in force at the time, so when I walked down to friends they quickly agreed I could join if I gave everyone a piece of toffee.

Heather Carver (nee Stradling)

THE KING ALFRED SCHOOL 1957-2004

The present King Alfred School (then named The King Alfred County Secondary School) evolved from Burnham County Secondary School which occupied a variety of sites in Burnham-on-Sea until November 1957. It was then moved to its present position in Burnham Road, Highbridge where it was ideally situated to serve the communities of the two towns and surrounding area. Pupils came from a large catchment area including Pawlett, East and West Huntspill, Brent Knoll, Berrow, Brean and, of course, Burnham and Highbridge. The Head teacher of the school at the time, and until 1975 when he retired, was Mr Norman Edge.

The official opening in June 1958 was by notable Burnham resident and former Commander-in-Chief, Plymouth, Admiral Sir Mark Pizey. At the opening of the school that was to provide the secondary education for 380 children with 12 staff, it was pointed out that the school stood on a site once owned by King Alfred. It had cost £98,000 and occupied an area of 16 acres. At the time it was considered to be an ultra modern design and travellers in Somerset may have observed that the West Somerset School in Minehead and Broadoak School in Weston-super-Mare (now a Sixth Form Centre) were based on the same design, although with extensions they now look very different.

Aerial view in 1965

In the 47 years since the school was opened it has changed beyond recognition. For example, there were two laboratories in the original building, there are now nine. The school's gymnasium was added along with some additional teaching rooms and woodwork and metalwork workshops in 1962. Now, in addition to this, there is a purpose built Sports Hall, fitness suite and squash courts

And the original two changing rooms will increase in number to seven when the next extension to the buildings is completed in 2005. These are but two examples of how King Alfred's has changed over the years.

Growth was relatively slow in the 1960s but the coming of the M5 led to a population boom in the Burnham and Highbridge area and more classrooms were added in a new building in 1972. This block was largely open plan, reflecting the style of the time (decided on by architects but not necessarily with the approval of teachers). The classrooms were built around two quadrangles providing a great deal of natural light, and two specialist music rooms were included. Between the two ends of the block there was a kitchen to replace one in the original block. Pupils were served meals from both sides of it and ate them in open plan areas created when the partitions between classrooms were removed at the end of morning school. Again, an architect's idea, which lacked practicality. Pupils who brought sandwiches for their lunch ate them in the new block too. Originally school meals had been served to children who ate them seated at octagonal tables in the school hall with sandwich eaters eating in the Sandwich Hall. This small hall immediately behind the main hall still retains the name 'Sandwich Hall' although the origin of the name remains a mystery to most who use the hall today. At the time language laboratories with banks of tape recorders where pupils were linked by headphones and microphones to their teacher were very much at the cutting edge of foreign language education and one such room in the block was fitted out with this facility.

Experience with the first building on the King Alfred School site suggested to the planners that it would be sensible to make any further developments single storey. Looking at the main entrance to the original building leaves one in no doubt of the reason why. The 'tower' to the left of the entrance and the small hall - the Sandwich Hall - on the right, were obviously too heavy for the underlying clay and windows were continually cracking and having to be replaced with plastic. In addition, the lintel above the three doors is decidedly bowed!

1976 saw another major increase in facilities when another teaching block was added. This contained a very large and pleasant library (replacing the one in the original building which became another science laboratory), a superbly appointed lecture theatre, a custom designed drama studio and a Sixth Form area, in addition to ten additional classrooms. At the same time an Art Block was built with 3 studios and facilities for pottery. Adjacent to this a Sports Centre with two squash courts (later extended to three to accommodate the rising interest in squash) and small fitness room was built. The Sports Centre, opened by Somerset wicket keeper, Derek Taylor, in 1977, encompassed a small swimming pool that had been provided by the school's PTA and which previously had been surrounded by a rather insecure fence. This pool had been used in PE lessons and because of its size the water level must have risen by several inches when a whole class used it. Past pupils tell of lessons where the whole class were instructed to walk in a clockwise direction in the water and then told to 'about turn'. Apparently, this was impossible to do because of the whirlpool effect that they had previously set up. Even with such a small pool the school had swimming galas although the more able swimmers did little but turns, as the length of the pool was rather restrictive. Nevertheless, many pupils will have learnt to swim in this pool and it was a sad day when it was filled in to provide an outdoor badminton court and barbecue area for the Sports Centre.

King Alfred Sports Centre was built with money from Somerset County Council and Sedgemoor District Council and then, as now, was managed by a joint management committee representing the school and the community. It was remarkably successful right from the start under the management of

Allan Pendleton, winning national awards for Sports Centre Management. It has developed over the years with the bar area (open in the evenings) being increased in size and one of the squash courts having a change in use as the squash 'fad' diminished. This now is the 'Spiral Fitness Suite' on two levels separated by a spiral staircase and is a popular facility for community use.

Additionally, at the same time, an administrative block was built. This provided the staff with a new common room and work area, a reception area and several offices to house the Head teacher, his deputies and the school secretaries and medical room. This released more rooms for classrooms and offices in the original block,

Tinkering with the buildings occurred in the years leading up to the turn of the century with Somerset's only state school Astroturf pitch being added in the late 1980s following the sale of a small part of the school's playing field now occupied by the Highbridge Medical Centre in Pepperall Road. This facility, opened by the then Minister for Sport, Colin Moynihan, was much envied by other schools and used a great deal by sports clubs in the local area. Brean Hockey Club regularly played national league games on the all-weather surface.

Facilities for the sixth form had been incorporated into the 1976 building but they were never able to cope with the increasing number of students who were staying on to study for their 'A' levels. The one remaining open plan area in the 1972 building was later used as a Sixth Form common room but again increasing numbers led to overcrowding and in 2001 a new Sixth Form Centre was opened by local MP Mr David Heathcoat-Amory. This incorporated a larger common room, an ICT room exclusively dedicated to 6th form use, offices and three additional classrooms.

At the present time plans are well advanced for yet another building. In 2003 the school gained Sports College Status. This followed a commitment of £50,000 raised by local people, parents and businesses that enabled the release of a larger sum of money by the Department for Education and Skills. Some of this money is being spent on a one million pound project to provide modern changing facilities, a multi-purpose hall for dance, also to be used as a much needed dining facility, new kitchens and yet more classrooms, one a sports science laboratory.

All schools evolve and the more successful ones grow. King Alfred's has been no exception. Numbers have increased from the original 400 to 1450 in 2004. Numbers increased at the end of the 1960s as more and more pupils were staying on beyond the statuary school leaving age of 15. 1972 saw King Alfred County Secondary School become a comprehensive school taking all primary school pupils from its catchment area with the more able pupils no longer attending Sexey's Grammar School at Blackford, Dr Morgan's Grammar School or Bridgwater High School. Numbers continued to grow in the 1970s to a maximum of 1500 as the local population increased. There was a slight fall in the 1980s when schools were encouraged to market themselves and many of the catholic children in the area were tempted to travel to the county's only ecumenical school in Taunton. This trend did not continue into the 1990s and now very few pupils in the area attend schools other than King Alfred's apart from those whose parents choose the private sector for their children's education.

Hand in hand with the growth in numbers of pupils has, of course, gone an increase in staff numbers. From 12 in 1957 there were over 80 teachers and about 15 learning support assistants, who help less able pupils both in and out of the classroom, in 2004. One of the welcome additions in more recent years has been the inclusion of disabled pupils and it has been a real pleasure to see these children playing with their able bodied peers in the playground. This benefited disabled and able-bodied alike and brought a new richness to the school.

The range of subjects taught in 1957 was rather limited in comparison with that in 2004. In 2004 the school had, for example, eight dedicated computer rooms and in total approximately one computer for every 7 pupils. Pupils are offered a range of modern foreign languages, have to learn biology, chemistry and physics up to GCSE standard, can do dance and drama and the old subjects of woodwork, metalwork, cookery and needlework became design technology, food technology, textiles and graphic communication. All subjects in 2004 are taught to both girls and boys, a change from the days when boys wielded the hammers, chisels and files and the girls the wooden spoon, rolling pin and needle. PE changed from the days of limited opportunity when the best were creamed off for the first fifteen and the rest were left to kick a ball about aimlessly. 2004 pupils got

the opportunity to try a wide variety of sports and were encouraged to make full use of the school's extensive sports facilities out of school time. Methods of teaching have inevitably changed over the last 50 years. Pupils were taught more formally in rows of individual desks. In 2004 they are encouraged to take more responsibility for their own learning and it is not uncommon to see pupils working together on projects in the library or in groups in the laboratory.

Pupils at King Alfred's were always encouraged to study and care for their environment. From the early days there was a farm unit and pupils were keen to look after the animals kept on the site. Mr Frost, a farmer from Brent Knoll allowed the school to raise some of his calves and trips to his farm, where he explained the ins and outs of dairy farming, were a highlight of science lessons. Many other animals were kept on the unit. Pigs were bred and a calf was born watched by excited pupils, spell bound as a rope was attached to the forelegs to pull the newborn animal into the world. Chicken roamed about and goats kept the hedges down. Pupils were shown techniques of hand milking. Persuading a nanny goat to stand on a bench to be milked in full view of a rural science class was one of the skills developed by the teachers! Latterly, even rabbits were bred for meat, much to the disgust of many of the girls in particular, who considered rabbits only for cuddling. They obviously had a word in their floppy ears as they seemed reluctant to breed – not what was expected of rabbits!

Sadly health and safety regulations and the advent of the National Curriculum heralded the demise of the farm unit although an emphasis on environmental education remained in science lessons and Environmental Science is one of the subjects studied at 'A' level.

School visits have always played a very important part in the life of the school. From the 1960s the school has had a minibus for school teams to attend fixtures and for small groups of pupils to visit places of interest. In the 1970s there were two minibuses and in the following decade an explosion in the school's transport fleet meant that in addition to minibuses the school owned its own small fleet of coaches. Nowadays, there is just the one minibus and coaches are hired. Foreign exchange visits have always been popular and the only real way to get the true taste for another country and its culture. In France visits to Morlaix near Roscoff in Brittany and more recently to Louvigny du Dessert and in Germany to Homburg, close to Burnham and Highbridge's twin town of Fritzlar, have encouraged language study and started many lasting friendships. In more recent years King Alfred's has been involved with schools in the Czech Republic, Spain, Germany and Finland and pupils have both attended and hosted international conferences. Pupils from King Alfred's have visited Natare School in

Uganda and a reciprocal visit by six Ugandan students took place in 1999. Pupils have always extended their education beyond the classroom. In the 1960s and 1970s much of their chemistry course was rooted in the local area. Oil shale collected from Kilve provided the raw material for lessons in the lab and led on to further work on the oil industry; lead ore from Priddy, iron ore from other areas on the Mendips and copper ore from Doddington, near Nether Stowey, led to work on the extraction, properties and uses of metals. Other materials collected from the local environment provided the springboard for other lessons. The Duke of Edinburgh's Award Scheme has seen pupils travelling to the Lake District, Snowdonia, Derbyshire, Dartmoor and Exmoor to take part in expeditions. In the 1970s the Ten Tors walk on Dartmoor provided the challenge for pupils. On one occasion three King Alfred pupils were badly burned in a tent fire as they unwisely changed a camping gas cylinder in their tent in the vicinity of a lighted candle. They made their escape through the flaming tent sides and were transported to the Royal Naval Hospital in Plymouth where, thanks to the skill of their doctors they made an amazing recovery, returning to school only a few weeks later, although still minus some hair, but fortunately without any scars.

The organisation of the school has changed over the years. When the school moved to its present site it was organised on a house system. The four houses, Brent, Mendip, Steart and Quantock each had their own House Heads who, in many ways, acted as Head teachers. There were, for example, four house PTAs which organised their own events, they had their own assemblies and were autonomous in many respects. Classes were organised on a half year basis so 1BQ1, 1BQ2, 1BQ3, 1BQ4,1MS1,1MS2,1MS3 and 1MS4 were the eight classes in the first year in 1972 (B=Brent, Q=Quantock etc). The blocks in the school were labelled A, C, D, E, F, G but without a B Block as B was used for Brent House. Generations of pupils have wondered why there is no B Block and many first year pupils have been sent on false errands in their first week to find rooms in B Block by mischievous older children. There now will be a B Block as the new building will carry this initial. This is to avoid a notorious H Block with connotations with Northern Ireland prisons and Prisoner Cell Block H, the television programme!

There have been many characters that have graced the school over the last 50 years. Mr Lloyd-Henry, Mr Strickland and Mr Phippin were Year Heads who moved with the school in 1956 and gave over 30 years service each. Each had a different style and all were equally respected for their care and fairness. Mr Henry is remembered by many for the slipper he kept ready to administer discipline in the old fashioned way. Mr Strickland was a well-loved member of the local community. He forged many links

with local industry and, as Careers Teacher, was responsible for putting many pupils on the first rung of their career ladder. Sadly, he died in 2002. The three teachers provided the stability needed as young teachers came and went as they gained promotion, many of them advancing to become Heads of their own schools. Every member of staff in a school is essential if it is to run smoothly and caretakers are no exception. Indeed, new entrants to the profession are advised to make friends with the caretaker a priority. Mr Danny Keeping was the sort of caretaker that all Head teachers would love to have caring for their school. He joined the staff in the 1950s when it used the Technical School buildings in Burnham. He retired in 1976; sadly to die without having long to enjoy his much deserved retirement. He was a fatherly figure to generations of pupils and was much missed. Following Mr Edge, Brian Smith took the helm for six years. It was his first Headship, having been Deputy Head of Hartcliffe School in Bristol. He changed the house to a year system and to the present day the school is organised in years, with each year having its own Year Head. He moved to his second Headship in Bedford before taking early retirement and dying at the age of 69 in Cheshire in 2004. He was succeeded by John Ellener. After his resignation, Dr Keith Diffey moved to King Alfred School from a school in Plymouth where he was Vice-Principal. He ensured that the finances of the school were run efficiently and masterminded the school's successful bid for Sports College Status.

Many past pupils will remember their teachers with a great deal of affection. Mrs Bacon, Mr Lloyd, Miss Hartley, Mr Endall, Miss Turner, Mr Lewis (whose claim to fame was the try he scored for the South West against the New Zealand 'All Blacks'), Mr Yeomanson, Mr Barwell; their names will all evoke memories of happy days. Lots of staff has been at King Alfred's for over 25 years. Mrs Palmer who looked after the Special Needs Department and went on to become a Deputy Headteacher at the school; Mr Whittell, who was Head of Geography and later became responsible for the increasing number of examinations taken by pupils; Mr Smith, who led many expeditions and became a Year Head, Mr Higman, an English teacher who took over from Mr Strickland as Head of Steart House; Mr Maddy, History teacher; Mr Deahl, who joined the school in 1972 as Head of Chemistry and then became Head of Science, then a Head of Year and latterly took on the Community Liaison role and is still at King Alfred's 32 years later; Mr Peek who would acknowledge his mild eccentricities as a Year Head; all these people have shaped the school into what it has become in the 21st century. Many will remember Miss Morrish, a physics teacher who taught with a rod of iron but underneath had a heart of gold, never failing to send a congratulatory card to her successful 'A' level students and a card expressing her commiserations to those who were less successful. She was keen to introduce pupils to the art of fencing and many pupils became proficient in this sport. Additionally, she was a keen horsewoman and the annual gymkhana was eagerly anticipated, although not by the staff that volunteered to help only to be dragged into a staff race aboard horses intent only on giving watching parents some entertainment by being either stubborn or galloping off in the wrong direction.

Ancillary staff has also shown considerable loyalty. Mike Hawkings was a pupil at the school and then became a physics technician, a position he held until his retirement in 2003, after 36 years. Mrs Thatcher looked after animals, plants and biology teachers as biology technician for more than 20 years and Mrs Downer attended to all the school's printing requirements for more than 30 years. Mr Nicholls, in Technology worked for a similar length of time as technician in the department formerly known as Woodwork and Metalwork. Headteacher's secretaries, now quite properly called P.A.s have also stood the test of time. Mrs Kitchen succeeded Miss Williamson and between them they have served all four Headteachers that King Alfred's has had over the last 47years

Over the years ex-King Alfred pupils have enjoyed a great deal of success in their chosen fields. Several are practising doctors, Melica Endall working as a GP in Staffordshire and Richard Hughes in the A and E Department of a Manchester Hospital are just two examples. Ian Wright is a veterinary surgeon in Hull and countless others work in the health service as pharmacists, physiotherapists and nurses.

Gabriel Clarke who is remembered for his performance in 'The Causasian Chalk Circle' in the school hall in the 1970s went on to regularly be seen on ITV Sport where he presents soccer programmes and interviews players and managers. Michael Knott was the youngest naval officer to command a warship and Jeremy Plant became a high-ranking naval officer. Other services have benefited from King Alfred's ex boys and girls and some have piloted helicopters and jet fighters in the RAF and

distinguished themselves on the battlefields of the Falklands and Kosovo. Susannah Hickling became a freelance writer whose articles regularly appear in the Times, and Louise Jury became a features writer for the Independent newspaper following her English degree from Oxford. Many ex-pupils have gone on to Oxford University, although fewer to Cambridge, probably because of the geographical proximity of the former. Many past pupils entered the teaching profession and lots returned to their home area to teach, some of them at King Alfred's. Academically, many students have done well with most English and Welsh universities conferring degrees on the young people from Burnham and Highbridge. However, academic success has never been the be all and end all of what King Alfred's has been about. Producing good citizens prepared for the world of work and able to fulfil their potential has always been a major aim of the school and one that it has prided itself in achieving.

King Alfred's has often been represented in the media. On two occasions the school has taken part in the 'Young Scientists of the Year Competition' on BBC television with filming on location around the school and in the Pebble Mill studios in Birmingham. 'Top of the Form' provided a radio challenge and the school hall was full to capacity in 1977 to hear the programme recorded with a radio link to a school in Bath. Sadly King Alfred's was pipped at the post and did not progress to the next round. In 1979 the school was involved in a series of programmes about comprehensive schools made by HTV West and transmitted nationally, called 'A Fair Chance'. There were six programmes in the series and King Alfred's' as a rural school, was compared with Filton High School from Bristol as a city comprehensive. Filming was great fun with cameras, microphones and clapperboards in 'normal' lessons. Gillian Reynolds, the writer and broadcaster visited the school to conduct interviews and these were used for voice over commentaries to accompany the pictures.

King Alfred School is a living community, constantly changing and responding to the local and wider community. No doubt it will change to reflect future technological advances and developments in teaching styles and strategies. What is certain, however is that it will continue to insist on high standards and to serve local children well into the future.

(Article written by Tony Deahl and supplied with photographs by permission of Dr Keith Diffey)

School Memories

The school was split into 4 houses named after surrounding hills – Brent, Mendip, Steart and Quantock. All houses had their own colour – I was in Quantock House and our colour was a yellowy gold. Each year, a number of individuals were chosen to act as "Prefects" to do so you had to be honest and trustworthy and be prepared to look after others. I was lucky enough to be a Prefect for Quantock House. Pupils were not allowed in the school buildings at break or lunch times the role of the Prefect was to " man the doors" to ensure no- one entered until the break finish bell had gone. Or to man certain areas of the school 'out door' areas to ensure pupils were generally behaving and looking after each other.

We had an excellent Library which served as a social meeting place, once you became a 5th former you were allowed to go to the library at break and lunch times – It served as a good way of keeping out of the cold and had an area where a quite chat was allowed! Can't actually remember reading a book though! We played different sports in the winter term and summer term –

In the winter we did gymnastics, Hockey and Netball and in the summer, Rounders and Athletics.

I had several teachers of whom I have fond memories Mr. Moore was our English teacher and he had a way of making stories come alive. On occasions he would read aloud – particularly when we had a new book, and he would speak in the character of the people in the story which **was** excellent – I particularly remember him reading "Of Mice and Men" - a story of 2 strong men – one of which however had the mental age of a child but enormous strength. Miss Bacon was a Maths teacher who was the only teacher where I felt I actually understood the Maths – Unfortunately she did her job too well and I got moved up a class only to then suffer again as no one could explain and teach the way she did! School dinners. I remember my favourite pudding – Chocolate crunch with mint custard – yummy!

Friends. I made some lovely friends – Liz Draper, Gillian White, Nicola Hancock, Rachel Gass and Katherine Riley to name a few and for whom I have very fond memories.

Paula Rawles

On a Monday morning we have Physics; Miss Morrish said "Mark, I want to see you at break". I thought I was going to get told off, for doing something wrong. John Lee was also there, we had orange and biscuits – we couldn't have been that bad! We were then called into Room 8; in there were about twenty young persons, both men and women, plus an older man. We couldn't understand what was going on, but we had been chosen to show the visitors around the farm unit. because we knew a lot about the farm and Mr. Endall said we had worked hard.

The visitors were student teachers from Cardiff University and wanted to know how a school farm unit was run. We enjoyed the morning off work but found we actually worked very hard talking to them and showing them around.

I think they liked our school very much: they gave us a cheque for £10.00 towards the farm unit .

Mark Lavis

Feeding the hens and collecting the eggs was probably the best job during a tutorial session. A couple of us would go down to the School Farm, it needed two as one person had to go in with a metal dustbin lid and corner the cockerel before it was safe for the other to go and collect the eggs! Getting the eggs back to the classroom unbroken could sometimes be a problem, especially the first day back after half term, there could be twenty eggs or more. We were never organised enough to go down with a container, so it was a case of fitting as many as possible into our blazer pockets and carrying the rest in our hands. Some did get dropped I remember, and Antony Jones once ended up with a broken one in his blazer pocket.

During 3rd year Maths, Mr Buttery treated us to a lesson with the school's new and only computer. This was wheeled in on a trolley, with a full size television as a monitor. Mr Buttery typed in the program, which was little more than a small series of basic calculations. We had to be suitable impressed when he then input a number and the computer came back with the answer. I think we all appreciated the potential of the machine; it was just that we all had our own calculators with which we could all have worked out the answer just as quickly. Anyway, the computer was then wheeled away again and kept in a storeroom (renamed The Computer Room) at the back of Mrs Keast's classroom, never to be seen again by anyone other than members of the Computer Club. This was only 1978-9, but looking back at it now, I feel like one of my Grandparents, retelling their first experience of seeing a motorcar!

Robin Halstead

King Alfred School - 2003

Teaching Prior to 1891 -
(Do you think you would qualify?)

Prior to the Highbridge Adult School opening in 1891, teaching appears to have been carried out by a jack-of-all-trades person, an advertisement inserted by Richard Locke in the Statement of Accounts of the Burnham Society in 1796 stated:

"Wanted (at the probable salary of £100 per annum and insured for £50) to reside in the large village of Highbridge, a person qualified to teach school, and to write grammatically for the press, the composition of an old invalid. He must be a proper judge of securities for cash, draw leases, make wills and undertake the clerkship of a large Benefit Society, with whom he must pray extempore and give lectures. He ought to be able to sing, play different instruments of music to teach pupils, to dance and to dress, and to shave a few gentlemen in the neighbourhood, bleeding, drawing of teeth, curing fire legs, agues and chilblains in children, will be considered as extra qualifications. He must have no objection to superintend a Sunday school and if called to, become the Parish Clerk, to copy the sundry tithing rates and collect them. To keep the Lords pound as Hayward and to have sole custody of the stocks. Finally if he has any time to spare of a Saturday afternoon, he will be appointed gamekeeper of the Manor of Huish-Juxta — Highbridge".

Highbridge Adult School/Public Library 1891 - 1991

One hundred years of service in this building was celebrated on April 25th 1991.

Nationally, the Adult School movement was a non-sectarian Christian educational group closely allied in spirit to the contemporary Y.M.C.A. and temperance movements. By 1888 classes had started in temporary accommodation in Highbridge. In 1890 these classes numbered around 90 members and the school committee felt confident enough to commission a new building, the land being bought for £60 from Thomas Cox. The building was to consist of one large hall 46 ft by 24ft, dividing into two classrooms each with a separate fireplace. A newspaper account has it that "the acoustics have been carefully considered and it is expected will be as near perfection as possible. " The estimated cost was "upwards of £500".

Laying the Foundation Stones in 1890 were two ladies, both the wives of benefactors to the Adult School. On April 25th 1891 Mrs. W. S. Clark of Street, officially opened the new Adult School and was "most pleasantly surprised by the spaciousness and by its lightness, cleanliness and purity." She thought one might imagine the town of Highbridge raised to a very much higher level, both morally and intellectually, and in every possible way." Almost prophetically she went on to state "what they wanted in their towns and villages was good reading rooms

The school was active until the 1930's. The committee arranged weekly classes and Sunday services. Other meetings were held, the political ones and a keep-fit class for men being amongst the noisiest! During the Second World War concerts were held, one memorable evening two German prisoners of war gave brilliant piano recitals, being escorted to and from the blacked-out building by armed guards.

The Adult School in 1913.

The building has had many uses during its life, an extra classroom for St John's School, a Library and during World War II a 'Rest Centre' for families and for service men following their return from action.

After the war St John's school used the hall as an extra classroom. By the end of the 1960's the building was in a rather neglected state being used only for the occasional function. In 1967 the County Library service took it over, the library, later re-decorated and re-carpeted did prove to be a well-used and popular facility for a time retaining the loyalty of its readers, even when the large library was opened in Burnham in 1985.

However, this did not last as the opening times of the library became less and less, eventually finishing up as one morning, one afternoon plus one day per week. Consequently people never knew when it was open, the library was then transferred to Alpha House, Market Street. After this occurred the Adult School stood empty for some time, later was re-furbished and became a private residence.

Sources of information: Bridgwater Mercury 26.11.1890. 11.3.1890. 29.4.1891. Conveyance Deeds 6.10.1891 Mr. & Mrs. C. Herniman, kindly gave information about later use.

Highbridge Adult School Centenary

The centenary week of the Adult School Building in Church Street, Highbridge had a flying start on Monday. Flags were flown from what is now the Highbridge Library and the first event of the week was acclaimed a resounding success.

The Lecture Theatre at King Alfred's School, Highbridge, was filled to capacity when Mr. Peter Wilson of Southend Gardens—- ably assisted by his wife Angela—-enthralled his audience with slides and tales of Highbridge during the past 100 years. On the screen Highbridge was once more the busy port and market town with the largest cheese factor in the world. In those days, apart from the odd horse and cart, the only transport was boat and train—-and what a difference there was then in Market Street and Church Street, with no snarl-up of traffic.

The Town Clock was much in evidence on the slides and it was noticeable that with the passing of time many alterations had been made to the clock tower itself, as well as to parts of Highbridge.

Teaching in the 1930's

Mr. Daniel Chant bases the following on letters to his fiancée Miss Elsie Scammell, during their courtship. He came from Stoke- sub- Hamdon had trained as a teacher at Winchester College; in the First World War he was an ambulance driver working in Sarajevo. His fiancée, Miss Elsie Scammell was a farmer's daughter, from Martock.

On returning to civilian life Mr. Chant applied for a teaching appointment at St. Johns School, Highbridge and his letters to Miss Scammell, which have been saved over the years, gave a picture of how things were in the 1930's. His interview was with the Headmaster. Mr. Burke, who was very sympathetic and said he would do all he could to help.

The members of staff, at that time were a Mr. Samuels, Miss Round, and Miss Knight (There were no married women teachers until W.W.II). Mr. Chant lodged with a Mr. & Mrs. Hardacre who lived at Highbridge Common Farm. Sometimes there were opportunities in the evening, for walks in the surrounding countryside; also jaunts with Mr. Hardacre in his car. This must have been a pleasant change from the ill-ventilated classroom at St Johns School.

Mr Chants' typical day in his school timetable: -

February 5th 1930 - At 6.55 a.m. the hooter of the Highbridge Bacon Factory, which is close by sounds; at 7 00 a.m. it sounds again and promptly a knock on the door produces Mrs Hardacre with hot water and a cup of tea. At 8 a.m. breakfast and then I set off for school. Having got the children inside, there follows a fifteen minute service, taken by Mr Burke, the Headmaster, then scripture and prayer book study until 9.45 a.m. which we have to take ourselves.

We leave at 12.10p.m.for lunch, and then school restarts at 1.45pm. Finished at 4.00 p.m.

They are very poor children, poor physique and low intelligence; they are almost like Victorian children, which I would not have thought possible today.

It was almost a year before Mr. Chant was recognised by the Board of Education and put on a more solid footing. Work was becoming much harder, Mr. Chant writes: -

"Mr Samuels and I are at our wits end to get in, all that has been pushed on us. There is a Church fete and as it has no supporters here, it seems to be left to the teachers to carry the fete on their backs. I shall be responsible for the gate, the skittles and the dance in the evening. Altogether, I shall be working from 2.00 p.m. until 2.00 a.m. Then we have the Sports coming along, the swimming to be organised, and the garden, not to mention the usual schoolwork. The Vicar came to me one day with his hands working convulsively and said that he had been asked by the County Authorities to discover whether, in the case of our school being turned into a senior school, I would be able to teach sciences. I told him that at my certificate exam, I had taken a distinction in science, whereat he seemed rather relieved."

In October 1930;a Mr. Snelgrove, who had offices in Weston-super-Mare, interviewed him and offered him a teaching post in Frome, Somerset. The Headmaster of the school was a Mr. Jordan who had been at Winchester College at the same time and welcomed the prospect of working with someone he knew. By the end of December 1930, Mr. Chant had concluded his Highbridge experience and was looking forward to living and teaching in Frome at the National School in Bath Street.

(Account supplied by Diana Crossman, daughter of Mr Chant)

HIGHBRIDGE PRE-SCHOOL PLAYGROUP

Cherry Daldry founded Highbridge pre-school in 1968, in the Methodist Chapel in Church Street Highbridge with helpers Jasmine Welch and Elaine Scadden it was subsequently taken over by Elaine in 1970, Barbara Derham had joined as an assistant. In 1975 Jasmine left to be replaced by Gill Foster, and in 1977 Barbara bought the business from Elaine, which by now was occupying the old Hauser hut at St. Johns School.

The Pre- School provided education to children from ages 3 to 5 years at a time when the education authority did not cater for this age group. This basic education comprised, learning the school disciplines of coming to class each day, leaving mum, learning how to play and to interact with other children. Barbara always had a good working relationship with the heads of St. Johns and Beechfields schools, and they were always pleased to receive children from the group. With the Hauser hut in the school grounds and siblings in the adjoining schools it provided a smooth progression for the next step up.

Barbara Derham is centre back, holding the child

On many occasions the groups' activities went way beyond the call of duty. For example in latter years there were several occasions when some 3 year olds and their parents arrived unable to speak a word of English. However, Barbara and her trusty band of assistants rallied round and within a year it was not unusual for the child to be interpreting for the parents. Barbara was a good team leader and natural mother; all the children loved her as she helped them take their first steps along the road to life in the big world outside of their homes. The playgroup was of course, very much a team effort and all credit must be given to the band of loyal hard working assistants, without whom the group could not have functioned. There was mother and daughter Margie (Nannie) Fielding and Gill Foster, Rose Marsh, Sharon James, Sylvia Dyer, Helen Stephens and Jane Morris, plus many others who came and went over the years.

Of course all work and no play makes `Jack a dull boy` and many annual events took place during the school year. In the spring there were trips to the Apex Park to plant bulbs, at Easter painting eggs and making hats. In the summer, outings to Red Road Farm, picnics on the beach, visits to Bristol Zoo during playgroup week, and an end of term sports day and party. Then in the autumn, collecting leaves and making collages. Christmas, of course was the `big one` with a visits from Father Christmas and Jean `Auntie Teapot` Whitehouse, a keen supporter of the playgroup. It all didn't happen just like that of course, many hours were spent at home planning all the activities. However, as is the case with all things these days, bureaucracy began to take its toll. Increasing mountains of paperwork and the cost of meeting new standards began to tell on the viability of the group. Furthermore with grants becoming available from Government, politics began to rear its ugly head, the schools naturally wanted to take over the running of pre-school groups. Barbara with loyal support from the faithful few fought and won a temporary reprieve to stay open for a couple more years. Eventually fighting `The System` became too much, so she decided to retire after 21 years and a thousand children. Barbara missed the children terribly but still enjoyed meeting them and their mothers around the town, watching them grow up. One of her greatest joys was seeing children she had taught returning years later to the group with their own children. After Barb `retired in 1998 the Highbridge pre-school playgroup merged with the Humpty Dumpty group and ran on for two or three more years, before the Hauser hut was finally demolished and pre school activities for three to five year olds passed on to the State system.

Barbara had intended to write an article about the Play Group but tragically died suddenly, only five years later in 2003, aged 61 years.

(Article and photo supplied by Barbara's husband Peter.)

St John's: Highbridge Out-of-School Club

An out-of-school club is flying high based at St John's V.C.School the club opened in September 2000, and 82 children aged 5 to 11 from St John's School and near-by Beechfield Infant School attend. They enjoy a variety of activities including football, tennis, arts and crafts, I.T., cycling proficiency classes and much more.

**Supervisors Sharon James and Sharon Mason
with some of the youngsters they take care of at the Club.**

Chapter 3

RELIGION

BAPTIST CHURCH

"Organised" religion as such came to Highbridge a little late. Until the early 1800's meetings were held in the homes of the people who felt religion had a place in the lives of the inhabitants of the town.

In 1817 however, the local Baptists, who used to gather in the homes of their members, decided that the time had come to find proper premises. The congregations had increased too, in numbers that made the gathering in people's homes impractical. 1819 saw the building of a Baptist Church, paid for as a result of subscriptions; it opened for divine worship on 19th April and became the first church in Highbridge and remained as such for nearly 40 years. Pastors were elected over the years, coming to Highbridge from local parishes like Minehead or Weston-super-Mare, with some coming from as far afield as Portsmouth or Saltash. Some were short pastorates, a year, with the average time being three to five years, although the Reverend Jesse Roberts from Creswell, Pembrokeshire stayed for twenty six years.

Prior to this time it was necessary for those wishing to attend formal church services to travel some distance to West Huntspill, Burnham or Mark. The new church was primitive in construction, the floor being in its natural state. The building was heated by a stove, set in the centre of the building and candles or lanterns provided light. Water for baptisms came from the village pump, which was the only water supply at the time. A Mr. Elliot became pastor of the congregation and on 18th May 1826 a church was formed; it had no constitution of its own with possibly Bridgwater providing the "parent" church.

In 1867, it was decided to rebuild the church due to the growth in worshipers and during the next two years, the Hope Baptist Church was rebuilt on its present site, it was opened on March 16th 1869. The first Baptismal Service to be held in the new church was on June 8th 1873 it was recorded that "The Audience were orderly and the service solemn" During 1885 it was becoming increasingly difficult to accommodate the congregation, so in November a gallery was erected to increase capacity. Further alterations took place in 1893 with a new schoolroom being opened. Following the departure of the Rev. Lemon from the church in 1894, he together with some twenty members of the church founded the Baptist Congregational Church that opened in 1895. The building can still be seem on the Huntspill Road next to the old West of England Creamery site. Records in 1903 revealed the congregation growing with a total membership of 104 and a Sunday school with 154 scholars. In 1914-16 with the outbreak of the First World War many young men associated with churches in Highbridge were called to active military service.

A house (the Manse) was purchased for the pastor in Church Street in 1918. In 1919 on 9th October a covenant was signed and Baptist Union became the appointed trustees of the church.

With the closure of the railway works in 1930 the congregation was depleted when families left the Highbridge area to seek work elsewhere.

Due to the National emergency in 1943, the church together with houses and the cemetery lost its metal railings, the church replaced these railing with a wall and wooden gates.

1946 saw the enrolment of the Boys Brigade Company, however, the Company was unfortunately

disbanded after several years due to a lack of officers. Its sister organisation the Girls Brigade which commenced about the same time continued to flourish.

A Church magazine "The Messenger" was published in 1963 to be issued monthly with a hope of increasing circulation. It was reluctantly agreed to close the Girls Brigade in 1969 after 23 years, through lack of leadership.

A new Manse in Highbridge was purchased for the Pastor in 1988. In 1991 four plots if land (Albert Cottages) adjoining the hall were purchased and now form part of the Church garden. The 175th anniversary of the Church was celebrated in 1992 with an evening of praise in music and song.

Alterations and refurbishment to the Church and hall were undertaken between 1995 and 1997 which led to the building you see now in 2004.

(Information and photo supplied by Angela Wilson)

THE PARISH CHURCH OF
ST JOHN THE EVANGELIST, HIGHBRIDGE

In 1855 it was thought that Highbridge would become a commercial centre for Mid-Somerset, and for the staple trade of the district that it must develop in importance and population. Highbridge had no church and was too far from Burnham to admit of the mother church being available, or, (looking to the future), supplying adequate accommodation for residents of Highbridge. Reasons such as these induced Mary Ann Ruscombe Poole to offer to build a church and parsonage here, for a new Ecclesiastical District, soon to become a separate parish.

The Foundress laid the foundation stone on October 29th 1856; the Bishop of the Diocese (Lord Auckland) performed the religious ceremony; a large body of clergy and laity were present; and subsequently a public luncheon was held at the "Railway Hotel".

St John Church

The work must have gone forward somewhat slowly, for it was not completed till late in the year of 1858. The Church of St John the Evangelist together with the parsonage was completed at a cost of £4,840.

It was of stone in the early English style consisting of a tower with tiles octagonal spire, containing five bells; the pulpit (now removed) and the font were of Bath stone. The choir stalls, now removed were of carved oak and the church held approximately 450 people. Miss Poole had by now married Mr Henry Acland Fownes Luttrell, who became a willing co-operator in her good works. Mrs Luttrell's gift to Highbridge was completed only with the building of the parsonage, which went on simultaneously with the completion of the church and was ready for occupation in November 1859.

The first incumbent, the Reverend J.H. Macaulay was appointed and remained in office until 1871. The Day of Consecration – June 20th 1859 – had long been awaited, and in a hearty simple way was much welcomed in Highbridge. Very shortly after the Consecration of the Church an "Order in Council" was published, legally defining the Boundaries of the new Ecclesiastical District. Unfortunately the southern boundary was still kept to the old bed of the River Brue and is so to this day although this is now dry land. The "island" containing Clyce Road and the building beyond "Canal House" are in the neighbouring parish of Huntspill. This now causes some confusion, as the parish extends to Alstone Road.

Church workers did not exist in those days and although it was ready for worship on the 21st June this beautiful little church did not have any churchwardens, bellringers, verger, organist or choir. Friends of the Foundress supplied him with an organist and singers for "The First Sunday". After two years (i.e. 1861) Reverend Macauley's wife arrived to share the Parsonage with him and became organist and choirmaster. A creditable band of singers, men and boys had been assembled and became the choir; they were soon put into surplices and were promoted to the Choral song on High Festivals and sometimes to an Anthem.

Mission Services for part of the parish more remote from the Parish Church - at Watchfield - he established a kind of Mission Service at one of the farmhouses. Nearer the church, the same kind of thing was done in New Town, then growing rapidly in population. School Work, there was no Day School and therefore no room in which to hold a Sunday School that is until 1863. Education then made rapid strides but there were not many parishioners in Highbridge who would have learned to read and write, had there not been fifty years earlier, a "village school" where, painstaking and useful work had not been done by the first Mistress, Miss Charlotte Coombes. Social Work comprised Social Gatherings in the schoolroom almost weekly during the winter, they called them penny readings, and there were musical pieces, songs, recitals and readings. They drew an audience that filled the room and afforded an opportunity for cheerful re-union of parishioners.

The parish was beginning to grow and new houses cropped up around us, so that the church was found to be inconveniently small. Visitors too, from Burnham, used to come over early and our own parishioners frequently could not find room, consequently, on Sunday evenings we closed the church doors up to a quarter of an hour before the service." It was therefore proposed that the church should be enlarged, by the addition of another aisle, which meant the completing of the original plan. The proposal was readily taken up at a public meeting in 1882, and before the meeting broke up, over £350 was promised. The aisle was built, paid for and opened before the following Easter, at a cost of rather over £1000, which was raised in quite small sums, £20 being the largest donation and there were very few people in Highbridge who did not give something. No sooner had this been finished than the parish had to face the problem of enlarging the school.

The death of the foundress Mrs Mary Ann Ruscombe Fownes-Lutterell was recorded on 8th March 1908.

The Renovation of the Church

(Extracts from the Parish Magazine of February 1904)

The front pew on either side of the nave needs to be bodily removed. This would have the advantage of opening up and giving greater dignity to the chancel, and of removing the choked up appearance, which it now presents. Our present font is unworthy of its high purpose and in such a position that the priest cannot administer Holy Baptism in the proper place. A fund was therefore started to make for these various improvements but they were about to have a great disappointment and a far more serious problem to face than the inconvenience of a small and unworthy sanctuary.

The Church with its steeple in 1905— it was removed a few years later

Ominous cracks began to appear in the fabric and it was soon apparent that the steeple was leaning outwards and the whole structure sinking and being dragged with it. The steeple had to be removed in 1911, but work was done to the fabric in that year and on later occasions, which made it a perfectly safe structure.

The Rev'd C.J. Heughan became incumbent in 1919 and remained until 1952.

The Rev'd Harold Saxby who had moved to Highbridge in 1953, left to go to Jarrow in 1960. During this period in years 1955 –59 renovations were made to the church.

The Rev'd Harold Saxby was succeeded by the Rev'd Herbert John Sutters who moved into the Vicarage on 24th July 1961. In 1973 the Rev'd John Sutters exchanged livings with the Rev'd Norman Wells who was licensed and inducted on the 7th June 1973. During his tenure of approximately eleven years, a period of which he was the Rural Dean, the Vicarage was considered to be too large and costly to heat, and it became a Diocesan policy to replace such buildings. In 1984 some months before the Rev'd Wells retired, the new Vicarage was completed (built in the grounds of the old Vicarage) and he moved into this residence.

The Rev'd Christopher Gerald Chiplin followed Norman Wells and moved into the new Vicarage in 1984, with his wife Diane. In his first year the Quinquennial Inspection of the Church was held and revealed some considerable wear and tear. This led to the Church being re-ordered and it was closed for services following evensong on the Feast of Epiphany, January 1987 until Palm Sunday of that year. Services were held in the Church Hall, whilst the work was carried out. Fortunately the Church was the beneficiary of the will of Mrs. Agnes Knapp and this bequest funded the Re-ordering. To commemorate this, a Statue was commissioned and Mr. Tom Preator of Taunton carved a figure of the Virgin Mary holding Jesus as a toddler, in lime wood, it stands in position in the South Aisle. Also new Stations of the Cross were installed.

During his time as Vicar of Highbridge the Rev'd Chiplin served a period as Chairman of Churches Together and helped to form a committee from which "Riverbed House", a house for the homeless was built in Highbridge. Rev'd Chiplin left Highbridge in June 1994 to be Vicar of Midsomer Norton near Bath, and on the 3rd February 1995 the Rev'd Mark Francis Wilson Bond was licensed and inducted. Mark Bond was known for his work in the Community, he was a very popular man in this respect. He represented the town as a councillor on Burnham-on-Sea and Highbridge Town Council. Also he served a period as Chairman of Churches Together, when the Credit Union was first muted, this is now working satisfactorily at the Hope Baptist Church. During Rev'd Mark Bond's ministry in Highbridge a "Frank Foley Day" was instigated and the Inaugural service was held in St John's Church, attended by Michael Smith the author of 'Foley-The Spy who Saved 10,000 Jews" and members of the Jewish community who were involved.

(Photo supplied by Collin Moore)

The Church in the winter of 2000

In 1998 Rev'd Mark Bond was asked to train a curate and Steven John Harptree *joined* the ministerial team and was subsequently ordained Deacon and the Priest. This period was a very rewarding time for the Church. In July, 2002 Mark was appointed Rector of St. Brelades, Channel Isles and the Church was again in an interregnum. During this time Steven Harptree worked hard in keeping the Church together and as a non-stipendiary priest for a twelve-month period until July 2003 he remained until 27th August 2003 when he was licensed to be Priest –in-Charge of Tintinhull with Chilthorne Domer, Yeovil Marsh and Thorne Coffin. On July 11th 2003 the Rev'd Robin Lodge was licensed and inducted.

This history of the church contains excerpts from the Centenary booklet 1859—1959 and excerpts provided by. Joyce Dunbavan covering the time from 1959 until 2003.

METHODIST CHURCH

The Methodist Church or Wesleyan Chapel in Highbridge was originally opened for services in 1865 owing its origins to two men. Thomas Hicks, a gentleman, and John Buskin a saddler, were named in the church deeds. Both men lived in Highbridge, Thomas Hicks, of about seventy years of age and worshipped in Burnham; John Buskin, who was about forty-five years old worshipped, with his wife Ann, at West Huntspill. John was the Sunday school attendant and continued in this position until Highbridge opened its Sunday school.

Although Highbridge and Burnham are but a few miles apart, they were grouped by the Methodist Church as being in different circuits; Highbridge is in the Bridgwater circuit and Plymouth District. But Burnham is in the Weston-super-Mare circuit and Bristol District. Thomas Hicks therefore approached the Bridgwater circuit with his offer of land on which to build a chapel and received a favourable response, the chapel becoming the second largest in the circuit.

(Photo supplied by Collin Moore)
The Methodist Church, Church Street, now comprises a number of flats

In 1864, on the 23rd April, Mr. Hicks conveyanced the plot on land on which the church and schoolroom stood, to the trustees for the sum of £80. Immediately after the conveyance the land was cleared and a meeting held to consider the cost of building the church, £600 was immediately made available. A diary entry of Robert Daunton states "Highbridge July 11th 1864 Thomas Hicks Esq. Laid the foundation stone of the Wesleyan Chapel, before a crowd of nearly 600 persons and a tea party was held in the Market House to mark the occasion. Mr F.J.Payne records that it was pouring with rain and this gave the caterers an anxious time finding sufficient food. Mr G Wilton of Bridgwater had brought 100 men from his brickyard as guests. The superintendent was a Rev J Aldis and the Rev Punshon preached in a large tent erected for the occasion. It was soon apparent that the plot of land was not large enough for the chapel, there was a road on one side of the site and Mr Hicks had sold to Mr Buskin the plot of land on the other side. Mr Buskin came to the rescue by selling to the trustees the required plot of land. The chapel was eventually opened on 25th May 1865 the preacher being the Rev Marmaduke Osborne. There is no record of any other events that day.

The first baptism took place a fortnight later but three years past before the first wedding since the church although registered as a place of worship on 5th May 1865 was not registered for the solemnisation of marriages until 15 January 1869. A 'new' Act in October 1964 made the presence of a registrar unnecessary. The need for Sunday school premises was soon apparent and at a quarterly meeting held on March 22nd 1870 it was recommended a schoolroom be erected at Highbridge, the cost being £140, this would leave a debt of £40. It was built at a cost of £161 and later extended as membership grew. The Society was growing quickly and in April 1887 an application was made for the Chapel to be enlarged at a cost of £298. The initial application was turned down, but the work eventually approved. When the work was completed the opening took place on a wild day the celebrations being held in June 1888 – and it snowed! Not much happened until about 1926 when the chapel was lit with the new gas lamps and it was claimed to be the best-lit church on the circuit. The building was also plastered and decorated, all for £100. Around this time the choir members started an organ fund and in 1931 it was installed, the electric blower came later. The earliest attempt to obtain an organ had been in 1877 again in 1897. Electric light replaced the gas in 1942.

Major changes in 1948/49 were the first for 60 years, the church roof was retiled, the organ cleaned and moved to the centre of the church. Both school and church were redecorated and a new boiler was fitted. The Church progressed over the years and its work was celebrated in 1965 with the Centenary of the Church. A project was laid down to provide more accommodation for youth work and provision for the Sunday school. Much work was carried out to the building and for the comfort of the congregation; a new electronic organ was also installed. The Centenary celebrations began on 9th October 1965 with a visit from the MAYC President and he led the services on the Saturday and Sunday. The main celebrations began at a service led by Rev. Michael S.R. Meech a former Minister and the Rev. J. Russell Pope, Chairman of the Plymouth and Exeter District. Celebrations continued until the 14th November when the Rev Frederic O. Le Sueur the Minister in Charge led the service. Whilst a new pulpit, reed organ and suspended ceiling plus carpets were installed in 1966 services were held at the Hope Baptist Church nearby.

Sadly the Methodist cause in Highbridge declined over the following years until it was not practicable to maintain the premises and a decision was made in 1987 to close. Chris Esgate, the pastoral assistant took the last service; it included Holy Communion.

The building was put up for public auction on Wednesday 1st June 1988 at the Highbridge Hotel and the site sold to Somervale Builders, Wedmore and converted in to six flats.

Mission Hall

The origins of the Mission Hall in Newtown Road are not known, it was possibly built as a Seaman's Mission- (date unknown); it did later become the Plymouth Brethren Gospel Hall and was in use in 1933 but was apparently closed by 1952. It did re-open again at a later date because by 1970 it was back in use; this was when the Reverend Thomas Black and his wife Verna arrived in Highbridge from America.

A Mr. Loach of Weston-super-Mare had run the hall, however, because of ill health he wished to retire. This gave the Reverend Black the opportunity to use the hall. In 1973 the South and West Evangelical Trust gave the Reverend Black the use of the building and over the next few years a lot of work was done on the building including roof repairs and the laying of a new floor. An attempt was made to purchase the land at the rear so that they could build toilets, but they were not successful. The hall had been renamed the Gospel Tabernacle Evangelical Church. During this time the Reverend and Mrs Black were holding meetings for children and, over the three years to 1976 this had grown to five meetings a week, some 60-80 children attending and by now adults were also starting to attend the meetings. In 1991 the Reverend Black retired and with his wife moved back to the States together with two of their sons. A third son, Kelton Black remained in England, moving to this area from Crewkerne where he had been living. He continued with his father's work at the Gospel Tabernacle in Newtown Road.

It was obviously going to be impossible to improve the facilities at the Gospel Tabernacle in spite of all their efforts. However, a new opportunity was about to come their way, this time to a more modern building that already had many of the facilities they needed. During the mid 1990's the Salvation Army Citadel in the old Burnham Road came on the market, being purchased by a builder. No development took place and at a later date the Citadel was again put up for sale and was purchased by the South and West Evangelical Trust. The Trust then gave Mr Kelton Black the opportunity he was praying for, a 'new' Gospel Tabernacle Evangelical Church. Kelton Black, with his followers moved into the Citadel, their first service was held on Easter Sunday in 1998. Since 1999 this building has been renovated, it now has new windows, toilets and a modern kitchen. It is used regularly for services; on Wednesdays coffee and lunches are served to local people. Various Community groups also have the use of the;

(Information supplied by Kelton Black)

Gospel Tabernacle Evangelical Hall

The 'old' Mission Hall in Newtown Road is now a forgotten building, except for its neighbours, who have to look at a building that is falling into disrepair. The porch is now (2004) covered with brambles and weeds, it is apparent that this old place of worship will eventually be demolished.

THE SALVATION ARMY

In 1883 on a Saturday evening the Salvation Army 'opened fire' in Highbridge and Burnham. Their first meeting in the Puzzle Gardens went off fairly quietly. People going to their places of worship on a Sunday were concerned that the Salvation Army turned out with a brass band. Not only did these strangers play loudly they also sang very lustily. They stopped at street corners, offered prayers for people of the district and held open-air services. There were rowdy scenes when they marched upon Highbridge; one Salvationist said he received a hard blow. Later in the day, they marched back to Burnham to a meeting in the Skating Rink, now the Pavilion.

Many battles have been fought for the souls of people, since those early days. However, the Army has never been very large in the district, although General Edward Higgins (the first General outside the Booth family) came from Highbridge and his leadership of a World Wide Organisation is something to be proud of.

In 1977 the Citadel that had been built in Old Burnham Road, Highbridge held two services every Sunday, also Sunday school under the leadership of Major Iris Mitchin, with the ladies meeting on Wednesdays at 3p.m. The Secretary was Miss Minnie Vowles. In June there was a change of leadership in Highbridge, Envoy & Mrs Tring took over from Brigadier and Mrs. H. Foster who had recently retired. The congregation numbers diminished and services were discontinued on the 1st Sunday in July1996, when Capt. Mike Loveridge took the last service.

The Salvation Army Citadel, which had previously been the scene of many rousing meetings and had in January 1937, welcomed General Edward Higgins, the local man who had attained the highest position in the Salvation Army, is no longer the meeting place where Salvationists could worship.

(Photo supplied by Collin Moore)

**Now the Evangelical Trust Gospel Hall, this building was originally
a Citadel of the Salvation Army, opened by General Higgins in 1937**

General Edward John Higgins

In the mid 19th century Edward and Martha Higgins lived at No 10 Church Street, Martha was the daughter of George Deacon, a Highbridge man. Edward was from a family of ardent Methodists and had a not too successful Saddlers business; villagers said that at one time he had rebelled and 'He had run rather wild'. On Saturday November 1864 Martha gave birth to her third child, a son; he was named Edward after his father and John after his uncle John Ruskin, the founder and prominent member of the local Wesleyan chapel in Huntspill Road.

In 1872, following the death of his mother, young Edward went to live with his maternal grandfather, whilst his father Edward senior, devastated by the loss of his Martha and his unsuccessful business, moved to Bridgwater. Young Edward was educated at a private school in Burnham and then Dr Morgan's Grammar School in Bridgwater where he was a boarder. Before he was fifteen year old he passed the Oxford local examination with honours, left school and started working for Nathaniel Harding, a Highbridge provision merchant.

In March1864; eight months before young Edward was born, a man named William Booth founded an organisation known as the *Christian Mission* later to become the **Salvation Army.**

Edward senior, who had chosen to become a Salvationist, arrived in London in January 1882 to take up his first appointment with the Salvation Army and over the years rose to the rank of Commissioner. William Booth visited Bristol from Sunday 4th to Tuesday 6th June using the Colston Hall Where a crowd of 2000 struggled unsuccessfully to enter what was an already overcrowded building. Young Edward was alarmed to see people fighting to get into church. He moved to Reading joined the Corp and on September 9th still only 18 years old entered the training home at Clapton; he rose through the ranks serving in a variety of places in the north of England. He had a nervous breakdown before he was 21.

In Wales a young lady of 14 years named Catherine Price was becoming interested in the Salvation Army and by the time she was 17 had entered the training home. She eventually became a Captain at Teddington, London; where the Divisional Officer was Staff-Captain Edward Higgins. They exchanged letters at the start of a courtship and Headquarters officially approved their engagement. Some advised her to wait for at least 14 months, as Edward was a delicate man and she could be widowed within a year; they were working apart, Edward at Oxford and she was at Winchester. On Easter Monday on 2nd April 1888 they were married. On 18th April 1896 Edward sailed to New York being alone for 6 months, later his family joined him, Catherine arriving with their children, the fourth of which had been born only seven weeks earlier.

William Booth the founder died in1912 and the constitution of the Salvation Army stated that a retiring General would appoint his successor, Bramwell Booth was to become the second General and he appointed Edward Higgins as his Chief of Staff. The General's sister, Evangeline booth, informed him that the Constitution of the Army should be changed so that all succeeding Generals should be elected. He was clearly not happy about such a change of policy; in May 1928 he had a serious breakdown. On February 13th 1929, the High Council of the Salvation Army adjudicated that Bramwell Booth was unfit for his office due to reasons of health. They then proceeded to elect a new General and it soon became evident that the choice lay between Evangeline Booth and Edward John Higgins, this Highbridge boy, who had, some forty years earlier been given just a few months to live. The result of the poll was to reveal that Edward had made it to the top; he was to be the Salvation Army's third General and the very first to be elected; he won by 42 votes to 17.

On Sunday 16th June 1929 General Bramwell Booth died; it was Edward's intention to retire when he was 65, but as he neared his 65th birthday, decided to give it 5 more years. He travelled extensively both at home and overseas improving much of the organisation of the Salvation Army. On the 1st November 1934 with some health problems, he resigned his position; the day of his retirement was marked by a farewell meeting at the Royal Albert Hall to which General and Mrs Higgins had been invited. Ambassadors and Ministers of 23 countries plus dignitaries and leaders of almost every denomination attended; the Duke of York, later to become King George VI, and the Duchess of York supported the meeting.In January 1937 Highbridge extended a warm welcome to General Higgins when he visited the town of his birth to open the new Salvation Army Citadel.

Edward John Higgins formerly of 10 Church Street, Highbridge.aged 83, died in the 14th December 1947. He was laid to rest in the Salvation Army plot at Kemisco Cemetery. New York.

Mrs Phyllis Walsh, resident of the Clyce, has written a book entitled "The Three Local Pioneers".
This covers the lives of General Edward Higgins, Major Frank Foley and Richard Lock

Chapter 4

INDUSTRY

THE SOMERSET & DORSET RAILWAY

SLOW AND DIRTY - SWIFT AND DELIGHTFUL

Highbridge came into being in the form we recognise today following a suggestion put forward at a meeting at Glastonbury on 16th September 1850 where it was proposed a railway line, about thirty miles in length, be laid to connect Bruton, Wells, Glastonbury and Highbridge. Preliminary surveys followed and the Somerset Central Railway was formed at a meeting at Hodge's Railway Hotel Bridgwater on 1st December 1851. Highbridge was chosen as the terminal point of the railway as it offered an entirely level route to Glastonbury, along the River Brue valley. Bridgwater with a population of some 11,000 was a more important town but this would have meant crossing the Poldens Hills. The population of Highbridge and Burnham combined was about 1,700 in 1851.

An Act of Parliament incorporated the Somerset Central Railway on 17th June 1852 to run from Highbridge Wharf on the River Brue to Glastonbury. On the 16th August 1852 work started on the 12 miles from Glastonbury to Highbridge line; the total cost including stations, surveying and Parliamentary expenses worked out at £6,560 per mile. Proving to be one of the cheapest lines. The railway pioneers laid the first bit of permanent way and its construction was completed in two years. There were bridges, tunnels or cuttings involved, but the peaty soil presented engineering problems when crossing the boggy moors. The problem was overcome by using a great quantity of bundles of sticks and twigs bound together these are called faggots, which were tipped into the bog until its appetite was sated and a firm foundation established for the new "iron" road. The railway was opened for regular traffic on the 28th August 1854 and the official link up with the Bristol & Exeter Railway was in December 1854. On the 1st September 1862 the Somerset Central Railway and the Dorset Central Railway amalgamated and became the Somerset & Dorset Joint Railway.

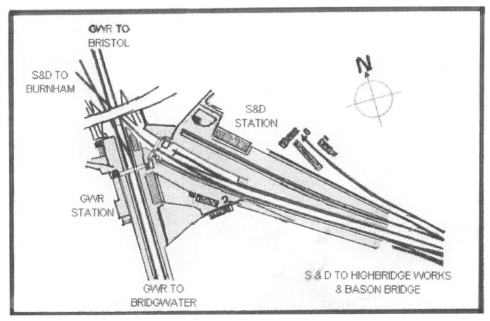

The layout of Highbridge Station in the mid 1920's

It was local interest in Glastonbury including the leather and shoe partners Cyrus Clark of Street, and his son James that the benefits of a railway to link their town with the Bristol & Exeter Railway was originally promoted and this obviously included the Somerset Central Railway.

The promoters of the S.C.R. had also had a grand vision, which was to link the north and south coasts by rail to a sea – train – sea route from Wales to France. It was gradually extended eastwards and in 1862 the Somerset Central Railway had amalgamated with the Dorset Central Railway that had started from Blandford in 1854; the two lines met at Bruton and thus the Somerset and Dorset was linked.

The opening of the Templecombe to Blandford line took place on the 31st August 1863, this enable the S & D J. R. to operate a service from the Bristol Channel to the English Channel. Between Burnhamand Poole (Dorset) there were four trains a day, the Highbridge to Poole journey took three hours fifteen minutes. Their original idea was to ferry passengers from South Wales to Burnham, then a rail connection via Highbridge, to the south coast where a service was intended to cross the English Channel to France. The half-day excursion ticket to Poole and Bournemouth in 1933 was 4/6d (23 p) unfortunately the original planning for the South Wales to Burnham and on to the South Coast had not been anticipated the building of the Severn Tunnel, or the coming of the motor car. The rail link with the South Coast although completed, was too late, because the coal and other products from South Wales were soon transported through the tunnel. Thus the coast link was only serving a thinly populated area and soon got into financial difficulties. A ferry service from Poole to Cherbourg did operate for a while, from about April 1856 to early 1857 it was then suspended due to its running at a loss.

S & D J R Locomotive Works 1910   *(S & D JR TRUST)*

Highbridge Station then had five platforms, a booking office, waiting room and toilets, also for a while, around 1910, a W.H. Smith bookstall. The single branch line from Highbridge to Burnham was opened on the 3rd May 1858; this ran along the course of the present Marine Drive, past Apex Park (the site of the Apex Brick & Tile Co.) passing the Highbridge Wharf. To avoid accidents/collisions when two trains needed to be on the same section e.g. a train at Burnham and a train at the wharf or brickwork's, a staff and tablet system was used.

The S. & D. J.R. Station at Highbridge in 1910

A view of the above station site as seen in early 2004

A familiar sight for local people was of the trains crossing Church Street, quite often carrying holidaymakers or day-trippers to or from Burnham-on-Sea.

The passing of freight trains to and from the Wharf was another regular occurrence.

The level crossing was, however, removed on 21st June 1968.

The first train entering the system was given the 'tablet' and was shown the 'staff', which was then given to the second train; thus both were aware of each other. The line continued alongside Newtown Road (now a cul-de-sac) to cross the A38 between Newtown Road and the neighbouring pub, where gates controlled the flow of road traffic. Pedestrians were able to cross the line by way of a footbridge. Signal Box 'C' controlled the crossing and lines to Burnham, the wharf and brickwork's.

The line then ran in a curve through a Goods Yard (now part of Bank Street Car Park) to cross the Bristol & Exeter Railway on the level and at an acute angle right underneath the iron bridge carrying the Wells Road (B3139).

To the east of the Highbridge Station on a piece of land bounded to the north by the line and to the south by the River Brue, the Railway Company had, around 1862 constructed a locomotive, carriage and wagon works comprehensively equipped to maintain its rolling stock. New railway engines were not built there but were maintained at the workshops where they would be re-built and have new boilers fitted. Wensley's of Mark and Day's of Mark Causeway carried out all foundry work. Heavy locomotive repairs were carried out at Bristol and ordinary repairs at Derby. Carriage and wagon repairs were undertaken at Highbridge, being a major part of the Somerset & Dorset Joint Railway network.

It was re-organised in the 1890's and from then until 1911 was the heyday of the works, all traffic in and out had to be moved by rail because of a complete lack of road access. Staff employed during the last quarter of the nineteenth century varied between 344 and 485, many completed less than a year's service but others stayed for forty one to fifty years, with twenty five achieving over fifty years with the Company. Changing circumstances led to a gradual decline after 1911, though the works remained in operation for a further two decades.

At the start of the First World War in 1914, a large number of railway employees joined the armed forces, almost one hundred and fifty of those employed in the locomotive and wagon works went off to fight. On March 8th 1922 a memorial was erected at the works in remembrance of those killed in conflict, it had been designed by a railway apprentice, made in the workshops at Highbridge, staff in the locomotive, carriage and wagon departments had subscribed for the memorial. It was then moved, firstly to the end of the station platform, near the booking office and later re-sited in 1965 in Southwell Gardens.

The locomotive works officially closed on the 31st December 1929 as the economic depression hit, 300 men were made redundant, and this was a major blow for the town as the population was approximately 2000. Jobs in hand gave further employment to the works until March 1930.

Passenger and freight traffic continued to operate as far as Evercreech Junction where connections were made to the remainder of the network. Subsequently the London Midland & Scottish (L.M.S.) looked after the railway engines and their operations whilst the Southern Railway took over maintenance of the track and signalling infrastructure. The works buildings were stripped of equipment but remained intact but semi-derelict for many years. That is until the United States of America entered the war and part of the original railway works were used as a government store and the American Army used them extensively as a large fuel depot, supplies from here were used by their Army during the Normandy D.Day invasion. It was the U.S. Army that finally constructed the missing roads that then provided access to the buildings.

The Highbridge to Burnham line closed for regular traffic on the 29th October 1951 although a special train did run from Glastonbury to Burnham-on-Sea on the 28th August 1954. The trip was a joint venture organised by C. & J. Clark of Clark & Son descendants of James Clark one of the chief promoters of the original Somerset Central Railway and Morlands of Glastonbury the Sheepskin Firm. The twelve coach train was hauled by a Johnson 3F 0-6-0 Number 43201 formerly the Somerset & Dorset Joint Railway engine No 64 that had been built in 1896. The train was packed with enthusiasts a number being dressed in Victorian clothes to commemorate the one hundred years of the railway.

(Photo supplied by Fred Faulks)
Children enjoying the Centenary Celebrations

Part of the original locomotive works was used to maintain engines using the local line and it was also a wagon repair depot; this facility gave employment until September 1955 when the building caught fire and was totally destroyed, it was never replaced. Passenger traffic was light, but excursion trains appear to have been well supported and there was also considerable freight traffic from Highbridge Wharf.

Workers from the Wagon Repair Depot assembled after the devastating fire in 1955

Named Alphabetically:

M. Bamsey, Bill Banwell, Walt Bennett, Walt Bishop, Les Brown, Ken Clapp, Mr Clare, Mick Clare, Dick Coleson, Alec Collins, Dick Conally, Dick Connaly, Ern Cook, Ray Cook, Ken Denham, Les Diamond, Cyril Dyer, Bert Fackrell, Jack Fisher, Reg Fisher, Ken Ford, Ern Goddard, Sam Gregory, Wilf Haggett, Cliff Heal, Doug Holly, Bob Hooper, Les Jones, Bert Masterman, Wilf Pugsley, Frank Smith, Larry Storey, Archie Taylor, Harold Taylor, George Thomas, John Thorne, Jeff Thresher, Jack Ward, Bert Warren, Ted Woodward.

Regular milk traffic from the Wilts United Milk Factory at Bason Bridge was one of the Somerset & Dorset Joint Railways best customers. The factory had two connections to the main line, one where the milk tanks were loaded or emptied, the other ran the full length of the factory and was used for incoming coal, sugar and tinplate (for making the tins); outgoing loads were boxes of condensed milk. The factory had three goods trains and one milk train each day, the service commenced in 1909 and was terminated in about 1970.

Into the 1960's the volume of traffic slowly declined there was less freight and fewer passengers were carried and eventually it resulted in the break-up of the network. The last passenger train into Highbridge from Glastonbury was on the 5th March 1966; this train was packed with railway enthusiasts.

The last passenger train arriving at the S & D Station in March 1966

One small remnant to survive from the old days was the milk traffic between Highbridge and Bason Bridge for which a new connection was made from the Western Region line at Highbridge. This was finally killed off by the construction of the M5 as the cost of providing a bridge over the railway line to Bason Bridge was considered to be unjustified. Paradoxically, the construction of the M5. Provided the last traffic for this particular line because 750, 000 tons of pulverised fuel ash was used to provide a firm base for the M5 across the levels (a modern substitute for the faggots used over 100 years ago).

This train is passing under Walrow Bridge carrying the first delivery of fuel ash on its way to the construction site of the M5.

Today, the Walrow Industrial Estate and in particular the Caxton Furniture Factory covers the site of the Highbridge Locomotive Works; the S. & D.J.R. Station site, will shortly become a housing estate. Development in Market Street has destroyed the track bed through Southwell Crescent across the A38 and beyond towards Apex Park. Marine Drive approximately follows the old line to the traffic lights in Burnham, where, if you stop at the traffic lights in Pier Street you are about where the trains would halt some years ago at Burnham Station

(Photos supplied by Peter Dyer)

Final removal of the track from the original S & D J R Station in 1971

The final closure of the Somerset & Dorset Joint Railway and its involvement with Highbridge saw the end of what was once describe as the "Crewe of the West", a true example of an English Branch Line, its associated industries and its involvement with the local people.

WESTERN REGION RAILWAY

The first railway to connect with Highbridge in 1842 was the Bristol & Exeter Railway. Initially built as a broad gauge railway. Many said this would have been more efficient, and arguably would have provided more comfort for passengers but would have been more expensive. Finance prevailed and the narrower gauge system we know today was introduced in the early 1890's.

The station buildings were erected from a design that was believed to have been by Isambard Kingdom Brunel, he had had a large influence on the construction of the railway and of the station buildings. By 1902 the railway had become the G.W.R. (Great Western Railway). Little had changed in the overall shape of the station, which comprised two platforms, between its origins and its demise. The up platform had a goods office with a rear entrance for the delivering and receiving of goods, a booking office for ticket sales. There was a ladies toilet in the waiting room (this had a well-kept coal fire in the early days) a gent's toilet was at the end of the building and a porter's room at the end of the platform, near Walrow Bridge. On the down platform was a slightly smaller building with a waiting room, ladies and gents toilets and an office for the Station Masters.

(Photo supplied by Mike Lawrence)

Highbridge Station (Western Region) Approach
***Left*: Vehicle from Isleport Farm owned by Horace Lawrence**
***Right*: Horse drawn wagon from Highbridge Bacon Factory**

In its early days the platforms were wooden and a canopy covered the footbridge between platforms, in those days it was a very busy station. Apart from large numbers of passengers, large quantities of goods of all descriptions went in and out of the station, there being a pick up and delivery service available. It must be remembered the town was growing fast, a typical market centre.

Between the station approach and the River Brue, which passed under the southern end of the station, the Station Masters house was built in an area that has recently become a housing development. The Station Masters house was the last of the original buildings to disappear, surviving some years after the station was demolished. Also on the station approach in the late 1890's could be found a G.W.R. horse drawn carriage, which would provide transport between Highbridge and Burnham. An imposing signal box was set apart from the station building, and was sited opposite the entrance to the main station. This box controlled the Western line, also the crossover from the Somerset & Dorset Line, which ran behind it under Walrow Bridge and on towards Church Street.

An up-line view of the station at Highbridge

At the southern end of the up platform, near the River Brue was a siding, and on the northern side of the down line, another siding that ran from Walrow Bridge to Springfield Road footpath crossing. This at one time had a spur running into the brickwork's, which lay, on the opposite side of the tracks, at the end of Grange Avenue. The station provided the normal passenger services, special price excursions trains to the south coast seaside towns or to London.

A Poster advertising the Great Western's Trips from Highbridge to London

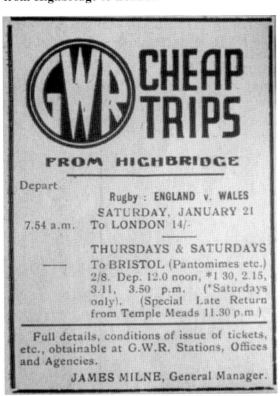

After the Second World War the character of rail travel started to change, the introduction of more car ownership meant less passengers, and more and more goods were being transported by road.

A highlight for the station and Highbridge was the arrival of Her Majesty Queen Elizabeth II on December 5th 1983 for her visit to the Maritime Radio Station in Worston Road. The station façade was transformed; the whole frontage was covered with large quantities of fabric and enhanced by ornamental trees, providing just the one entrance to the station

There had been many changes by now; the G.W.R. had been overtaken by the Nationalisation of the Railways. British Rail had taken its place, passengers and freight continued to decline, and then on one Sunday in November 1983, the 27th to be precise, the end; certainly for the station buildings came suddenly. The buildings were demolished on that Sunday morning, just a few local people knew about the demise of their station, a move which some felt, was far too hasty.

What a sad end to a station that once had life and character, a station remembered by many for all sorts of reasons, a station soon to be modernised – whatever that is!

The Highbridge station is still in operation with two platforms and a footbridge, small open fronted shelters on both platforms. It became just a halt station on the main line to and from the South West.

The Station buildings just prior to demolition in 1983

Also linked to the station at the end of the Recreation field was a goods yard with a couple of sidings alongside the main line north out of the station. Here large goods were dealt with, the yard was reached by a roadway at the bottom of Walrow Bridge in Market Street. Part of this is still visible alongside the Kwik Save Supermarket. A level crossing was needed here because the road crossed the S. & D. Line, which had itself, crossed the Western line and continued on towards Burnham, after the level crossing the goods yard opened out into a large area where any heavy goods could be received or loaded ready for despatch.

During the war, live cattle for transportation to other parts of the country were received and penned before loading; they had been driven through Market Street from the cattle market. On at least one occasion, when there was a shortage of pigs for the Bacon Factory in Huntspill Road, the problems were solved by a delivery of pigs at the goods yard from Ireland. These too were driven through Market Street over the River Brue Bridge and on to the factory.

On the north bound track a short distance from the station was a footpath crossing at the bottom of Springfield Road, and here at around 6.00 p.m. on weekday evenings, children would gather to watch the Royal Mail train 'pick up and drop' as it sped past. On the mail carriage was a net that was positioned to pick up a mail bag hung from a platform at the crossing and, from a lever positioned low down on the carriage was hung the bag for dropping into a large rope net positioned at the crossing. The 'pick and drop' would be simultaneous and over in seconds as the train roared past. Mail from this and many other 'pick up' points on the line would be sorted on route, this system was discontinued during the 1960's.

The local lads watching the Mail Train collect the Mail as it sped through Highbridge

"Roast Beef by Rail"

On a Friday night in April 1940 a train carrying the meat ration for the families of Plymouth was passing through Highbridge when smoke was seen coming from the goods van. The train driver shouted to the signal box operator as they passed his box and by the time the train pulled into Highbridge the staff were ready.

The van was uncoupled and the fire was attacked with fire extinguishers, luckily the insulating material in the van protected the contents. With the fire extinguished the van was re-coupled and the meat was on the way to Plymouth, the Sunday joints had been save

---

Also, in 1948 a Tile worker aged 37 from Grange Avenue, Highbridge. Was, at a Burnham Magistrate Court was fined 5s for trespassing on the railway line near Highbridge Station. The Detective Inspector said that when stopped the defendant said he did not realise he was committing an offence, by crossing the line he could get to working in less than 2 minutes, whereas it was 1 mile round by the road. It was a great temptation to cross by the line.

(Burnham Gazette & Highbridge Express Reports)

HIGHBRIDGE WHARF

Following the completion of the drainage plan at the end of the 18th century ideas were formulated to provide Highbridge with a wharf. Originally the land belonged to the Dean and Chapter of Wells Cathedral who were responsible for the sea wall repairs up until this time. The River Brue with landing facilities at Highbridge had provided the Abbey and town of Glastonbury with a convenient link to the sea. Trade in corn, fish and wine, was carried by ships to this point and continued on boats up the river. Highbridge had been ideally situated to make the most of its position, having a navigable river.

A wharf together with the Glastonbury Canal had opened as early as 1833. Then in 1842 the Bristol and Exeter Railway had arrived with a station at Highbridge and some twelve years later the Somerset Central Railway arrived from Glastonbury. It was in 1854 that contracts were given to J & C Rigby to construct berths to enable the unloading of goods. At the new wharf, land was purchased to permit the enlargement of the Somerset Central Railway's sidings. The wharf was taking shape and by about 1858 the area was being further developed, the old Road Bridge, from which the town got its name –"Highbridge", was at the head of the wharf. Under the three-arched bridge flowed the course of what was left of the original River Brue where there was a sea lock. The course of the river now flowed under a new road bridge and through the "new drain" at the end of which was a new Clyce, this controlled the flow of water off the levels.

In 1860 the Burnham tidal harbour was incorporated for the purpose of converting part of the River Brue into a tidal harbour. Up until now the harbour at Highbridge had come under the control of the Port of Bridgwater. According to Kelly's Directory in 1872/5/9 the timber yard and saw mill of Cuthbert Ritson were most extensive and had caused a great increase in work for the accommodation of the employees.

Throughout the early days much remedial work was carried out between the harbour and canal, the lock gates, wharf wall, etc. all required attention. Also, with the increase in harbour usage the wharf and sidings available had to be extended, plus the purchase of additional cranes.

One major problem was the silting up of the wharf area; this was the cause of prolonged correspondence with the owners of the wharf and the various users. The Somerset and Dorset Joint Railway had become responsible for the canal and wharf areas and had inherited all the problems. The increasing quantities of mud caused the Company and its 'customers' untold grief. Drainage of and the controlling of water on the levels had been the responsibility of the Commissioners of Sewers, following the Drainage Act in 1877 the Somerset Drainage Commissioners were to take over and the two (S & D.J.R. and S.D.C.) did not get on. The Act required that the wharf/harbour must be kept clear of silt, many methods were suggested and used but to no avail, the mud kept returning; in 1910 a company removed thirty truck loads of mud in one week.

It has been recorded that for some reasons unknown the New River had been cut four feet deeper than the existing River Brue. This had caused the wharf to silt up much more quickly because the flow of water passing through the wharf entrance caused eddying and thus the mud had not dispersed.

The Steamer 'Julia' in Highbridge New Wharf around 1920's, the town and bridge
can be seen, with Island House visible on the right.

This view is taken from a similar position in 2004, it is now the Cattle Market
Vehicle Park and the site of a very successful Sunday Market, Island House is visible on the right.

(Photos supplied by Chris Handley)

As late as October 1947, the Burnham Gazette & Highbridge Express reported that a ship had to be re-directed due to serious silting problems. The case of a ship destined for Bridgwater, which was re-directed to Bristol, as it could not berth at Highbridge wharf owing to silt deposit. The vessel was stated to be of approximately 600 registered tonnes. It was resolved that the Town Clerk be requested to communicate with the London Midland & Scottish Railway Co. drawing attention to the serious effect which occurrences such as these had upon the port and upon traders and urge them to arrange for the wharf to be cleaned. That he also communicates the facts to any other authority that might be powered to take action on the matter.

In Quieter Times
An area that once had been a thriving port seeing Colliers and Sailing Ships loaded with timber etc.

One of the earliest ships at the wharf was the "Julia" a wooden ketch of 69 tons (1873 – 1904). A regular vessel at the dockside and the last ship built for the Highbridge coastal trade was the "S.S. Radstock" (190 tons, built in 1925 by J. Crighton & Co. Ltd., Saltney, Cheshire.) At its height around 1910 the wharf was a busy place with its shipping and railway sidings.

John Blands' timber mills, which were adjacent to the wharf, were busy unloading Russian timber ships. The timber was raised from the holds to a platform where men "Timber Runners" with shoulder pads, carried it across the railway sidings along planks and into the timber yard. Mr. Fred Luke recalled in 1989 "It was hard, unremitting toil, in summer you would be running with sweat soon after starting work. Two beer boys would trot to the local pub for beer, with some men drinking twelve pints a day". The men 'ran' their load up timber "skids" and slid it off their shoulders onto a growing pile of lumber. The men had to be nimble, as the skids used to whip under their feet and they needed to dance to the bounce or be thrown off. Pay was good - £6.00 per week. (In 1930's) The last timber vessel to make use of the wharf was the "Jola" in June 1948.

'Timber Runners' unloading timber from a ship and carrying it into J. Bland's Yard

Private sidings at the wharf during the 1920's included those of John Bland & Co. (Timber), Highbridge Anthracite Fuel Works Ltd., Norris Siding (Coal) and Willetts Cake Mills.

Ships were loaded and unloaded by steam cranes, there being two types – Winch and Hydraulic. Their carriages ran on broad gauge (7ft. 0 1/4in.) rails that gave more stability than the standard gauge (4ft. 81/2 in.)

At one time Highbridge Wharf was yielding good profits on the exchange of cargoes between South Wales and other Bristol Channel ports, in fact the services were maintained until 1933. Outgoing boats carried dairy and other Somerset products and ships brought back coal, both for domestic use and for the railways, hundred of tons of rails for the extension of railway systems in the West were landed and despatched from Highbridge. The little trading ships continued to do their cross Channel journeys from Highbridge Wharf; there was the gallant "Julia" which the Somerset & Dorset bought in 1873 and which was in service for over forty years mostly bringing rails and coal from Newport. "Julia" was replaced by a new "Julia" in 1904; in one year the old "Julia" and the "Alpha" had brought over 7,960 tons of rails between them.

However, the shipping interests of the Somerset and Dorset were wound up and all vessels were disposed of by 1934. The wharf continued to be in use, but things changed in 1939 with the outbreak of World War II. Suddenly there was an increase in imports, mostly coal plus some foodstuffs and stone for road making. There were times when the wharf was quite busy, boats arrived from Scandinavia loaded with timber, and there was the local sail and steam traffic.

Later parts of the wharf were taken over by the American Army for the storage of war materials, particularly the large grey concrete building once used by the Eclipse Fuel Co. and later the Anthracite Fuel Works. Unfortunately, although the wharf had been kept active, lack of maintenance brought back the old 'silt' problems. These were to remain and the indications are that it was an insurmountable problem. The tug "Rexford" was used to keep the wharf from silting up, but when this was finally scrapped in 1950 the wharf ceased to be available for private mooring in 1964.

The Somerset and Dorset Joint Railway had signal (Box 'C') that controlled the level crossing in Church Street in the town, the branch line to the right went to Burnham, and the left branch went to the wharf. This was convenient to Highbridge Cattle Market; the market that originated in 1851 covered an area behind the "Highbridge Hotel" roughly where it is today.

Wharf facilities included a weighbridge and house, Willett & Son had a corn and cake feed mill and store with stables attached, near the town end of the wharf. Rail traffic ceased to use the wharf from November 1964 with the wharf line closing in March 1965. By the 1970's buildings had been abandoned, some had stood idle for years.

In 1990 plans were being considered which called for the Dunball Wharf to be moved to Highbridge, Sedgemoor District Council had set aside a sum of money to cover a feasibility study. A project under consideration at the time called for the creation of a barrage at Dunball, but the scheme came to no avail.

Mr Fred Wiltshire, who lived in Bertha Terrace became Berthing Master and retired in 1947 at the age of 70 after over 47 years working at the wharf recalled at the time "When I first started at the wharf it was a busy place and we had plenty to do. Ships came from all parts with coal, timber and general cargoes. Some came from as far away as Liverpool; I have often seen eighteen ships berthed there. We did plenty of work in the war too, mostly with coal, tons and tons were brought over to be stacked in different parts of the South West".

Mr. Wiltshire was berthing Master for 21 years, he had started as a goods porter with the railway that owned the wharf, and then became a driver in connection with shunting wagons by horses. Horses were used for shunting until the Second World War years. Local men who were young lads at the time, recall happy times helping with the horses. Fred was once asked if it was not time he retired; he replied that he had stayed on after the war because things had got into "a bit of a muddle". He said, "The place'll stop when I go". Little did he realise, that what was said as a joke, proved to be the case, as the wharf closed shortly after his retirement.

Incidentally, the large grey building, known by some as the "Winkle" lay derelict again after the war and became a challenge to local lads with 'mountaineering' tendencies. One lad, upon being caught by his father climbing into the uppermost reaches of the building and being duly admonished – "Don't let me catch you up there again my lad, it is dangerous" was surprised by the reply "I saw your initials up there at the top, Dad".

The Highbridge Seafarer

Mr. A.E. Buncombe was a man who loved the sea; he had a powerful frame and a ruddy complexion and was for years, a familiar sight in Highbridge. He used to be seen every day sat on a bench outside his home, wearing an engineer's suit of well pressed blue, a sailor's cap and observing life as it passed by 24 Church Street. Albert was born in December 1871 and his affection for the sea began, when, as a lad of sixteen, he used to travel across the Bristol Channel to Wales in one of the canvas sided boats known as 'Trows'. A 'Trow' used to carry up to 150 tons of coal, and he sailed in and out of the busy port of Highbridge regularly.

He joined the Royal Navy when he was twenty-one and in 1899 sailed from China in the four funnelled cruiser HMS 'Powerful' to take part in the war in South Africa. A year was spent sailing between Durban and Simonstown performing duties which helped the army in the problems it was experiencing inland. One of his memories was transporting 800 Dutch prisoners of war to St Helena where Napoleon spent some years.

At the outbreak of the Great War, being a member of the fleet reserves, he was recalled to the navy and posted to a cruiser H.M.S. Talbot. An exciting experience was sailing up the Gallipolli Peninsula during the campaign against the Turks, his ship also covered the East coast of Africa that was at the time, occupied by Germany and the Royal Navy carried out many activities including sailing to Dar-es-Saalem. In 1918 he was paid off but was not going to leave the sea; buying his own tug, which he named the 'Rexford' and that tug with its master sailed the local waters up until 1948. Big timber boats used to anchor out in Bridgwater Bay and Alfred's tug used to guide them to the Fairway buoy and see they were brought safely up river to Bridgwater, Dunball or Highbridge. Mr. Buncombe was the engineer of his tug so he used to hire pilots to undertake the navigation; they included the late Fred King and a well-known man from Burnham, Mr. Albert Woodward.

The last job the 'Rexford' and its master performed was bringing in and out the last ship to come to Highbridge the Phoenix. Mr. Buncombe retired soon after and then spent his days chatting to old friends and watching the world go by, happy to talk about events that have passed, plus those of the present. He was a man of strong independent views and a typical old British 'Seadog' a man from this great seafaring nation. Albert Buncombe died on 14th August. 1956.

Kimbers Boat Yard

The Highbridge wharf was approached through, what was called the River Brue Channel. When the tide was high this area provided anchorage for a number of cargo ships, waiting loading or unloading.In this area, Mr. Harold John Kimber, or 'Kim' had established a boat building and repair yard in 1927 it was in part previously called the Clyce Wharf.

Many small boats were built, including some for the Admiralty, particularly during World War II. A local lad John Meader, upon leaving school, took up a six-year apprenticeship in December 1949 at the boatyard and remembers being involved in the repair of boats for the Admiralty, Lloyds and R.N.L.I. They also built private boats and although being a small family owned business it carried out a wide variety of work, in the early days, it was mainly timber and woodcraft. Fibre Glass, which was soon to become a much-used media in boat construction, was not, as yet, used in boat building.

One of the largest yachts built at the yard was "Fresh Breeze" designed by Uffa Fox a leading boat designer, the yacht being for a Mr. Morrell of Porlock Weir.

Kimber's Boat Yard around 1949-50. The Troon Lifeboat is receiving a re-fit. Workers include Gordon May, Dave Blake, John Meader and Trevor Maslen.

(Photo supplied by John Meader)

MARKETS

The earliest record of there being a market in Highbridge was in the mid 19th Century when a Post Office Directory of that time stated that a market had been established and was held on the first Monday in every month. It was apparently the largest market for cheese, oxen, sheep etc. in the neighbourhood.

Again in 1902, Kelly's Directory confirmed there was a good market house for cheese and dairy products, still on the first Monday each month. There was also a weekly cheese auction held by F. Body & Son every Tuesday throughout the year. Cheddar and Caerphilly cheeses were consigned from this auction to the Highbridge Market and to the markets in several adjoining counties. The cattle market was then held on the first and third Monday each month, with a calf and lamb auction every Tuesday. The markets were well attended and were considered to be the largest in the West of England.

The Kelly's Directory of 1939 re-affirmed the success of Highbridge markets and it appears that there was also an auction every Tuesday for calves, sheep and pigs.

Highbridge Cattle Market

Highbridge Market established in 1851, was held on the first and third Monday of the month, with calf and lamb auctions every Tuesday. The Market has been extended twice; the first time was when J.H. Palmers bought part of the old River Brue from the Council. They, the Council, had bought it from some authority for 10/- and Palmer's bought their section for £1.00, but it had to be filled in. This was done by filling the whole of the riverbed with wattle hurdles and then placing great big stones on top of them, then it was filled in with quarry waste and some more wattle hurdles, it made a firm surface. Over the years all the movement has virtually ceased and the market area now takes large articulated lorries loaded with cattle. More recently a piece of land, the old coach house and paddock that adjoined the old "Highbridge Hotel" was added to complete the main entrance.

If a farmer had not got his stock into the market by 6.00 a.m. he might just as not bother, in the early days there were no pens, cattle was tied to a rail. Before the last war stock arrived in a horse and cart or, if local were often driven in, that is where the name 'drover' came from.

(Photo supplied by Maurice Wall)
Cattle Sales at Christmas 1954

The busiest time for the market was up to 2001, before the foot and mouth outbreak, it was one of the, if not **the,** largest fat stock market in the West of England in recent years. Up to the foot and mouth outbreak anywhere between 200 and 400 fat cattle and about 2000 sheep passed through every week. Cattle sold at the market were for slaughter. Taunton Market was bigger and probably had more cattle and sheep but they would have been for store, as were those from other markets.

Meat Rationing

Up until the time meat was de-rationed after the war, the market as such was called a 'collecting centre' and it had to advise the Ministry of Food in Cardiff what had been entered for sale. The 'entrants' had to advise the market what cattle they were sending by Thursday, we had to tell the Ministry on the Friday and the market was given allocation instructions for the following Monday week. Trains from the old Highbridge Goods station then dispatched all the cattle. Cattle were driven from the old cattle market down Market Street to the railway station; cattle by law are domestic. Therefore

Sheep sales in the 1950's

they are not considered 'wild' and as long as you had got a drover at the front and a drover at the back it was deemed to have been adequate precautions. Fifty or sixty at a time, sometimes even a 100, were sent for transporting and they used to go down to the station where there were proper pens for loading them onto the cattle trucks, the pens being approximately where Kwik Save is now. On the way down they bumped a few people's cars but they could not claim compensation off the Ministry, because cattle are domestic animals. Highbridge market had priority over the whole of England for cattle trucks, it used to have a special train and because there were so many cattle entered for a particular week, (normally on a Monday), but sometimes needing two days, the market still had priority for cattle trucks. A lot of them went to South Wales to be killed, some to the Midlands, a few to the South and London. The train would have been 100 yards long, perhaps even more. It caused quite a disturbance getting the cattle to the trucks, because they were on the A38, then had to be diverted where the clock used to be; someone had to stop the traffic by the market and then by the clock to send them down Market Street. Someone else to prevent them going over the Railway Bridge, and to divert them down to the pens in the station yard. People often complained that there was a mess in the roads, especially if it rained.

Auctioneers

In the cattle market we were the auctioneers we did not employ anyone. There is a lot to it, of course, I can always remember my first time, I can take you to where I did my first auction sale, a little house in Jubilee Street in Burnham, which was for furniture.

W.H.Palmers & Son Auctioneers in Bridgwater are no relation to J.H. Palmer. J.H. Palmer was my grandfather, there were three sons Percy, Hugh & Jack, when grandfather was still in the business, Percy ran Weston office and Hugh and Jack my father ran Burnham office and Highbridge. When grandfather died, things had to be sorted out, Percy went on his own in Weston and the firm was called Percy Palmer. We kept the name J.H. Palmer & Sons, then fairly soon after, I came into the practice, Hugh retired and I bought his share of the business, or rather father bought it for me. Then father more or less retired, it was 1939 and at that time it was mainly father; Hugh took a chap called Fred Cross into partnership, he was a 'Bridgwaterite', his father had a fish business in Bridgwater called Cross and Co. Immediately war was declared, Fred was called up because he was a reservist, he was away in 1939, he was only in the firm about six months and he was gone. He was a prisoner of war having been captured by the Japanese, he didn't come back until about 1946,but he did stay in the firm, up until about twenty years ago.

When he decided to retire, I invited Maurice Wall to join me and then I decided to retire and it is now Maurice Wall and Jeremy Bell. There are no Palmers to carry on, my son is a solicitor and not interested. So it is the last of the line, because John has no children, so when John dies it is the end of the line, but there you are, these things happen.

Calf Market

The calf market was situated between the cheese market buildings and the river it was where the calf and pigpens were, occasionally if you had conditions of a high tide because the Clyce gates were shut for a longer period and heavy rain, the river would flood. It would come over the top and flood; in less than five minutes you could have a foot of water all through the calf and cheese markets. Just after the war when I (David Palmer) came back from the Air Force, it did flood and you had to move the calves very quickly. If river conditions were high you needed to watch it, especially if we had had a lot of rain, and it was a high tide. The bank is not very high at that point and the river would come over very, very quickly and cover virtually all the pens, it never got to the cheese market building.

"I remember the Wharf, at the top end Russian timber ships would come in and unload their cargo. Behind Canal House is the bed of the original River Brue, this used to be the boundary between Highbridge and Huntspill. The Highbridge Hotel was not in Highbridge but in Huntspill; I was connected with Freemasonry and our lodge in Burnham was established in 1793, its original meeting place was the Highbridge Hotel. The First Master was John Jennings and he is buried in West Huntspill churchyard."

(The foregoing is a transcript of an interview with Mr David Palmer in 2001.with additional details from Maurice Wall)

Highbridge Cheese Market

(Photo supplied by Miss Monica Board)
**The Cheese Market, owned by Mr Alan Board.
Auctioning the cheese is Mr Jack Palmer**

The Highbridge Cheese Market was the largest cheese auction in the world? An article in the "Farmer & Stock Breeder" somewhere around 1936 –8 stated it was the largest cheese auction; it used to sell 100 tons of cheese by auction, every week, all local cheese. It was a most wonderful system, because all the farms around here, they were all dairy farms, milked their cows and most had a cheese maker, they turned the milk into cheese, the whey was fed to the pigs and the pigs went into the bacon factory. You could not wish for a better system, all self contained no transportation all very logical. Of the cheese that was sold, I think, say 80% was Caerphilly and most of it went to South Wales for the South Wales miners, a little bit of it went up to the Midlands but by far the greatest proportion of it went to South Wales.

The original Cheese Market was on a site near the Coopers Arms.

The market was held weekly, cheese would be put up for auction with buyers and agents arriving from all over the country. However, it closed in 1940 because at the outbreak of the war cheese was rationed. Some cheese production continued but this was for personal consumption, but apparently this also, soon came to an end.

There were Cheese factories in Highbridge, these included F.A.Chubbs and Mr A.Board

F.A.Chubbs had a shop next to the George Hotel in Church Street. The only bomb to fall on Highbridge during the war hit their shop. The reports are that the town smelled of toasted cheese for some days.

Local Cheeses were mainly Caerphilly and Cheddar. The Welsh preferred the former because it maintained its moisture under ground and did not break up like the firmer Cheddar.

Caerphilly is semi soft, slightly acid, with a mild flavour; white in colour. Seven gallons of milk is needed to make seven and a half pound of cheese; with no bandages or greasing it could be sold within 7 days. Highbridge Market frequently sold 15 tons per week.

Cheddar is harder with a buttery texture; darker than milk cream it is neither acid nor sweet, but nutty in flavour. A good Cheddar deserves 6 months or more to mature.

(Photo supplied by Mike Lawrence)

**Inside the Cheese Room, Horace Lawrence (right),
Cheese Maker, Jim Tewkesbury (left)**

Isleport Farm

The farmhouse is a Grade II listed 19th century building and was one of a number of local farms producing their own cheese in the years 1910 to 1940.

Horace Lawrence first occupied the farm in 1901 and for many years employed Jim Tewkesbury as Cheese maker, quantities of cheese was produced, Caerphilly, which was typical of the area and some Cheddar.

A bookkeeper was employed together with three or four casual workers and members of the family, cheese mainly, but also butter was produced on the farm. Later Norman Moxey took over the position of cheese maker. Some milk for the cheese process came from the farm itself, the remainder being bought in from smaller farms in the area.

When the required amount of milk had been processed, any excess would be transported in churns, by horse drawn flat wagons (later motor transport) to Highbridge Western Region Station for despatch to a depot in London.

Most, if not all of the cheese manufactured at the farm, would be taken to Highbridge Cheese Market (The area is now a housing development) the buyers and agents in the town to buy cheese would stay at the 'Railway Hotel 'that was where Alpha House now stands.

In the 1920's, usually in July/August, the haymaking time, a wagon would be taken to the Somerset & Dorset Railway Works and would wait outside for employees to finish work for the day. Those who wished, would then volunteer to help with the haymaking and make some extra money; this continued whilst there was daylight, they were supplied with ample quantities of bread, cheese and cider during the evening.

Some cheese production continued at Isleport Farm for a short period during the war, during this time Austin Lawrence joined his father on the farm. After his father died the farm remained in the family when Mike Lawrence, the grandson, occupied the farm. Being an enthusiast of vintage tractors and farm machinery Mike had gathered together quite a large collection, with the view of setting up a Working Museum in the future. As a preview to this he has, for several years, organised around August time a Vintage Hay and Harvesting Working Show, where much of his current collection can be seen in a working environment.

(Information for the above article provided by Mike Lawrence)

Mike Lawrence of Isleport Farm recalls that a Mr Thomas Moss Heal of Worston House, near Highbridge was an 'Engineer Extraordinary'.

Thomas Moss Heal, Engineer Extraordinary

The Second World War was well known as a period when people were encouraged to 'make do and mend', and nowhere more so than in agriculture. The shortage of new tractors in particular, led to some amazing feats of improvisation, with redundant passenger cars being converted into pick-up trucks, tractors and even self-propelled mowers.

One man began improvising in this way a decade or so before hostilities broke out, he was Thomas Moss Heal, and he lived at Worston House, near Highbridge. Born in the United States, to which his parents had emigrated, he came to England when his parents decided to return. As a young man, he became a farmer, raising pigs, but at the same time, using his fertile imagination to produce equipment for his farm.

Photographs in the collection kept by his daughter, Mrs. Rosemary Hawkins (who still lives at Worston Farm) indicate that at one stage he appears to have converted at least three cars – two were probably Austins – into small tractors, whilst another was made into a mower, the type of machine for which he is best remembered. He also produced a small lorry from a Model T Ford, and possibly another from an Austin 12. Nick Jones who lives at Cannington near Bridgwater regularly rallied a 1927 Austin 12 pick-up that was once owned by Mr. Moss Heal.

Mrs. Hawkins said her father was a great improviser, and also something of a magpie, collecting cars and other items that 'might come in useful' (We all know that feeling!). He disliked and mistrusted horses; this probably led him to consider ways of replacing them for work on his farm. Of course, cars of that day had 'real' chassis with easily detachable bodies, so conversion into working machines was made much easier than it would nowadays. He broke up a number of old cars, keeping the engines, gearboxes, axles and other parts that might be useful with his projects.

The "*Farmer and Stockbreeder*" of November 19th 1946 detailed some of his inventions:

"Home-Made Hoist"

For lifting heavy bales and the like, Mr. T. Moss Heal, of Highbridge has made a portable hoist. It would deliver a bale to the door of a 17 foot high Dutch barn and for unloading a wagon; the hoist would go between the wagon and stack. The very simple hoist with its four stays would not tip over as there was never more than a few pounds difference on either end of the cross beam."

Mike Lawrence, of Isleport Farm, recalls this hoist being sold at auction. Mrs. Hawkins has a fascinating cutting from the *Evening Times and Echo* of Friday July 18th 1930, which tells much about the inventor and his machine:

"Highbridge Farmer's Home-Made Motor Mowing Machine

The season has been remarkable for the heaviest hay crop for thirty years, and a novel mowing machine, constructed by Mr. Tom Heal, a young Highbridge farmer, has proved a highly successful aid in cutting the grass.

The motor mower is well known in connection with the maintenance of large lawns, but so far it has not been adapted commercially to haymaking. Mr. Heal has, therefore, had to rely entirely upon his own resources in constructing his machine. He has gone on improving it until this year it has practically reached perfection, having cut some thirty acres of grass without a hitch. Mr. Heal is very modest in his claims for the mower, but those who have seen it working are loud in their praise of the machine. Its constructor's chief claim is that it has freed two horses to do other work, but actually it will do the work of two horses in half the time – and do it well. It takes approximately half a gallon of petrol to cut an acre of grass. The machine, as previous photograph shows, somewhat resembles a "Heath Robinson" contrivance, and certainly to watch it lurching across an undulating hayfield belching out smoke from its exhaust, and combining the well known rattle of the mowing machine with the characteristic noises of the motor, is somewhat amusing.

The car that forms the basis of the machine was originally bought for £5!

Mr. Heal has retained the back axle of the car, but has fitted the wheels of a mowing machine, whilst the knife, with its working parts, is attached to the side of the chassis in a similar manner to an ordinary mowing machine. All the necessary constructional work has been done by the owner, who is a very clever mechanic and the proud possessor of a fully equipped workshop with a fine lathe."

It is fortunate in that Thomas Moss Heal's demonstration mower has survived in his daughter's ownership. This particular version has a Bamford horse drawn mower, linked up to the engine and gearbox from a Morris Cowley, but sporting a Humber radiator, necessitating a steeply sloping bonnet to connect it to the scuttle panel on which is mounted the petrol tank with gravity feed, just as it would have been on the car.

The actual car chassis is virtually unaltered at the front, though it is cut off short at the rear where the Bamford mower is attached. The front axle appears to be set further back than it would have been as a car; whether this was accidental, or intentionally done, to give a smaller turning circle, we can but guess. He devised his own steering arrangement, and his plans for the adaptations needed on the chassis still survive. The steering column was, apparently, from an American car. The prop shaft from gearbox to rear axle was shortened, and the drive to the mower was taken from sprockets on the end of the original half shafts, by roller chains to larger chain wheels on the mower. The chains were specially made for him at a Midlands factory.

Mrs. Hawkins still has the original metal templates for the sprockets and chain wheels, carefully marked out in pencil, and quite clearly meticulously cut out and filed to shape by hand. One rather interesting comment addressed "To Irish Customers" is that "Carriage paid to all orders to Ireland if chain is ordered with sprockets. There is no duty on chains and sprockets entering Eire if they are used for work solely on the land."

The surviving Humber-radiator mower was taken round to various shows in the area to advertise the conversion. Clearly the 'demonstrator' did its stuff, for soon Thomas was not only making mowers, but marketing gear and chain kits and sets of instructions for others to do the same. Advertisements were put into papers and he appears to have built up quite a business. It also appears that others copied the designs, because they were not patented. Bearing in mind what Mrs. Hawkins said about her father's dislike of horses, it is interesting to read a section in his mower building instructions how a farmer can reduce the number of such animals on his 'workforce'.

Finally, Mr. Moss Heal stated his own position:
"I have been designing, making and using car motor mowers and tractors since 1926 and from the vast amount of experience I have gained, I have designed a chain drive which is adaptable to nearly any make of car and mowing machine. This will enable the machine to cut an average heavy crop in second gear, leaving the lower speed for emergencies and cutting uphill."

Thomas Moss Heal was a fascinating man, of great ingenuity, who, as well as improvising cheap and simple, yet efficient, machinery to operate on his farm, he also made it possible for others to acquire the same kind of equipment for their own use. His mowers are true memorials to British inventiveness and ingenuity at its best.

(This article written by Mr John Reeves of Trull)
(Photographs supplied and permission for reproduction of article, provided by Mrs. Rosemary Hawkins)

BRICK AND TILE PRODUCTION

The production of bricks and tiles in Somerset got under way around the 17th century. Early brick makers used limestone, sandstone and clay, all found in the area. Initially, temporary kilns were constructed close to the area where the raw materials were to be found. Straw and wood, also readily available were used to fire the kilns. Alluvial clay deposited along the coastline during the Roman occupation, when the area was inundated by seawater proved to be invaluable to brick manufacturers.

In the 17th Century there were many small-scale brickfields and the earliest example of brickwork in Somerset can be seen at the Grays Almshouses, East Street, Taunton, dated 1635. By the 18th Century the localised brickfields were superseded by permanent brickyards and the inexhaustible supply of clay enabled the brick and tile makers to respond to the opportunities of mass marketing during the industrial revolution of the 1840's and 1850's.

By the 19th Century the local brick and tile industry was thriving with over 250 manufacturers in Somerset. A trade directory lists nine companies in the Highbridge area in 1859 – Apex, Thomas Basten, Abraham Board, Colthurst Symons, Cox & Company, John Prior Estlin, Johnson & Griffin, Arthur George Pitts, George and Frank Pitts. The biggest of which was Colthurst Symons who had six other sites within Sedgemoor.

Working conditions were hard and this led to a number of strikes, the worst being in 1896. Police got heavy and in one incident a man called Joel French was pulled off his bicycle and roughed up whilst returning from picket duty in Highbridge saying "The men are sticking together as tight as those bricks in the kiln down Highbridge". Due to the strike wages increased, from 12 to 15 shillings per week and hours reduced to 12 per day.

To make ends meet whole families had to work and a bylaw had to be passed to protect children under the age of 13. It was as late as 1947 before this was raised to 15.

In the early days clay was dug by hand with a spade, put into a wheelbarrow (about two cwt); pushed along planks of wood to the clay store heap, that was about twenty to thirty feet high, then left to weather. This process was later replaced with a multi-bucket excavator, which made this stage of production much easier. Different clay was used for different products – hard brown for land drainpipes – soft brown for twenty hole bricks – blue for roofing tiles.

Drying Room for Bricks, Tiles and Pipes

The next job was to load it onto a wheelbarrow again and push it into the millhouse for grinding, two or three shovels of sand were added and this mixture was put into the pug mill. The grinder was steam driven and in the mid- 1940's a very young worker fell in and was killed, as it was impossible to stop the machine. Electricity was introduced later, which made it much safer. This mix was then cut into pieces for making tiles, pipes or bricks. The cutter and his helper would then load onto a barrow and push to the drying racks.

The worst job in the works was clinkering which had to be done four times a burn and was carried out with a large iron poker and rack. However, in the olden days a young lad (before the kiln was lit) had to wriggle through on the fire bars with a lump hammer and chisel knocking clinkers off as he crawled along.

In the early 1930's Colthurst Symons had two squares and two pinnacle kilns that were replaced over the years by downdraught kilns. These took 84 to 90 hours to burn using ten to twelve tons of coal with a brick capacity of 45,000 to 48,000.

At a later stage Colthurst Symons were asked by Calor Gas of Southampton to participate in the use of Gas (propane) to burn the kilns, which took seventy-two hours on four and a half tons of gas. The advantages were cheaper burns, with no coal wheeling, no clinkering and cleaner burns.

Originally the goods were moved locally by horse and cart, progressing further afield by road, river and railway. Colthurst Symons owned three clippers, which used the Highbridge Wharf. A list of tolls, this quotes fees charged for bricks and tiles of 4d per 1,000.

The Somerset & Dorset Railway provided two private sidings, one for Colthurst Symons and the other for Apex Tile Company. The former eventually bought the latter. The First World War interrupted trade and marked the

Tile Display Framework, towed by a Buncombe Steam Roller

beginning of the decline of the industry. After employing eighty-five men in the 1950's Colthurst Symons finally closed the Highbridge Works making ten men redundant, bringing to an end the brick and tile trade in the Highbridge area.

The durability of the product was illustrated recently by the discovery of Somerset blue bricks found in the sunken wreck of an old wooden sailing ship located off the coast of the Americas.

(This information was obtained from research carried out by the late Tom Cornish, who was employed by the brickyards for most of his working life; the photographs are from his collection plus details obtained from the Brick and Tile Works Museum. Bridgwater)

APEX LEISURE, HIGHBRIDGE

The Apex Leisure and Wildlife Park is situated on the Highbridge border, on land acquired by the local Council from Colthurst Symons in 1969. A scheme for the future use of the area was proposed and it was decided to use the site as a leisure and wildlife park.

The land was a derelict brick and tile-making site, including kilns and buildings that were demolished. The name Apex was the name of the previous Brick and Tile Company on the site that was bought out by Colthurst Symons. The flooded clay pits were pumped out, but before work could start on the scheme the Highbridge Angling Association had to re-home fish, and a Royal Engineer Squadron removed bombs, mines and grenades. The first phase was completed in 1971 by W.A.H. Crotty Ltd., a Cornish firm specialising in China clay. They moved clay and shaped the land into a car park, and landscaped the lakes creating an island in the middle, which was duly called Crotty's Island. The 42-acre site was seeded and planted with 5000 trees by Richard Berry of Highbridge.

In 1993 it was decided to enhance the park with mounds and slopes. The work was carried out and a new causeway from the park to the riverbank was built with an all-weather footpath.

Sedgemoor District Council manages Apex Park for the benefit of the community, visitors, and to encourage wildlife. The park benefits from many varieties of fauna including a beautiful display of daffodils in the spring from bulbs planted by local schools and organisations. The wildlife is quite varied including swans, mallards, coots, moorhens, Canada geese and grebes.

(Photo supplied by Collin Moore)

An afternoon in the park enjoying the radio controlled boat races.

The Apex Park is used by various organisations, including Highbridge Angling Association, B.M.X. Biking, Radio Controlled Boats and Dog Obedience Classes. There is also a Skate Park, Trim Trail Circuit and a Play Area for Children. The park has benches and picnic tables situated at various points.

The Apex Park is enjoyed by numerous visitors and local residents; and as stated by a local councillor in 1974 "I don't think I have seen, anywhere in Sedgemoor, a more imaginative scheme of reclamation of a totally derelict area".

HIGHBRIDGE GAS WORKS

An Act of 1860 gave authority for Highbridge to provide gas lighting for the town or "hamlet" and as a result ' The Limited Company' was formed during 1870 and the first supply of gas began in 1878. The Gas Works was located adjacent to the Great Western Railway line at the end of Springfield Road, (formerly known as Gas House Lane.)

The share capital paid amounted to £3500 with a dividend of 9%. At the first A.G.M. it was reported the cost had exceeded that anticipated due to the requirement to provide a gas supply to the Midland & South Western Railway Co. Works and also to their wharf sidings.

A few interesting details surviving from 1909 are:

> Cost of coal for making gas, per ton approx. 12 shillings (60p)
>
> Annual production of gas 9,000,000 cubic feet, using 900 tons of coal.
>
> Number of street lamps – 60   Number of cooking stoves - 50
>
> Number of consumers   - 100 with the cost of gas at 3 shillings and 9 pence (19p)
>
> Per 1000 cubic feet, there was a reduction for gas engines.

Manager - Mr. A. E. Tulk   Secretary - Mr. T.F. Norris

Ownership of the Works passed to the Weston-super-Mare Gas Co. in 1933 – and Gas production ceased at Highbridge two years later.

(Information supplied by Mr. Eric Lynham).

Railway "Oil" - Gas Works at Highbridge

An Oil Gas Works was built for the Somerset & Dorset Joint Railway Company in 1895. The oil- gas produced was used solely for the lighting of railway carriages and a specially designed gas making plant was used. It was located in a building on an approach road to the Locomotive Works on the Walrow side of the Walrow Bridge. The oil gas was first stored in a traditional gasholder before being transferred to cylinders 6ft. to 8 ft. long, at a pressure of 100 – 150 p.s.i.

The cylinders were suspended beneath the railway carriages; the gas was then piped to a number of gaslights within the carriage roof; this was at a lower pressure, (below 1 psi). This system replaced the existing individual lamps that used rope oil.

However, following a railway re-organisation in 1921 the works closed and gas production was moved in its entirety to Swindon.

(Information supplied by Mr Eric Lynham)

HIGHBRIDGE BACON Co. LTD

A bacon curing business was established in 1890, the factory covering an extensive area in Highbridge, South. The factory was situated off the Huntspill Road; its entrance was just beyond the garage over the River Brue Bridge, the premises being behind the garage with a driveway off the A38. The factory site adjoined an area once occupied by the towns' waterworks, which was established in 1886, this was replaced in 1906, when mains water supply came to the town.

Standing in over three acres of ground and fitted with the latest machinery for the curing of bacon, the Company gave employment to the town. On average 140 employees worked for the company, including a number of van salesmen for distribution and retail outlets.

Piggeries (pens) attached to the main factory received the pigs upon delivery and these were retained in pens overnight prior to slaughter. This took place on Tuesdays, Wednesdays and Thursdays; local pigs were also killed here. Pigs arrived in cattle wagons, by road, from Devon and Cornwall. Some deliveries were received from Ireland, transported by sea and rail, and then unloaded at the Western Region Goods Yard (this used to adjoin the Recreation field), for delivery to the factory. Ownership of the factory eventually passed to C & T. Harris (Calne) Ltd. Their green coloured vans could be seen making their deliveries around Somerset, Devon and Dorset.

A salesman (Mr. John Soloman) employed at the factory, recalls: -

"Work commenced at 7.30 a.m. when the vans were fuelled and loaded with the orders for the day, depending upon the length of the journey. There were five vans out each day.

My journeys covered Somerset; Mid Dorset (an area covering Gillingham, Shaftesbury and Blandford with many villages in between. Also North Devon: - Barnstaple, Ilfracombe, Bideford and Westward Ho.

Vehicles were serviced every other Saturday morning and every two years were returned to the Calne workshops for a complete overhaul and repaint. They were very well maintained and were kept for ten years. I started working for them in 1951 and remained there for ten years".

OUTLINE OF PROCESS

After the animals had been slaughtered the carcasses were processed and then weighed by the factory staff and check-weighed on behalf of the farmer by the Ministry of Agriculture, Fisheries and Food Representative. Following which they were then examined and graded by the M.A.F.F. official grader.

PRODUCTS

Pork cuts of all types, Bacon, Ham, Trimmed meat – Pork Pies-Sausages (some bacon smoked in original wood chipping smoke house). Offal, – Kidney, – Liver, – Bath Chaps, – Chittalings, – Faggot casing, – Sausage casing.

Bi-Products:-   Bones for glue and fertiliser, hair for brush bristles, blood for fertiliser.

The Factory had its own shop in the town, selling the factory produce. This was situated next to the "George Hotel". "The Highbridge News" now occupies the premises.

Closure of the factory eventually came in December 1963. However, for a period after closure, van deliveries were still made from the site to outlets, including the town shop. Bulk deliveries were made to the depot from other factories within the group. In 1969 the closure of the town shop ended the association of the factory with the town.

An employee (Margaret Brown) who worked at the factory in 1940 for a short time recalls their working conditions.

"I started work there early in 1940 but left in July 1941 to join the Women's Royal Air Force. We started work at 6.00 am; had ? an hour for breakfast, I think it was at 8.30am. a tea break mid-morning, also lunch and tea break. We worked overtime; usually finishing between 6.00p.m.to 8.00p.m.we made and packed sausages for the Forces. Orders came in and had to be done quickly. We worked on long wide marble-topped tables, with a conveyor belt down the middle; we weighed the sausages, (1lb packs) put them on the belt and they were packed at the end. Sometimes we put our name and address in the boxes, didn't get many answers.

It was very cold and wet, we wore Wellington boots, to warm our feet we put them in buckets of hot water. I had a happy time there, a good gang of girls. We did not like the days then the pigs came in on their last journey; I would not do it now. We could order extra meat and spare ribs, sometimes in the shop. Mr Needs, the baker, used to supply us with buns, etc."

WEST OF ENGLAND CREAMERY

The creamery was part of the Harris Bacon Company that was situated in the Huntspill Road.   It was an important creamery for local farmers, their milk, in churns, was brought in by horse and trap or van each morning. It was checked for quantity and quality, a large quantity was bottled; the remainder was used for cheese. Tankers from other parts of the country delivered milk for cheese making.

Six large vats were used for the making of Cheddar and Caerphilly cheeses. It required six hours to make a vat of cheese from start to finish. At peak times twelve vats were made each day, whey was put through a separator to make cream and then made into whey butter, the remaining whey was then sold back to the farmers for pig feeding. The Cheddar cheese was stored and turned every day, a grader would test and inspect for maturity.

About twenty staff worked at the creamery, the cheese makers had to start about 6 am. Finished cheeses were delivered all over the country.

(Information supplied by Ray Reddish)

JOHN BLAND & Co. LTD

One of the earliest references to this Company was in about 1881, it states that 'the timber yards and sawmills of John Bland & Co Ltd are considerable'; previously Cuthbert Ritson who is referred to as early as 1872 had operated the yards. John Bland & Co Ltd who had previously been trading in Cardiff, where they had their registered office, took over the old Cuthbert Ritson premises that were situated within the Highbridge Wharf; the buildings and area being an ideal site for their business. The River Brue and the Highbridge Wharf were navigable for ships of 150 to 200 tons burthen; these were carrying cargos of Coal, Salt, Cake, Bricks and Tiles.

John Bland & Co Ltd being importers of timber and slates found the Highbridge Wharf perfect for their business and over ninety years of trading in the area a work force totalling seventy was built up. It had a good reputation for its quality and service. Employees of Blands still remember and talk about the past, of the ships that came to Highbridge and how hard the men who unloaded the timber worked until their hands bled.

(Photo supplied by Mr D Besley)

J.Bland & Co Ltd. Employees in 1930's

The site housed quite a large business, comprising: - weighing machine, stable block, assorted sheds of brickwork and wood, an office block and engine house. Additional buildings housed a variety tanks, tubs, pits, a smithy, a Cabon Engine and a boiler house. There was over 1000 yards of railway sidings complete with cranes –one fixed and one mobile.

Large sailing ships were arriving from Finland, Sweden and Russia with their cargoes of timber that was then carried by the workmen over the adjoining sidings, railway trucks and into the workshops. John Bland & Co Ltd was a Sawing, Planing and Moulding Mills. Timber was imported and then dealt with as necessary, supplied to the building trade or was moulded by Blands for such items as skirting boards etc; their designs could be supplied in Deal, Oak, Mahogany or any kind of wood desired.

There were discussions early in 1923 concerning some of the 'old sheds' at the Highbridge wharf; John Bland & Co. Ltd., apparently wished to replace some old sheds on the wharf, as they were not suitable for their use. Having paid rent on the sheds for between forty to fifty years, John Bland felt that the owners (the Railway Board in Derby) should foot the bill. Due to the passage of time the buildings were in a sorry state and proposals were put forward to effect their replacement with a new building at the cost then of approximately £ 258.8.4. The cost today (2003/4) has been estimated at being about £19.365.24.

The London and South Western Railway and the Midland Railway Company had previously owned the original buildings and wharf area however, following successful negotiations a contract was eventually signed and J.Blands & Co Ltd moved in. Later, in 1928 the Company leased additional buildings from the Southern Railway and the London and Scottish Railways (the old S.R. and L.M.S. Railways). The buildings were needed to house the new equipment and business was booming.

Also during the war the wharf and the timber yards were constantly under pressure to meet the urgent needs of the nation and to show its appreciation the Ministry of Supply-Timber Control Department wrote to John Bland's in June 1942 praising them for their war effort, the letter reads:-

" I am not without pride in the way the Timber Control has been able to "deliver the goods" after Saturday nights raids, but neither do I lose sight of the fact that the speed and efficiency which our organisation can be brought into existence on Sunday mornings depends on the co-operation of the Wharf mongers within whose districts raids occur.

I want therefore, to thank Mr Tindall and those members of the staff who so promptly responded to the call which we made upon you yesterday morning and to pass to you the credit which was to the Timber Control for the immediate deliveries of supplies for first-aid repairs."

During World War II, in 1942 the Defence Department (Southern Command) requisitioned part of the timber yard, but in 1945 the same Command transferred its rights to the Ministry of Works. In June 1948 John Bland's got the yards back when they were 'De-requisitioned'. The Company was doing well into the 1960's when planning approval was given to allow for alterations and extensions to the site in order to provide showrooms, offices and toilets. In 1962 with the Nationalisation of the Railways, their landlord changed again, namely the British Railways Board. Unfortunately, this also saw the end of John Bland & Co Ltd, because in 1972 their lease on the wharf passed to Shepherd Bros (Lancs). In August of that year a Jeff Plant of Shepherd Bros. was transferred to as Branch Manager and major changes took place. A Builders Merchants department was opened and stocked items for the building trade. In 1975 Shepherds was sold to International Timber, over the years many more changes took place and eventually all the various companies within the Group became JEWSONS. This latter company was also involved with the local firm of John Tyler Ltd.; details of that exercise are covered in the history of Tylers later in the book.

A Highbridge man who worked for John Bland & Co. Ltd. recalled the following: -Timber used to arrive at the wharf on ships from Sweden and Russia. The men would carry the wood across the planks from the boat straight into Blands yard on the high trestles. They were paid by the cargo, and would need to go to the "George Hotel" to get paid off, it was good money. You might have to work long hours, to eight, nine or ten o'clock at night. You had to empty the hold so that the ship could get out on the next tide. A lot of men did not take much money home because they would spend it on cider when they were unloading the cargo. There was a pub by the Blands entrance "The Somerset Vaults" and old Mrs Baker would come in three or four times a day with a wicker basket, full of bottles of cider. That's why some men did not have much money; they owed it for the drink they had consumed

In 2004 there are still a few ex-employees of John Bland & Co Ltd around and they have fond memories of their working days on the Highbridge wharf.

(Information supplied by Fred Faulks, photograph supplied by D.Besley)

PORTISHEAD RADIO - LOOKING BACK

For more than 70 years Portishead Radio in Worston Road. Highbridge has served the world's shipping, providing two-way long-range communication both on long and short waves. Today we have undoubtedly witnessed vast and undreamed of change in maritime communication techniques and it is perhaps timely to pause for a brief reflection upon this important part of maritime history.

EARLY YEARS

At the close of the Great War, the General Post Office reopened its short-range coast stations for commercial two-way ship-shore traffic. Although broadcasting had been directed to ships from the great long-waves stations like Poldu and Caernarfon, no formal long-range two-way service existed. Late in 1919 the GPO agreed a contract with the Marconi Wireless Telegraph Co. to convert a redundant Imperial Wireless Chain receiving station at Devizes for long-range maritime use. Comprising a receiver and a six-kilowatt valve transmitter, GKT opened for service early in 1920 with a guaranteed range of 1,500 miles.

(Photo supplied by Collin Moore)

The Radio Station in Worston Road

Housed in old army huts, its service advertised telegrams to and from ships up to five days from any British port at 11d (old money) per word. A small team of operators manned the station and radio traffic was keyed to and from the London Central Telegraph Office. This two-way long-range communication proved both successful and popular and by 1924 it became necessary to expand Devizes. The GPO constructed a second long-wave transmitter at Devizes and built a separate receiving station in Somerset, to which most of the operators transferred. By 1926 the value of short-wave communication was being proved by Marconi and Franklin and their confidence in the cheap and effective worldwide means of communication was fulfilled in their building of the Empire Beam Wireless System. The GPO in the same year constructed at Devizes the first maritime short-wave transmitter, keyed, like the long-wave transmitter, by operators with receiving equipment in Somerset. Tests were carried out with the SS Jarvis Bay and quite outstanding global results were achieved. By 1927 long-range two-way communication had become so firmly established that further expansion became necessary and a completely new transmitting station was built at Portishead near Bristol comprising initially of three long-wave transmitters and by 1929 a new shot-wave transmitter resulting in the final closure of the old

Devizes station.

Throughout the 1930's the long-range service expanded with a gradual decline in the use of long waves and rapid growth in short wave. Early in the thirties a new form of maritime customer was heard on the short waves, the flying boats, and their radio operators passing telegraph traffic to Portishead by Morse from as far as South Africa and India. The great liners, who had relied heavily on long-waves for their two-way communication, were making much greater use of short waves. By 1936 Portishead Radio, using three long-wave and four short-wave transmitters with its control and receiving centre handling well over three million words of radio traffic per year with a staff of sixty operators.

WAR YEARS

In common with all technical services, the war years brought great changes to the Portishead Radio. The station's role of two-way communication changed to broadcasting to ships without acknowledgement of receipt. However distress calls, enemy sighting reports, and news of the North Africa landings, the sinking of the "Scharnhorst" and clandestine signals from Europe also kept the station busy.

Early in 1943 work had grown to such levels that naval operators from HMS "Flowerdown" augmented the civilian staffs. Many of Portishead's civilian staff was seconded to Government services at home and overseas not only to man the radio station but also to train the many new additional radio officers required for convoy work. A special aircraft section was constructed for communications with patrol aircraft in the North Atlantic (Catalina's).

PEACE

Peacetime brought once again a return to commercial activities with an almost overwhelming demand for long-range communications. Largely from wartime experience the Area Scheme was set up in 1946 to enable British and colonial registered vessels to use naval station around the world with free relay of their traffic to Portishead.

Nineteen forty eight saw the opening of two new operating rooms with a landline room and a central control room with a steel plotting map of the world measuring 36 by 16 ft. A bureau file of both ship and aircraft positions were maintained and many were plotted with magnetic indicators. During the late forties and the fifties the transatlantic liners provided high volume traffic, particularly when VIP's were amongst their passengers. Throughout this period all communications were still telegraphic, largely hand keyed by Morse code. The development of the shore telex service at this time enabled customers to deposit and receive messages direct from the station, with high traffic users installing their own private circuits.

On the morning of 5th December 1958 Her Majesty Queen Elizabeth II visited Highbridge to tour the Radio Station and to receive a demonstration of the transmission and receipt of messages.

The sixties saw a continued expansion of the station, as a result of ever rising traffic and the introduction of new services such as the first experiments with telex over radio (TOR) and a Morse news press transmission. By 1965, eighty-six operators were handling more than eleven million words per year and communication with more than 1,000 ships each day.

In April 1970 the long-range radiotelephone service previously operated from Baldock Radio was transferred to Portishead Radio. Using transmitters at Rugby and Portishead, this service expanded so rapidly, it became necessary to operate temporarily, an additional control centre from Somerton Radio. By 1972 the Area Scheme came to an end and with it went the remaining Royal Naval presence. The demise of liner traffic had little affect overall, the oil trade and the deepwater fishing industry more than compensating for its loss. The advent of world yacht racing and single-handed events probably did more at this time to bring Portishead to the notice of the public at large than any other single factor. 1974 handled almost twenty million words of traffic by 154 operators and still traffic continued to grow.

Further major expansion of the service within the existing buildings in the Somerset control centre was impossible and in 1976 work commenced on a totally new building together with a computer-based message handling system. Radio telex continued to increase in popularity and by the late seventies it was obvious that no further expansion of the manually operated system was feasible. The advent of satellite point-to-point communication resulted in many short wave transmitting stations having spare capacity and in the late 1970's it became necessary to rationalise the terrestrial services, resulting in the closure of the Portishead transmitting station.

The Somerset control centre remained using transmitters at Rugby, Leafield, Ongar and Dorchester but still announcing itself over the airwaves as Portishead Radio. In May 1981 the new control centre in Somerset was opened, initially for telephone and telegraph services and by 1984 for fully automatic radio telex. A new aircraft service was inaugurated in January 1985 providing a 'phone patch' and flight information on a worldwide basis.

Visitors to the town of Portishead, near Bristol will now find little trace of the old transmitting station, a beautiful building now sadly demolished. In its place stands the new Avon & Somerset Police Headquarters (with aerials) but the name Portishead Radio still echoes around the world – as a signal of service to mobile users on land, sea and in the air.

With many services transferred to Satellite via Goonhilly, BT will close virtually all of its commercial terrestrial radio services, in July this year (1999), bringing an end to Somerset's involvement in Maritime and Aeronautical services.

Phillip Lewis retired from the post of Operational Manager at Portishead Radio a few years ago and his article, above, was written for "Seaways" the Journal of Master Mariners and was originally published in 1987.

ALL SHIPS ALL SHIPS ALL SHIPS

THIS IS

PORTISHEAD RADIO PORTISHEAD RADIO PORTISHEAD RADIO

THIS IS THE LAST BROADCAST FROM PORTISHEAD RADIO. FOR 81 YEARS WE HAVE SERVED THE MARITIME COMMUNITY. WE SAY THANK YOU TO ALL WHO HAVE SUPPORTED AND USED OUR STATION. WE PAY TRIBUTE TO MARCONI WHO MADE IT ALL POSSIBLE. HIS FIRST TRANSMISSIONS ACROSS WATER WERE MADE FROM NEARBY HERE AND SO STARTED THE RADIO ERA. WE ARE PROUD TO HAVE BEEN PART OF THAT ERA. AS THIS HISTORIC TIME IN THE COMMERCIAL MESSAGING WORLD COMES TO A CLOSE THE MANAGER AND RADIO OFFICERS WISH YOU FAREWELL FROM PORTISHEAD RADIO/GKB

Operator Mr Pat Dear transmitted this Last Message on 30th April 2000

W.W. Buncombe (1879-1935)

Walter William Buncombe will be remembered for Steamrollers. He was born in Highbridge on September 27th 1879 and died at Pawlett June 16th 1935. During his adult years he brought to the town a thriving business.

The first was at 34 Huntspill Road, Highbridge in the late 1890's/early 1900's; this was Bicycle and Motor Cycle Engineering; selling and repairing machines. (Selling bicycles at £2.00) In 1908 he purchased the Congregational Chapel opposite 34 Huntspill Road with the view to turn it into a garage and eventually to sell petrol and run a taxi service. With the motorcar becoming a popular means of transport it was increasingly obvious that road conditions would need to be improved. He therefore founded the Steamroller firm early in the 1900's, the roller yard was situated on the Huntspill Road near the River Brue, and a garage now stands on the site. During the 1930/40's he sometimes had as many as 150 rollers in the yard, these being available for hire to help with the construction of the countries roads.

Companies like Aveling & Porter, Wallis & Stephens, Marshall, Babcock & Wilcox, Clayton & Shuttleworth, Thomas Green & Son and John Fowler manufactured the majority of these vehicles. Names that have, like the 'giants' they produced, now disappeared from our roads. Steamrollers were often exported by Buncombe's to aid road construction overseas; the Air Ministry in Singapore (in 1927) and to India were such examples, they were not returned.

During World War Two the rollers were in constant use for many purposes; where their weight was essential, including building a railway marshalling yard for the American Forces near Newbury, Berkshire. Making barrack squares at Ashchurch(Glos), and other Army bases, plus runways at Weston Zoyland, Ilton, Wroughton, Yeovilton and Colerne there was also work in Savernake Forest for a munitions site. Come the end of the war the Steamrollers were again in demand all over the country to help reconstruct the nation's highways; County Councils in the South West and East Anglia constantly used this local firms' vehicles to improve its road networks. When a roller was needed a long way from its base the driver went with it, usually in his own little home, this was a caravan (perhaps primitive by today's standard) that contained his bed and a small kitchen. On some occasions the driver would take his family with him and thus they would be together during his time away from Highbridge. One roller went from Somerset to Northumberland on a job, it took three weeks and three days to get there, later low-loaders were used and these obviously drastically reduced the 'travelling' time.

Steamrollers needed a supply of coal and this was delivered to the Buncombe Siding at Highbridge Station and stored until required by the roller out on the road.

It was during the early 1960's that diesel started to replace coal as a means of producing power on the rollers and the familiar steamroller soon started to disappear. There was certain glamour about the steamroller that diesel would never replace, but with diesel all you had to do was press a button and it started. The days were gone where you had to build up steam first thing on a cold frosty morning before you could move. Buncombes' kept up to date with the changes and these vehicles were at Hinkley Point Nuclear Power Station helping to lay roads etc, also with other construction companies that were carrying out similar work.

When more modern units were introduced to the construction industry, many rollers were scrapped due to replacements and parts became difficult to obtain. Some became the prized possessions of the enthusiastic fans that were prepared to pay from £250-£300 for a good model. A few went to Preservation Societies and can now be seen at Steam Rallies about the country, such as the Great Dorset Seam Fair.

A Buncombe Steamroller, an Aveling & Porter unit No 44 built in 1922 was featured in the Channel 4 Film "Salvage Squad".

Mr Walter William Buncombe had three sons Sidney, Norman and John, who later helped run the roller business. He was also a councillor, on the Highbridge Urban District Council.

(Information and photographs supplied by Gerald Buncombe)

MAJOR'S TRANSPORT

E.A. Major & Sons business started in the early years of the 20th century at 11, Newtown Road, Highbridge, when Edward Arthur Major took over the carting business of a Mr. R. Channing, (his uncle). Initially work was of a local nature – materials for Council road works and cheese haulage from farm to auction, or to railways for despatch to distant points. Work continued along these lines with Edward's sons Harry and Reginald joining their father as they became old enough. Harry still a teenager running the business during the latter years of the First World War when Edward was in the army.

The first lorry came in 1925, an ex W.D. chain drive Albion which Harry drove, followed later by a second-hand A.E.C. which Reg. drove. The first new vehicle was a 3 – 4 ton Leyland in 1928. All these vehicles were on solid tyres. Edward was able to handle the heaviest horse and cart but had no inclination to handle these new fangled vehicles, never having learnt to drive. Many new customers were acquired over the ensuing years. Grain was collected from Avonmouth for milling at Harold Brown's corn store in Church Street; cattle food from the same point was collected for Willett & Son and delivered to many local farms. Timber from John Blands yard was delivered over a wide area. Tinned milk from the Wilts United Dairies at Bason Bridge was carried country wide – Rowntrees of York being a regular trip. The Highbridge Bacon Co. employed the Company to collect pigs from surrounding farms and to deliver sides of bacon.

To these customers must be added the needs of Colthurst Symons brick and tile yards. Furniture removals were also included together with many smaller customers; obviously there was never a shortage of work throughout the thirties.

The first diesel engine – a Crossley vehicle – came in 1934, followed by Albions in 1936-7-8 these being the preferred marque from then on. One of these vehicles is owned by a North Country enthusiast and is still on the road having been preserved.

At the outset of WW2, two Company vehicles were put under the control of the Ministry of War Transport and one compulsorily taken over by the Military. The remaining vehicles hauling for existing customers, plus any wartime requirements, one of which was collecting Prisoners of War from a camp at Goathurst and taking them to work on local farms and then returning them at night.

On the cessation of hostilities, normality returned to the transport industry. Harry's son Jack and Rex joined the Company, Jack initially as a driver and subsequently was put in charge of the workshop and Rex on the office staff. In 1949 the depot at 11 Newton Road became a B.R.S. Depot under the Governments nationalization policy.

This lasted for some 4$1/2$ years until a change of Government saw free enterprise return to the industry, and E.A. Major & Sons (Transport) Ltd., was formed. Trade flourished in the booming post-war years, many new customers came along, the most important being the Somerset Wire Co. at Bridgwater. Unfortunately, the brick and tile trade was wound down and was almost completely ended by the mid 70's.

A.E.C. Lorry (circa) 1956

Many of the drivers had a long association with the Company, including Philip Stark who started pre-war. Reg Stokes, a long time employee, on retiring became caretaker living at 11 Newtown Road. Jack Chedzoy and Gordon Blake were also with Majors pre-war, Jack being chiefly concerned with the sand pit and the delivery of sand to the many local brick yards, while Gordon, after returning from war service, was engaged on long distance trips. Jack Gamblin made the change from agriculture to road transport and joined the firm in the late 1950's, he continued until its closure in 1988. His knowledge of things agricultural earned him the nickname of "Farmer Jim"! Stanley Crandon joined the Company as a driver on completion of his National Service, but in later years became a member of the workshop staff until the Company's closure.

Jack's wife Ruby took over the accounts in the early 1970's and Harry took a less active part in the Company, finally retiring in 1978. Reg had died in 1974. During the next ten years Jack and Rex with Ruby's assistance ran the Company, but with the biggest customer leaving the area and with ever increasing difficulties in trading conditions the Company closed in 1988 and sold part of the premises for development. At this point Jack bought a lorry and operated from the remaining part of the premises as a sole trader; Rex did similarly with a Transit van. In 1997 the remaining part of the premises were sold and the Major family's association with transport and Highbridge came to an end after almost 100 years

(Information and photographs supplied by Rex Major and the late Jack Major).

PARLATEX

The site, in Walrow had, originally been a milk factory and was then used as a pound, where cows were held awaiting transport. The cattle had been purchased at Highbridge market; then delivered to the pound and were held until a train arrived to take them to their final destination.

Parlatex was established in 1936 and after the war made mallets and rollers for the flax industry; they had previously been in premises in West Huntspill. Richard Wright had come to the company at the start but had been transferred to Bridgwater during the war to be employed in engineering. . Some of the directors were members of the Wills Tobacco Co and when Wills retired Robert Hobbs and another man ran Parlatex. A Mr. Jones joined the company in 1975, as maintenance fitter and foreman and, the firm soon expanded.

The production of flax rollers was gradually reduced so this prompted the firm to look for other work in order to maintain production; the development of additional mallets for firms such as SMC.FKI Crypton plus some work for Cellophane resulted. At one stage in production they developed mud flaps for Vauxhall cars, but not for the Company direct, mud flaps were also designed and manufactured for cars made by Opel. Around that time Upton and Scott were at Sealed Motors Co. where they produced mud flap moulds and Vauxhall wanted flaps for their new Cavalier. David Gwilliams required milking machine rubbers and arrived on the scene with a representative from Avon Rubber Co. who needed machine rubber items. At this time there was about 25 employees plus quite a number of out-workers.

Sealed Motors Co. found they required "O" rings for pumps that were made by Dowty, these were produced in Malta, (500 a week). SMC needed 3,500 a day and would send a car to Heathrow to collect the 500 a day needed. It was decided, by Palatex to buy the machine, from Italy, to cover the new contract with SMC; the machine to arrive in London in 6 weeks time for an exhibition. In the meantime they would use a sample to make the tools needed so that Parlatex could start production of the "O" rings, the suppliers kept their word, and they worked 7 days a week producing the required rings. Mr Jones was promoted to Works Manager. Orders for mud flaps increased for Vauxhall to a lorry load a week, so Parlatex built a new factory to cope with the increased production, that building is now "Hill Leigh", the old building was demolished. Later another factory was built behind where the original one had stood; this is now "Flight Pumps".

By now Mr Jones was Works Director, this was a man who had started out as a farm worker. He left the Company and set up on his own factory at St. Lukes. Walrow. Parlatex continued for a further 2 years, a firm from Weston-super- Mare bought it out and quickly closed it down.

(Article supplied by John Jones)

MORLANDS

The Morlands business started in Highbridge, at 15, Market Street in 1946; fourteen women were employed to make pram canopies from parachute silk, pram rugs were also made. Demand for their products grew so in 1948 they moved to a purpose built factory off the Burnham Road. The Morlands Housing Estate soon followed.

On May 4th 1951 Googie Withers a well-known film star at that time, visited the Morland factories at Glastonbury and Highbridge. She was entertained to lunch and afterwards was given a tour of the factory at Glastonbury, she then moved on to Highbridge to be shown through the various departments. The youngest employee at Highbridge, Margaret Smith presented a bouquet to her.

It was also in 1951 that a National magazine asked the Morland Company to relate the story of one of their girls during a typical working day in the factory. Joan Peddy a seventeen-year-old machine operator in the canopy stitching section was selected, and an article was based on her typical day.

"Once upon a time, an English country girl had the choice of either drifting to an industrial town and thereby losing the bloom of youth by working in a factory; or, alternatively she could remain where she was, isolated and alone, unable to make a living for herself, as did her city sister.

Today, however, Joan Peddy and hundreds like her, are now able to live at home in the country and by taking a short cycle ride to work and can earn about £5 or £6 a week by the time they are eighteen. Joan, who left school at fifteen, has worked at the Morlands factory in Highbridge, Somerset, where they make fringed canopies for baby's prams. She was trained from the very beginning to work a sewing machine, she now operates a taping machine and coming up to eighteen, is now one of the factory's best canopy machinists.

Her life at work is easy; it provides her with companionship, a good living wage and the happy conditions of a modern factory. Her benefits include, a first rate canteen, pleasant working conditions and sports (she is a member of the hockey team). Her employers also provide entertainment, dances and lectures, etc. At the same time, she is still able to live with her parents in the Somerset village of Huntspill, where she also enjoys work in the community doing her nursing duties with the St. John Ambulance Brigade

(This article appears with the kind permission of Joan Peddy(Mrs Joan Rowden))

(Photo supplied by Doreen Reddish)

A Christmas Party at Morlands in 1951

With their product range growing to include footwear, an extension to the factory was built, into which they moved in 1956. In the 1960's sheepskin rugs were added to their production line and later in the 1960's sheepskin coats appeared. It was inevitable that foreign manufacturers would attempt to do better than the U.K. and eventually this hit production at Morlands.

Regrettably the factory closed in 1981.

At the time of the closure the Manager was Herbie Edgar, (past Managers included Mr.Williams, Pip Lockyer and Danny Weeks). The original fourteen "girls" who worked under forewoman Doris Leek and Manager Mr. Smurdon (affectionately known as "Dad") included: -Chris Stanbury, Kath Coles, June Cook, Norah Coombes, Phyllis Tippetts, Dorothy Dean, Edwina Clare, Violet Kidner, Rose Pepperall, Phyllis Wells, Joyce Wells, Gwen? and Joan? Other employees at later dates were: - Dennis Coles, John & Betty McCleary, Joe & Gladys French, Mark Browning, Joyce Parsons, Jean Sandiford (Packing Coat, Inspector).

WOODBERRY BROS & HAINES

It was soon after the Second World War, that in 1948 Jack and Cecil Woodberry, together with Cecil Haines, set up their first workshops in Coronation Road.

There was a need for someone to produce furniture; because during the war many families had lost all their possessions in air raids, also with men returning from the forces and wishing to set up homes again there was the inevitable a shortage. Woodberry Bros & Haines saw this need and they decided to start producing pieces of furniture from redundant ammunition boxes. With orders starting to build up it was not long before larger premises were required and in 1949 the first bay was opened in Springfield Road. It was built on the site of an old Gas Works, with a labour force of six. Over the following years building

work continued on the adjoining site of the brickyard once owned by Cox's, it was in these workshops that **School Furniture** was produced.

A view of one of the Workshops at Springfield Road

Due to experiencing some bad debts on the joinery side of production, that had caused a few problems, it became necessary for the Company to take stock of the market for school furniture. The decision was therefore made to produce school furniture only for the County Council where the money was safe. This proved to be a wise decision and it soon paid off, orders were received to cater for the supply of furniture on a national basis. Woodberry Bros & Haines were the first manufacturer to produce a bent laminated school chair, and, because other companies could not supply these, they had the monopoly on school furniture.

(Photos supplied by Collin Moore)

Works Entrance at Springfield Road, with some of the Staff.

It was whilst in this production that the business decided to invest in the first machine of its type to 'print wood' and **Caxton Furniture** was born. —William Caxton had invented the first printing machine; so it was agreed they call their product **Caxton.** Boards that were printed on this machine were supplied to the caravan manufacturers for the internal decorative panels. This business was further developed, so that they may enter into the production of **Domestic Furniture,** the prices were very competitive. Again their eye for future business had not failed, as this became a successful venture.

Many times it is said, "Why did'nt I think of that"—Jack Woodberry whilst looking through wallpaper books spotted patterns of decorative wood paper. He decided to develop a machine that would put wood patterns onto the panels they were producing; the cost of manufacturing domestic furniture was cut and demand soon outstripped production.

It was around this time that County Councils were suffering severe cutbacks from the Government with regards to educational spending and the orders for school furniture diminished. Obviously this caused a decrease in its manufacture but this gave them the opportunity to increase the manufacture of domestic furniture and, in 1972 the manufacture of school furniture ceased. Eventually the Springfield Road site was not able to cater for further expansion, and due to the increase in demand, it was necessary to look for an alternative site. In 1988 the negotiations with British Rail to purchase land in Walrow were successful and additional buildings were provided.

Woodberry Bros & Haines now also produce kitchen and bathroom furniture; they have 350 employees. In 2002 the Company moved to the Walrow Industrial Estate to a new factory and office block.

(Information supplied by Christine Woodberry and Ben Griffen (an employee for 55 years)

WILLSHER & QUICK LIMITED

Willsher & Quick Limited was founded in 1956, with the two Directors – Mr L.G. Willsher and Mr N.S. Quick and was originally intended as a general sheet metal producing unit, working from premises in Market Street.

In 1958 the two Directors realised the difficulty being experienced by the electrical industry in enclosing their equipment. With the acquisition of larger premises the production of control gear enclosures commenced. The growth of demand for these enclosures was so rapid that it soon became apparent that further expansion was inevitable, and in 1962 plans were made for a modern factory

Visitors being shown completed Consoles

unit, specifically designed for enclosure manufacture. In November 1963 all production was transferred to the new factory at Walrow, it was the first on the estate. In 1970-71 a building expansion programme was complete extending the works area and building a new office block.

The work force gradually grew over the years with the increase in production and in the late 1970's employed 130 personnel. The Walrow estate was chosen, being the only one available. The Company commenced supplying custom-built enclosures for West Germany through an agent in 1964. It had seen that there was a potential in this market, so consequently in 1965 Willsher & Quick (GmbH) was formed in Kaldenkirchen, West Germany. Following this Willsher & Quick (Northern) Limited at Blyth, Northumberland was formed for the production of enclosures mainly for the electronic industries. Since the companies have moved into new and larger premises. Willsher & Quick have had a major share of the enclosure market but competition is very keen and with today's conditions, maintaining deliveries and a high standard is essential.

Visitors here being shown completed Custom built Enclosures

In 1956 Cooper B-Line Ltd. began trading as a partnership in the name of Willsher & Quick Ltd., and it was incorporated in 1959, being subsequently sold in November 2000 to Cooper B Line that is a wholly owned subsidiary of Cooper Industries Ltd. The U.K. and European headquarters of the American Company is at Walrow Industrial Estate Highbridge Somerset TA9 4AQ

Walrow Industrial Estate

This Industrial Estate was established in 1963, it is thought that Willshers & Quick were one of the first to occupy the site, they were followed by a number of companies including: - Hill Leigh Joinery Ltd, Keedwell RT Transport Ltd, Peter Evans Storage Systems Ltd, Walrow Tyre Services, Ltd, Henri Studio (Europe) Ltd, plus many other smaller businesses; the latest to arrive being Woodberry Bros & Haines.

Isleport Business Park

This Business Park was set up in 1990; this includes Tycom Ltd, Yeo Valley, Brake Bros.Food Service Ltd, Jewsons Ltd Builders Merchants, Isleport Foods Ltd, David Salisbury (Conservatories) Ltd, and more recently Crabtree & Evelyn Ltd. plus a number of others companies.

Chapter 5

SPORT

Within the community sport was an important social event, whether it involved individuals or groups. Representing their hometown or place of employment brought pride and for many the first taste of discipline, that was tinged with excitement lifelong friendships were formed.

Through the generations various activities have come and gone. The following articles give us a glimpse into sport in Highbridge over the years.

Recreation Field

After the death of Dr. Reginald Wade in 1932 Southwell House and land, and the area called "The Home Field" was sold to the then Highbridge Urban District Council for the sum of £550, the area to be used for public walks and a pleasure garden.

The Council officially opened the Recreation Field to the public on March 29th 1933. A month later in April 1933 the Council was dissolved and amalgamated with Burnham under a Somerset review; but in 1974 when Sedgemoor District Council was formed it took over responsibility of the Recreation Field.

Angling Association

This is the oldest Angling Club in Somerset, it was formed around 1878 and was the result of anglers meeting in a public house and deciding to hold a match to find out who was the best angler.

The "Rose and Crown Inn" which was then situated at the corner of Market Street and Market Terrace, was closely associated with the start of the Highbridge Angling Association (H.A.A.). Later the "Cooper's Arms" became its headquarters, in 1985 the Committee moved it to the "George Hotel". However, in 1988 came a move to the "Highbridge Hotel" returning after two years to the "Cooper's Arms" which is the current headquarters. Committee meetings were held about four times a year, Mr. F. Young was Secretary during 1920 and 1948 but ill health caused him to resign and he became a life member. In 1948 Fred Avery (from Mark) took over as Chairman from Len Chick who became Secretary.

Membership in the late nineteenth century, comprised, mostly, the employees of the Locomotive Works, Bacon Factory, Bland's, timber yard and about four brickyards. The fishing rights were on the River Brue from the Locomotive Works to the New Bridge and this is where all the contests were fished. The River Brue was fished freely up river as far as "Blackbull Bridge". The membership fee in 1900 was Adult 2/6d, (12 1/2p) junior 1/3d (7 1/2p) and the old Avon, Brue and Parrett Licence was 6d. (2 1/2p).

Fish were plentiful for most course species Pike, Carp, Roach, Perch, Tench, Dace, Gudeon, Eels, but no Bream. These were introduced after the worst pollution ever known, when millions of fish died between 1918 and 1922. At that time the cause of the pollution was not publicised, unlike today's health and safety rules. Four contests were held each season – three Club Matches and the Annual Tradesmen Contest when all the prizes were donated by local tradesmen. All contests were on Saturday's, fishing from 3 p.m. to 7 p.m.

The event of the year was the Annual Supper and Concert held on Saturday evening following the Tradesmen Contest when all the prizes, both Club and Tradesmen, were presented to the winners. This was held in November at the "Coopers Arms Hotel", price 2/6d. After the supper there was a concert, all the artists, being members of the local Minstrel Party, who also gave concerts to full houses during the winter months at the Town Hall and surrounding villages.

These past memories bring to mind some of the well-known officers of the Association – John Tyler and his sons, Archie and William, Mr Mundy, Editor and Proprietor of the old "Highbridge Echo", Mr. Perkins, his son-in-law and Reporter Tommy Came, Auditor and Pianist, Fred Young, Secretary.

Tim Hand, Chris Fear, John Hand, Maurice White, Violet King and Peter Pengelly

Coming to the later years one of the most coveted prizes to be won annually is the Harry Thompson shield. During the 1940's, Mr. J.T. Lewis, then Secretary received a letter from New Zealand written by Mr. Thompson saying he would like to make and present to the Association a shield for competition. The offer was accepted and it is now one of the Associations best trophies. Mr. Thompson also informed the Secretary that he had given the Auckland Museum a Carp in a glass case, which his father had caught in the River Brue. Mr. Lewis kept in touch with Mr. Thompson for many years and sent him numerous photographs of the Brue at different spots, also views of Burnham-on-Sea and Highbridge, the photographs had been taken by Harold French who was Chairman of the Association. Harry Thompson's father was a craftsman working at the Locomotive Works and Harry also apprenticed as a fitter and turner, and after working in the Midlands emigrated to New Zealand.

(Information and photograph supplied by Maurice White)

Association Football

In the early days the arrival of the railway brought prosperity to the town and as it grew industry arrived in the shape of the Railway Works and Brickworks. There were also factories associated with the agricultural life of the area, such as a Bacon Factory, cheese making and a creamery.

Sporting activities were soon to spring up and football was probably one of the most popular. Employees from the various businesses soon formed teams and football matches between them became a regular pastime.

In 1906-7 there was evidence of a team called Highbridge Rovers and a reserve team in 1911.

**Highbridge Bacon Factory Team
1937**

Back row: 1st left - Bert Hill
2nd left - Bert Besley
4th left - Reg Slocombe
5th left - Horace Ham

Front row: 4th - Charley Cross

**The lady is Mrs Kidley
(Manager's wife)**

(Photo supplied by Mrs G Besley)

There was also another team, the Highbridge Athletic, but little is known about it. In those far off days, Highbridge Rovers played in the Bridgwater and District League, whether or not this was their introduction to a full competitive league is not clear. It is known that the Highbridge Town association football Club was first registered with the Somerset Football Association in 1932. Records and reports of matches are sparse and little is known of where teams played **their** home matches. It is possible "Daunton Field" now Poplar Estate, provided pitches or perhaps the Recreation field, previously known as "The Home Field" off Grange Avenue that was officially opened in 1933.

**Highbridge Town Youths A.F.C.
Season 1948-9**

Back row
T.Pepperall, P Baker, D.Bird,
W. Evans, B. Hooper, D.Coles,
B.Seabourne

Middle row
D.Hale, R.Childs, J.Norris(Capt).
B.Rowden, C.Simmons

Front:
R. Moore, D.Came

(Photo supplied by Brian Rowden)

The "White Hart Hotel" in Church Street, had by now become the clubs headquarters. In 1949 the club attained its highest league status when Highbridge Town A.F.C. joined the Somerset Senior League.

The team's shirts were in the colours of claret and blue quarters. The team had a good regular following, the supporters coach was full for most away matches, a few of those being held at places such as Chard, Winscombe, Watchet, Ilminster, R.A.F. Locking and Frome.

Home matches were played on a ground off the Bristol Road, opposite the entrance to Poples Bow.

In the 1952 –3 season a match was played against Mount Hill Enterprises (Bristol) this was in the Football Association Amateur Cup at the local Bristol Road ground. Highbridge was defeated 3 - 2. The team shown below.

Back Row:
F. Palin, B. Chiffers, W. Sheils, D.Marsh, D.Coles, C.Close, T.Smith.

Front Row:
K.Tonkin, T.Raynor, H.Cox, J.Bidgood, L.Trickey.

Highbridge Town A.F.C. 1952 Pictured at the Bristol Road Ground

Highbridge having played at the Bristol Road ground for some years returned to the Recreation ground in January 1953, for home matches and have continued to play there until the present day.

Matches played against the old rival Burnham during the 1950's were for the Fred Thomas Challenge Cup these always provided a lot of interest, supporters of both towns turned out in force to cheer their team and the result always caused much discussion afterwards.

Highbridge Town A.F.C. Late 1960's

Back Row:
F.Popham, N.Barrett, T.Hoyland, W.Sheils, B.Hooper, P.Hooper, D.Faulks, R. Stuckey

Front Row:
J.Holley, M.Dyer, D.Saunders, H.Williams, A.N.Other

Highbridge Town played in the Somerset Senior League with some success but by the end of the 1950's times changed and in September 1960 the team left the League to join the Weston-super-Mare & District League until around 1970 when they joined the Taunton & District Saturday League where in 2003-4 they are in Division Two. There have been good and bad seasons but the team continues to get local support and many enjoy watching 'their' team on the 'Rec'. A small celebration was held in 2003 to mark "50 Years of Football" at the 'Rec'

(Photo supplied by Mike. Lang)

Highbridge Town (2003/4 season)
Back Row: S Pople, S.Woodberry, W.Hand, J.Picton, S.Wills, K.Watts(Manager), D.Johnson, R.Catterall
Front Row: J Hicks, B King, M Thresher, A Chedzey, M Flanagan, A Donavon

(This article has been compiled with additional information and photographs supplied from previous research by Tony Smith and Bill Sheils)

Footnote - *Many followers of football will remember a certain Brian Clough, who it is learned played for R.A.F. Watchet at the Recreation Ground on January 14th 1955; he scored in his team's 2-1 victory over Highbridge Town in the Somerset Senior League*

Badminton

The Jubilee Badminton Club was formed in the mid 1950's by an enthusiastic group of players. Competition Matches were played in the Town Hall, also club nights were held for all members to participate. Amongst teams played were Cheddar, Morlands and R.A.F. Locking. The club continued for a few years but eventually disappeared at the end on the 1950's.

Boxing

In the late 1940's after the end of the Second World War, an interest in boxing emerged in the local area. Young lads were encouraged to attend keep fit and training sessions at the scout hut in nearby Burnham-on-Sea organised by Billy Parsons who later fought as a professional boxer known as "The Highbridge Hurricane" (See separate story).

Eventually a club was formed in Highbridge, the headquarters and training area were at the "White Hart Hotel" in Church Street. Mr Bill Tyler was President of the club and with the support of a committee the club was very successful for a number of years. Trainers with the club throughout its history were believed to be Taffy Smith, Ivor Yard and Johnny Popham.

Competitive matches took place at the Town Hall in Market Street, Highbridge where prior to the boxing, entertainment was provided by a dancing display by the Erin Fay School of Dancing.

Members, Committee and Boxers, outside the "White Hart Hotel" in season 1949-1950
Front row: Taffy Smith (Trainer), Clive Young, John Cornish, Bobby Pocock, Bill Tyler (President)
Dennis Howard, John Toomer, Peter Teal, Johnny Popham (Trainer)
Front: Len Cornish

Amongst opponents for the matches were teams from National Smelting (Avonmouth), Tiverton, Weston-super-Mare, Radstock (National Coal Board) Swindon and Bridgwater, also individual contests on separate bills at other venues were organised. On boxing nights the Town Hall was well attended by the public, eager to cheer on their local lads. During the life of the club many successes were achieved in both the Southern Area (National Association of Boys Clubs) and the Somerset N.A.B.C. It is believed the highest achievement was by Bobby Pocock who became the All England National Association of Boys Clubs champion at his weight in 1950.

By the mid 1950's the boxing club had disbanded, the reason for this is not clear, it could have been financial or perhaps lack of interest, either way a boxing club was to be lost to the town. However the facility for young lads to keep fit and train continued at the "Bristol Bridge Inn", where Billy Parsons

(The Highbridge Hurricane) who had finished his professional career became landlord. He encouraged lads from groups in the town, such as the St. John Ambulance and many other individuals to use the gym.

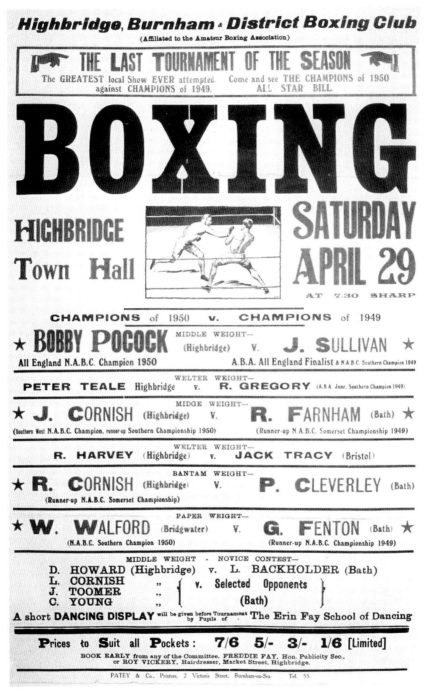

(Original poster supplied by Ralph Cornish)

Years were to pass and in October 1998 a new boxing club was formed, the King Alfred Amateur Boxing Club, founded by Andy Churches a qualified Amateur Boxing Association coach who had been a member of the Sydenham A.B.C. (Bridgwater) from 1991 to the formation of the new club.

Initial funds for the new club were obtained by an organised sponsored walk to Brean Down and as fifty years previously Billy Parsons ("The Highbridge Hurricane") was there to take part in the walk aged 77 and give encouragement to the new endeavour.

Training nights were held at King Alfred School, Highbridge, until 2001, when a move was made to facilities in Love Lane (Burnham-on-Sea). The club is now flourishing under the President Roger Cross and the hard working supporters and Committee, organising their own tournaments, the third of which took place in 2003 at the Burnham Holiday Village.

Club members are matched against opponents by age, weight and experience, from other clubs in various parts of the country e.g. Bristol, Dagenham, Bideford and South Wales. Members also travel to other club tournaments to gain experience and further develop the club.

In memory of Billy Parsons who died in June 2002 the family has given the title "The Highbridge Hurricane" to the club and is now carried proudly for the club by Rob Boardman.

From the details obtained the new club appears to echo what had taken place all those years ago, it is hoped the King Alfred Amateur Boxing Club has continued success.

Information for the Original Boxing Club – Ralph Cornish – Peter Teal
Details King Alfred A.B.C. from Andy Churches and Roger Cross

"The Highbridge Hurricane"

A young Billy Parsons at school in West Huntspill showed little interest in the art of boxing. Yet who would have imagined that this young lad would eventually spar with Don Cockell who was preparing for his World Heavyweight title fight with Rocky Marciano, who ruled the world of boxing from 1951 –1955?

On leaving school Billy attended a keep fit class run by a couple of local builders, and although not keen at first was encouraged to box, and eventually he climbed into the ring against an opponent, was successful it was fairly obvious he was a natural. At the age of eighteen, his first amateur bout was in Weston-super-Mare, where he quickly beat his opposition with a knock out, this was to be the pattern for his amateur days, with thirty two wins from thirty six fights – seventeen by knock out.

The Second World War put his boxing career on hold, as he became a fireman on the Somerset and Dorset Railway at Highbridge, although he was still training and boxing with American servicemen stationed in the local area. All of which paid off when he turned professional in 1945, that young lad at school in West Huntspill was now nine stones of granite with dynamite in both fists as he knocked out his first opponent.

A year later in 1946 Billy married Joyce Manchip at West Huntspill church, back in the ring the "Highbridge Hurricane" in his first fourteen fights knocked out ten of his opponents. By the age of twenty six his amateur and pro record showed twenty four knock outs and twenty two points wins, out of fifty three fights. Promoters from London were chasing the boxer who was now described as "The greatest prospect for British Championship Honours the West Country had produced for years". Billy finally relented and spent some time training at Jack Soloman's famous gym in London.

Even though he was now training alongside the likes of Don Cockell, Jack Gardner, Randolph Turpin and Freddie Mills he still found time to return to Highbridge and encourage the local youngsters in the towns amateur boxing club. Several promoters wanted Billy to move to London, where they promised him he would be fighting in world-class bouts. But the pull of the West Country was too strong and his boxing career came to an end.

After keeping a guesthouse for a short period with his wife Joyce, they became Licensees of the "Bristol Bridge Inn" on the Bristol Road where Billy continued to support and train the local amateur boxers. He and his wife later worked at Morlands Sheepskin Factory until being made redundant when the factory closed. By now there were three children, Carol, Terry and Jeanette.

On June 8th 2002, Billy "The Highbridge Hurricane" a grandfather and great grandfather died at the age of eighty.

(Information and photo supplied by Carol Barnes (Daughter)

Cricket

The first reference to cricket in the town appears to be a recollection of a field near "Sandyway Farm" on Burnham Road owned by Mr. W. Hatcher. This was used for a short time; however, there are no further details available.

Highbridge & District Cricket Team, together with a Somerset County XI in May 1937

During the 1930's a cricket field did appear on land (believed to be part of "Dauntons Farm behind Church Street, now the area covered by housing (Poplar Estate).

The club was well established and achieved a high enough status to attract a benefit game for a Somerset County player Wally Luckes (wicket keeper), who brought a County eleven including Arthur Wellard, Harold Gimblet and Horace Hazell. The game took place on May 5th 1937, the County fielding eleven players and Highbridge fourteen. Unfortunately no details of the final scores are available. No official records show the end of the club, it is known the club was still playing in 1940 when Harry Norman (fishmonger) was Captain and Jack Dyer was amongst the players.

In 1951 a club was formed playing their home games on a pitch at Bristol Road. Alongside an area used by the football club, also at some time games had been played on Burnham Road. (Now the site of King Alfred School Grounds). At this time no leagues had been formed, but the games were "friendlies", some opposing teams were Stonehouse, Wells, Timsbury and Bridgwater "A". The club eventually moved to "Ashford's" field, situated on the left of Walrow Bridge between the bridge and the brickwork's. The playing area here was not ideal as Groynes (gullies) spread across the field making a flat pitch area difficult to provide, efforts were made to fill in certain areas to provide a better surface. The changing area too, was less than adequate, a cow shed in the corner of the field being pressed into use.

Visiting teams did not take kindly to the facilities provided both by the changing rooms! and the playing surface. However, games did take place and at the tea interval, a leisurely stroll over Walrow bridge and onwards to the "Constitutional Club" next to the "Railway Hotel"(now the site of Alpha House) where teas for the players were provided by a band of helpers.

The club eventually disbanded in 1952 and some players continued their interests by joining Burnham Cricket Club.

Darts

This is another sport which started many many years ago and was a very popular game during the war, many hours were spent playing darts to overcome the tiring hours spent "fire watching" or "on guard". Unlike skittles, darts was a game that could be played in the home and this increased its popularity.

Combined Darts Teams from George Hotel and Artillery Arms in Season 1973-74

V. Plews, M. Soloman, M. Butt, J. Akers, R. Moore, B. Short, V. Draper, P. Love, G. Pole, D. Bagshaw

(Photo supplied by Vernon Draper)

Public houses formed dart teams and players strove to do well in order to get in the pub team; leagues were formed and continue to be competitive. Friday night being darts night. The Somerset County Darts Team was at the Highbridge Social Club in October 2003 to play the first of four home matches.

Highbridge & District Racing Pigeon Club

This club was founded in 1939 by six or seven local pigeon fanciers, who until then had raced their birds with other local clubs, namely "The Huntspill Homing Society" and two clubs from Burnham, at the "Crown" and the "Commercial".

On the suggestion of a well-known local (bobby) P.C. King the "Globe Inn Pigeon Club" was formed, and in later years was joined by members from Burnham and Huntspill to make one club, which is still going today. Over the years we have seen a lot of changes, in 1966 we moved from the "Globe" to the "George Hotel" and then in 1980 The "Highbridge Social Club" became our headquarters, where we are today.

The strength of the club is now only eight racing lofts but in its heyday the 1940's and 1950's, nearly every back garden on the Clyce and in Grange Avenue had a pigeon loft, as well as many others. In those days the birds were taken to race points by rail, when thousands would be released at a given time. To keep the club ticking over during the 1950's whist drives were held in the Old Railway Club hut, this was at the bottom of Walrow Bridge near where "Kwik Save" is at present.

Other clubs in the country would send to Highbridge, these were liberated in John Bland's yard opposite the "Top House" Pub, (quite a spectacle!) The birds were later taken by road transport, they go to the South Coast for some races and then on across the Channel to the South of France for races of up to 500 miles. Homing pigeons have varying degrees of ability, as some would not find their way home from Highbridge town clock.

Pigeon Club 1980's
Left to Right
Back Row: R. Puddy, O. Crandon, J. Burridge, C. Greenslade, T. Dredge, C. Bale, W. Haggett,
Front Row: C. Clapp, W. Haggett, K. Haggett (Hon Sec), J. Andrews (Chairman), E. Baker, W. Crandon

Mr. Wilfred Thomas Haggett (Keith's father), when interviewed by a local newspaper in 1991, told how, as a lad he took up pigeon racing and won a number of prizes. In those early days (1940's) Highbridge had a bustling Market Square and as a boy he remembers how a pub there had a long veranda where the post ponies that pulled the mail carts used to be hitched "just like the cowboy films".

When racing, pigeon fanciers would remove the rings from the legs of the pigeons and "run" them to the judges table outside the "Cooper's Arms". Later when they had a recording clock at Burnham they were allowed only three minutes to get the rings there. So Keith his son used to set off on his bike, to get it there in time and a certain Police Officer would hold up the traffic to let him through. This practice obviously ceased when the club could afford to purchase its own clock.

Between the two wars pigeon racing was the sport of the workingman and birds could be purchased for one shilling and sixpence (7½p) or two shillings (10p). Today it is rather different; in 1991 a pigeon was sold for £77,000 and its eggs for £2,500. Mr. Haggett worked for the Somerset and Dorset at Highbridge, in W.W.II. serving in the infantry and looking after a pigeon loft used by the Commandos. He went with them on small cross Channel patrols, later serving with the Desert Rats in Egypt. His son Keith carried on the family tradition, his grandson Brian, was also an enthusiastic pigeon racer.

Regrettably, in October 2003, after 64 years the Club decided that due to lack of support (only 4 members attended the meeting) it should be dissolved.

(Information and photograph supplied by Tony Dredge and Keith Haggett)

Footnote - *During the 1939-45 war, some of the better birds were donated to the National Pigeon Service and performed many great feats; the owners of these courageous birds were given a special corn allowance, which was collected from Mr Bert Cann on the Cornhill. (Where Tyler Way is now located)*

Article from the Highbridge, Weston, Bridgwater and Somerset Advertiser dated December 22 nd 1945.

It was reported from the local Homing Pigeon Society, owners were now scrounging food for their birds. Corn rations are now only continuing to owners who gave birds for Special Government Service in the war. Rations will affect long distant racing, it is hoped normal feeds will be resumed soon.

Rugby Football

Rugby football was played in Highbridge between February 1885 and November 1896. During its lifetime the club appears to have had two headquarters, one being the "George Hotel" the other the "Railway Hotel" on the Town Square.

Games in 1887 took place in the Burnham area but home games mainly took place in Highbridge at various venues including Walrow and Bristol Road, also on the outskirts of the town, land offered at Huntspill and near Mark. The underfoot conditions of many of these grounds were appalling, sodden conditions, pools of water in groynes (gullies) and of course games were cancelled when conditions made the pitches rock hard under severe frosts, remembering that pitches were not immaculately prepared grounds but simply farmers fields.

Teams visiting during the clubs lifetime would have included – Bridgwater 2nd XV, Wells, Westward (Taunton), Shepton Mallet, Weston-super-Mare "A" and Bath plus many others. Social activities were organised by the club, during 1892 to 1895 a regular event was a Rugby Ball held at the Town Hall, an annual dinner was also well attended at the end of each season. In 1895 a smoking concert (a convivial evening) was held at the "Railway Hotel" for members and friends of the club.

In 1892/93 season, Highbridge played a team at Huntspill, a match organised for the newly inaugurated Huntspill Rugby Football Club.

November 1896, rumours of discord were rife amongst the Highbridge Rugby men and it was considered doubtful whether the team would again appear in public, this appears to have happened and the club dissolved. The club did surface again briefly in 1898, under the name of "Highbridge Veterans".

One very interesting item that was found in the records was that during the very hard winter of 1890/91, in fact, people skated from Highbridge to Bason Bridge along the frozen River Brue.

(These extracts were taken from a publication of Highbridge Football Club (Rugby) –1885 – 1896. Compiled by the late Herbert Howell in 1991)

Skittles

The nine wooden pins, wooden balls and a pitchboard are the type of skittles played in pubs in the West Country. However, an alternative type is played in Weston-super-Mare and some other areas where they have cambered alley and rubber (or vulcanite) balls.

When the game took off locally has been lost in the mist of time but no doubt it arrived when the public houses first came to Highbridge. Because of the competitive nature of this sport it was not long before contests started between teams and soon a league was formed; the Highbridge and District Mens Skittle League.

Local pubs taking part in the league comprise teams from the "Cooper's Arms" "Bristol Bridge" "George Hotel" and the "Social Club".

Pubs from the surrounding area also taking part include; "Brent Knoll Inn" "Berrow Inn" "Pack Horse" Mark, "Royal Artillery", and the "Crown Inn" and "Victoria Inn" from Burnham. Many players may recall attending away matches at such places as the "Railway" (Burtle) now the "Tom Mogg" when they had to go across the levels on pitch dark nights, in fog, sometimes snow, and on icy roads.

Local leagues were once well supported and competitive. There is also a Burnham, Highbridge and District Ladies League. Many of the team's leagues continue today but with pubs closing there are fewer alleys, however, skittles is still followed with the same enjoyment and enthusiasm as it always was.

Speedway

A fairly recent development took place in 1999 with the arrival of speedway to the Highbridge area, previous to this and some while ago the nearest speedway would probably have been at Bristol with "The Bristol Bulldogs"

So for many people in this area of Somerset, there was excitement and anticipation at the thought of speedway being established in the locality.

The "Oak Tree Arena" was built just off the Bristol Road, heading towards the Edithmead roundabout, it was opened in 1999 and the first action was watched by an estimated crowd of nearly 2000 spectators some of whom had travelled some considerable distance to get involved again with speedway. The team who raced under the name "Somerset Rebels" gathered riders from various parts of the country and with the crowds in the first three years averaging 1200; it soon became the top sporting attraction in the Sedgemoor area. Now as action moves into the 2004 season home matches on a Friday evening continue, the club is established and the track itself has become a popular venue praised by many of the visiting riders.

Swimming

The Highbridge Amateur Swimming Club used the River Brue at a point between the station approach and the Calf Market alongside the river, this is now a housing development opposite the "Cooper's Arms".

The club was formed in the early 1900's and taught many children and adults in Highbridge to swim. A wooden platform was constructed for use as a diving board and being adjacent to the bank made for easy access to the river.

Competitive races were held, boats would be moored at different distances on the bank with a rope across, to form the start and finish line. There is still in existence, a silver cup, which was presented for the 120 yards championship and was given by Captain George Sanders in 1907.
Winners were: -

1907	W. Marsh.	1919	C.J.Sparks.
1908	A.J.Forward.	1920	R.Andrews.
1909	J.T.Hardacre.	1921	R. Andrews.
1910	H.Roberts.	1922	R. Andrews.
1911	F.Luke		

By 1930 it appears the club was beginning to struggle for both members and support, as the following report will show:-

An early Water Polo Team

APATHY – *Swimming Club to close down unless further interest is shown.*
There were half a dozen members and two pressmen present at the annual meeting of the Highbridge Swimming Club which ought to have taken place at the "Cooper's Arms" on Wednesday evening. The meeting was due to commence at 7.30 p.m. the press representative arrived at 7.20 p.m. while the club members turned up at 7.40 p.m. and 7.50 p.m. The hon. Secretary Mr. F. C. Dyer failed to put in an appearance at all, no apology received either. As he was in possession of the Minute Book, the few interested members were unable to proceed with the business, and there was no meeting. The hon. Treasurer, Mr Cecil Sparks, moved a resolution that the club should be closed down due to the apathy displayed. The meeting had been widely advertised and yet only six members had put in an appearance. Mr. Howell seconded the motion. However, Mr. Berryman the sports secretary said this was a pity to close the club down. Mrs Pepperall said the children were very keen and that there were some promising swimmers in the junior section. It was finally decided the club should close, Mr. J.C. Sparks and Mr. H. Howell were appointed as trustees.

After the closure of the club it became apparent that local people were concerned by the loss of a facility that had given an important service to the community. However, by 19th July 1930 the situation seemed to have improved as the Burnham Gazette shows.

Swimming Club.
A month ago it was decided to revive the Highbridge Swimming Club, two volunteers have patched up the men's changing quarters. The women are hoping to use a shed near the river for changing, a temporary measure. In the meantime the Secretary, acting on the instructions of the Sub-Committee had invited tenders for the repair of the men's quarters, on average this was £40. After consideration it was decided that due to a low bank balance this would not be viable at the present time. The intention was to hold a dance and other fund raising events before embarking on such expenditure. The hon. Secretary would be pleased to receive any donations towards the erection of this pavilion.

Reports show that the club did reform, but unfortunately not for long, because in late 1930 or early 1931 the swimming club finally closed due to the Local Authorities banning the use of the river.

Footnote - *Anthony Stephens aged 17 from Burnham Road has qualified for the Paralympic Games of 2004 to be held in Athens. He was entered for the 200m, 100m and 50m freestyle events having already broken five world records; setting a new record in the 200m freestyle event at the British Swimming Paralympic Trial.*

Chapter 6

SOCIAL LIFE

Celebrations

The townspeople of Highbridge has always been ready to celebrate special occasions and the reports that we have unearthed, together with a few photographs, show that everyone has been prepared to, not only dress up themselves, but also to bedeck the town with flags and bunting. An early celebration was that for the Diamond Jubilee in1897 of Queen Victoria, as shown in the picture below

This picture shows the residents of Cuthbert Street assembled beneath the garlanded arch that expressed their feelings by pronouncing "God save the Queen"

Following the death of Queen Victoria in 1901 the Coronation of King Edward VII was held in 1902 and this was another occasion when Highbridge could show its patriotism.

In 1911 there was another Coronation, this was for King George V and Queen Mary.
The people of Highbridge dressed in their Sunday best gathered on the Town Square for the planned celebrations.

There were a number of occasions when Highbridge celebrated over the intervening years, for the Coronation of King George V and Queen Mary in 1911 the streets were again a blaze of colour, a picture in the Town Square section illustrates the fervour shown by the townspeople. The next Royal Celebration was for: -

The Coronation of King George VI – 12th May 1937

Major Sutherland called a meeting in January 1937, to discuss the best way of celebrating the coming Coronation, how much money would be needed and how it should be raised. It was agreed by twelve members of an Executive Committee (six from Highbridge) that a penny on the rates should raise the money. This would be allocated to the Burnham and Highbridge wards, with a portion to Berrow.

The committees were elected to cater for: - Luncheon, Children's Tea Committee and Sports and Decorations. In all 140 people formed the united Committee.

The whole town was beautifully decorated; streets, roads and houses, both electricity and gas were being adopted in many pretty designs. They were kept up for more than a week and much admired by those passing through the town.

At 10 am. "The Warmley Silver Military Band" marched through the town.

10.15 am. A large number of people assembled at the Town Square, where a Religious Service was held and the Chairman Mr W.H. Hatcher gave a Loyal Address.

The vicar then took charge of the United Service, supported by the Revd J. Roberts, Rev. E. De Ville and Captain Kirkwood (Salvation Army). The service was concluded with the blessing and the National Anthem. Mr Victor Dyer, conducted the singing, led by the band and several choirs.

By 12.30 the elderly townspeople were entering the Town Hall that was decorated with the National Colours, the tables decorated with vases of real flowers, catering for 250 people, never had the Town Hall looked better. The Committee had arranged a fine menu consisting of roast and corned beef, ham and tongue with bread, pickles, cheese and sauces followed by mince and apple pies, beer and minerals to drink. A toast was given with great enthusiasm to their beloved King & Queen. Cigarettes, which had been presented by Messrs. Wills of Bristol, were handed to all that needed them and were very well enjoyed and greatly appreciated.

At 1.30 pm. a programme of sports commenced in the Recreation Ground, the children's events numbered 16, these were watched by a large number of townspeople.

By 4.30 pm. the children's procession had formed up in Grange Avenue, all the children carried either flags or bannerettes. Companies of Girl Guides, Cubs and Brownies, with their banners led a splendid procession; accompanied by Ministers of several churches, Magistrates, Members of the Highbridge ward. The children were received at the Town Hall, each child's place had a Coronation cup awaiting him or her; the whole affair went without a hitch; the children would remember the importance of this occasion for many years to come.

The sports programme was continued after tea when a large crowd watched ten events for both men and women. At the conclusion of the sports Major Sutherland presented 7 silver cups and 7 silver teaspoons to the tug-of-war teams, together with a silver cup presented by Mr. F. G. Dyer for the highest individual score for skittles.

At 7.30 p.m. was the ceremony of planting a Commemorative tree, (kindly given by Mr. W. H. Hatcher) in the Recreation Ground.

The Warmley Military silver band brought this excellent programme of the day to a close. The carnival dance, arranged by the Entertainment's Committee was held in the Town Hall, a large number of people had a most enjoyable time this went on until the early hours of the morning. The Red Star band, leader Mr Jack Webber, supplied the music.

A final account showed a balance of £10.11s.0d with recommendations that it go towards a drinking fountain being erected in the Recreation Ground.

Finally - 66 unemployed persons within the Highbridge Ward were supplied with a voucher each, to the value of 2/-(10p) to be exchanged by Highbridge tradesmen.

Local people or the press probably photographed the activities, but we have not been able to locate these, it must be borne in mind however that cameras were not so plentiful in the 1930's.

Many people probably remember the next Celebration, this was: -

The Coronation of her Gracious Majesty Queen Elizabeth II 2nd June 1953

Highbridge, on this momentous occasion, was a riot of colour; the streets of the town had been gaily decorated. It had been difficult to discover where the centres of the decorations were, because the streets had been liberally swathed in red, white and blue. Flags and bunting had been stretched across the streets from the famous town clock, making it look like a giant Maypole.

A large congregation attended the Civil Service that was held on the morning, singing and praying under a canopy of colour. The Town Hall normally a rather drab building, had been festooned with bunting and the shops nearby in Market Street were draped with hundred of flags. The "Railway Hotel" was nearly hidden beneath flags, the colourful display being carried across the street.

For many days prior to the celebrations the residents had spent hours bedecking their streets with flags, bunting and streamers. The ingenuity and perseverance shown by many was cruelly tested when on the eve of the celebration wind and rain tore the decorations apart. No matter, next morning out came the ladders and within a very short time the loyal greetings were once again blowing in the breeze.

Residents of the streets of Highbridge had been making plans for months to ensure that everyone, especially the children, remembered this great occasion. To many it would be a 'once and only' opportunity to demonstrate their patriotic fervour, barely a single house had not got some decoration of its own. Whilst houses not only vied with each other to express their loyalty, but whole streets attempted to be the most spectacular. The organisers had taken special care of the street celebrations to make sure no one was forgotten, young folk, old folk, and people of every class. This was going to be a day to rejoice and rejoice they would.

The religious and serious part of the Highbridge Coronation Celebrations ended with the final words at the United Service at the Town Square. Within a short time of the service ending the be flagged streets in the town were nearly deserted, people had hurried home to join in their own or street celebrations, the jollity continuing into the night.

Owners of that rare commodity, a television receiver, quickly took up their positions in front of the screen, not wanting to miss the pomp and pageantry-taking place in London. Because of television they were now able to feel "They were part of the Coronation" proper.

Those less fortunate, not having access to a T.V. queued at the "Regent Cinema" where there were six large screen televisions; four in the stalls and two in the balcony. The cinema owners, and "Sheppard and Sparks" of Market Street, earned the gratitude of the townsfolk for providing them with the opportunity to view the Coronation Procession and Service. People had queued from 9 o'clock to take up their seats, some waited for seats throughout the day, and many stood at the back of the stalls and in the aisles to obtain a view. Those watching the television in the cinema echoed both the solemnity and jollity of the crowds in London.

Street parties abounded in Highbridge everyone having their own special programme, entertainment, fancy dress, and tea parties were the most popular. Fancy dress parades were very popular events in Highbridge, some Coronation Festivities were held on the Saturday, most of which were held indoor due to the inclement weather. We have obtained details of some parties and have referred to them alphabetically.

ALSTONE ROAD

There was a fancy dress competition for adults with entrants parading along the road; the winner Jack Ward as "Town Crier" led it. Heading the children's procession was four-year-old Peter Hand, who drawing a miniature Coronation Coach, this won the first prize. About eighty adults and children sat down to tea in Mr. M. Duckett's shed, this was in the field where the sports had taken place, children were presented with a Coronation mug, the old folk also received a gift.

BERTHA TERRACE

Residents of the Terrace and of Market Street found it necessary on the Tuesday to erect a sacking and canvas screen to protect the children from a stiff breeze. A large Coronation cake, the ingredients were given by the residents, was made by Mrs. Bishop. At their party each child was given a mug full of sweets plus a shilling. Games and sports were held in the street.

BRITISH LEGION

A Coronation treat that had been arranged by the Highbridge British Legion for over 80 children of members on the Saturday was a memorable occasion. A programme of sports had been arranged and was held on the Recreation Ground. An iced Coronation cake was the centre of attention at the tea party held in the Town Hall. To round off the day there was a programme of films comprising "The Tonto Basin Outlaws", Laurel and Hardy in "The Housetow" and two coloured cartoons "Mary's Little Lamb" and "Sunshine Makers".

BURNHAM ROAD

Because of uncertain weather the organisers accepted the offer of Mr. Bert Redding and used his garage on the Monday afternoon. The residents from Half-way House to just beyond the Burnham Road Post Office enjoyed this party. Sports for the children were held in a nearby field, over the entrance, there was an arch of red, white and blue. Mrs. Brookfield had made the Coronation cake for the 52 children; a miniature coach and horses given by Mrs, Clayton, topped it.

The other section of Burnham Road, from near the Post Office to the Old Burnham Road held its party on the Saturday on the lawn of Mrs. Davey's house. The centre piece was a magnificent cake, each of the 21 children was given a cup, saucer and plate, plus sixpence, bag of sweets, an orange and ices. Sports and games were held after tea and prizes given.

CHURCH STREET

The "White Hart Hotel" hosted the party for Church Street, the licensee Mrs. M. Harwood dressed up as Queen Elizabeth I. Printed invitations had been sent out to 90 children to attend this gay party, most of them wearing fancy dress. A huge iced Coronation cake brought sparkle to their eyes and there was great excitement shown at the moment this lovely cake was cut. Mr Freddie Fay amused the children at this party, which was held in the skittle alley and he led them all in community singing. There was a charming dance display by pupils of Erin Fay, the dance teacher. Prizes were awarded for the best fancy dress and, before reluctantly, making their departure everyone joined in singing the Coronation song "Golden Coach". Children received a Coronation beaker filled with sweets, plus a new shilling, together with an orange and an ice cream.

CLYCE ROAD
Dr. J.S.W.Little gave permission for the party to be held in his surgery, this had to accommodate 38 children as well as the many helpers. Everything went well, the chief feature of the table being a lovely iced cake, decorated in red, white and blue and inscribed "ER II Coronation. Long may she reign". The children each received a Coronation mug with toffees, one shilling, a paper hat, and streamers, teaser and a flag – so had plenty to take home. The old age pensioner's egg and spoon race was held during the adult sports, this was followed by an adult meat supper at the home of Mrs. Lovibond. A tug-of-war between 25 women and 8 men took place and, after much hilarity, in a win for the former.

CUTHBERT STREET
Mrs. Mason and Capt. Brittan of the Highbridge Salvation Army judged the fancy dresses of sixty-four children who attended the party for Cuthbert Street and Newtown Road. Children under 11 received a mug and sweets, those over 11 years old, had two shillings. The less than 11 years and babies also received National Savings Stamps. After tea the children went to the home of Mrs.Cook at 41, Poplar Estate to see on television the Coronation Newsreel, they returned for community singing and dancing.

EAST AND SOUTH AVENUES
Mr. F. Parsons, the Vice-Chairman of Burnham Urban District Council, wearing a crown of cardboard and paper, presided over the Coronation party given to 75 children on Saturday. Each child received a Coronation beaker. Two iced Coronation cakes graced the party and the children also received confectionery, apple, orange, stick of rock, chocolate, crisps, ice cream, a paper hat and a balloon. Following the sports all joined in the community singing.

GRANGE AVENUE
Possibly the last of the Coronation street parties took place on the Thursday when about 46 children were entertained to tea near Mr. F. Morgan's home. The centrepiece of the table, being a cake weighing eleven pounds, this was accompanied by another cake shaped like a crown. Whilst the children were being photographed the adults sat down to tea. Next came the grand march past of the children to receive their souvenirs, every child from 5 – 16 received a souvenir pen. All children under 5 received beakers filled with chocolates, an orange, plus a shilling. Older people were presented with Coronation souvenir tins of tea. An Old Time dance was held during the evening.

HIGHBRIDGE ROAD
That part of the road between Worston Road and the Territorial Army H.Q. held their party on the Monday afternoon. It was a delightful setting on the lawn at the rear of "Brewery House", by permission of Mr. & Mrs. Porter. Pride of place was the Coronation cake, surmounted by a crown, the residents had given ingredients and Mrs. Porter made the cake. Souvenir brooches were presented to 38 children together with sweets and balloons; games and races were held.

The section from the Territorial Army H.Q. to Half Way house held its party on the Tuesday, 22 children were entertained at the table where the centrepiece was a two sided cutout of the Queen mounted on a revolving turntable. Mrs Tales had loaned her garage for the event and had also made a Coronation cake surmounted by a crown. Each child, in addition to being given a silver spoon also had a National Savings stamp in a souvenir folder, a bag of sweets, a teaser and a coloured balloon.

HUNTSPILL ROAD
Fifteen children living in this road held their party on the Wednesday in Dr. J.S.W. Little's surgery, each received a cup (filled with sweets) a saucer and a plate. There was a tremendous amount of food and everyone had an excellent time at the games that followed.

KING STREET
A gay little party was held 40 children and their parents in the large garage loaned by Mr. Tucker. The children each received a souvenir mug, presented by the oldest resident Mrs. Saunders. A Coronation cake given by Mrs. Scaddon, was the highlight of the festivity. The souvenir mugs were filled with sweets and each child received a pencil engraved with their names. The party ended in the evening with a concert and singsong.

MORLAND ROAD
On Tuesday afternoon one of the largest parties took place in the canteen of Morland's Factory. Over 125 children from families living in North and West Avenue and Morland Road received a souvenir mug. Oranges and sweets were received, plus prizes from the sports held nearby. The parents tucked into the food left by the children; there had been a mountain of food supplied for all.

OLD BURNHAM ROAD

This celebration started as early as 10.00 o'clock, on the Tuesday morning when Mrs Hatcher installed a television set in her garage. Everyone was invited to watch the Coronation. In the afternoon 30 children attended the party, each receiving a souvenir cup, saucer and plate for under 7 years old; older children received an engraved mug. A Coronation cake was made by Mrs. Wells.

(Photo supplied by Stephanie Wynn)

Crackers, sweets, balloons and paper hats were given to each child, plus an orange. Sports and games were enjoyed after tea.

POPLAR ESTATE
A different celebration was presented to the 47 children from one half of the estate, leaving Highbridge at 11.00 a.m. on the Monday morning they went in two coaches to Bristol Zoo. Accompanied by their parents they saw the Coronation decorations in Bristol before going to the zoo. Arriving back at Highbridge at 5.00 o'clock they were soon sitting down to an enormous spread in the Scout and Guide headquarters in Coronation Road. There were two Coronation cakes and each child received a mug of sweets, money and ices. The remainder of the day was spent in games and sports at the headquarters.

Children from the other half of the estate also held their party in the Scout and Guide headquarters but on the Tuesday afternoon. The hut had been gaily decorated and over 90 children sat down to an enormous spread, the tables piled with food. Again each child was presented with a mug filled with sweets and was afterwards entertained with sports and a firework display. There was dancing during the evening, the adults joined in the fun with a party and games

SOCIAL CLUB

Most of the members had spent the morning and afternoon helping to organise various street parties but come the evening it was their turn to celebrate, again on the Tuesday evening. The skittle alley had been festooned with flags; streamers and other decorations made especially for the occasion. Sixty members and guests sat down to a supper of home cooked ham and salad. After the meal and a loyal toast the members watched a newsreel of the Coronation and scenes around London, and saw the Queen switch on the illuminations over the City.

JOHN STREET

The youngsters of the street enjoyed a fireworks display at their Coronation party held on Saturday. They were lucky to be able to have their party in the street where Mrs. Dinham the licensee of "The Globe Inn" presented each of the 23 children with a souvenir mug, plus ice cream and a orange. A fancy dress competition caused some fun, more adults joining in, although not to receive prizes. Old age pensioners each received a gift of three shillings and sixpence. Supper for the adults followed in the evening where there was dancing and singing.

WALROW

The children had their party on the Tuesday afternoon and after a tremendous tea, each child was presented with a mug filled with toffees and a two-shilling piece. Celebrations continued into the evening with sports and games.

WORSTON LANE

Children living in the Highbridge end of Worston Lane held their party on Coronation day in the afternoon, 75 sat down at 3.00 o'clock to begin the festivities. The 3rd Burnham Scout Troop had generously loaned two large tents, a third was provided by Mr. T. Heal. The proceedings had been opened by a fancy dress parade, each child receiving a small gift. Rain prevented any sports before tea, the highlight being a Coronation cake made by Mrs. Giles. All children were presented with a mug filled with sweets. After the sports and games took place, a skittle match for the adults followed.

Footnote - To many readers - it may be strange to read that the children at the parties received a mug, cup or beaker filled with sweets, plus the gift of oranges, balloons, 'teasers' etc. It must be remembered that following World War II there was still rationing until 1953 the year of the Coronation. The sweet ration had been 2ozs per week for a very long time and fruit was still not plentiful. Therefore to receive all these sweets at one go, plus fruit and paper hats, streamers, balloons etc. the children in June 1953, thought that all their Christmas's had come at once.

Also it will be noted that part of Highbridge Road and Worston Lane were included in the Highbridge Coronation street party reports. At that time the boundaries were not as they are today and residents of those areas were included in Highbridge. The most outstanding feature of the decorations in Highbridge, were the premises of Mr. P. Griffin (Fishmonger) Church Street, for his shop window display and the decorations over the shop.

Finally, it is appreciated that during the celebrations many photographs were taken of the various street parties; we have attempted to obtain copies, but without any great success. Photographs that appeared in the local press at that time were not suitable for reproduction; therefore, regrettably, we were not able to include them.

ROYAL VISIT BY HER MAJESTY THE QUEEN

On the morning of 5th December 1958 Highbridge came to life with growing excitement in anticipation of the visit by the Queen and the Duke of Edinburgh.

Bunting, pictures and flags adorned Market Street and Church Street the route the Royal party were to take to the Radio Station. Highbridge Station buildings, where the Queen would arrive were unrecognisable with a façade completely covering the front entrance. Flowers and shrubs also added to the colourful display.

The Royal train arrived at 10.00 a.m. onto the platform stepped Her Majesty to be welcomed by the Lord Lieutenant of Somerset and Mrs E.E.J. Herring (Chairman of Highbridge and Burnham Urban District Council). The Queen was alone, the Duke of Edinburgh who had been on a visit in Europe had been delayed by bad weather and could not make the visit.

The Royal party travelled through Market Street and Church Street, which by this time had filled with people eager to see the Queen whose destination was the Radio Station in Worston Road. Here she was greeted by the Postmaster General Mr. Ernest Marples and introduced to members of the Radio Station and the local M.P. Sir Gerald Wills. There followed a tour of the Radio Station to demonstrate how messages were received and transmitted to shipping in all parts of the world. After the tour, which last some forty minutes, the Royal party left to return via the town, to the railway station. The Royal train left Highbridge at 11.00 a.m. for Bristol where a four hour visit had been planned for the same day.

The day before the Queen's visit .... **And awaiting the Queen's arrival**

The Queen's visit had been short, but it was exciting and enjoyed by many of the local people.

The next Royal celebration was for the Queen's Silver Jubilee in 1977 and to mark the occasion the people of Highbridge had, at a Public Meeting, discussed what arrangements they should be make to celebrate this special day. Several people had agreed to serve on the organising committee and produce a programme of events for Jubilee Week.

Highbridge Jubilee Celebrations 1977

At the "Queen's Jubilee Party" in the **Morland Estate** over 120 children from **Queen's Square, West Avenue, East Avenue and South Avenue** had an enjoyable time. The organising committee under Mrs Skuse had produced a programme of party games, egg and spoon race and sack and balloon races. Tea was for the twelve's and under followed by a competition and, upon leaving every boy and girl received a mug, bag of sweets and a balloon. Later a disco was held at the Social Club for the 13 to 16 year olds and Committee members.

Another 'high spot' was the Jubilee Celebrations prepared by the ladies from **Grange Avenue**, **Church Street** and **Springfield Road** areas. Among beautifully decorated surroundings the children enjoyed well-organised sports and a superb tea; every chid receiving a jubilee mug, crown and a bag of sweets, plus a ball. The event was held on the Recreation Ground with Dr & Mrs Creamer judging the fancy hat competition.

Grange Avenue bedecked ready for the Jubilee Celebrations the next day.

The **Clyce Road** held an event for 80 residents and former residents at a party on the Wednesday night, the party for chiefly adults, was held at the top of the road. The organising committee comprised Mrs Lovibond, Mrs Mitchell, Mrs Sully, Miss Lynham, Miss Fackrell and MissWall.

About 130 children from **Huntspill, Clyce and Alstone Roads** had their party in a field belonging to Mr Duckett on the Bank Holiday Monday. Each child received a jubilee mug, the older children a jubilee plate and those up to six years of age a silver-plated spoon; Mrs Ladd was chair of the organising committee.

Celebrations on the **Poplar Estate** were organised by Mary Picton, Dianne Wharton and Myra Spice. For months prior to the party raffle tickets had been on sale for a box of groceries. A jumble sale and sponsored skittle match had raised funds for the party under an estate decorated with flags. On the day, a party was held in the Town Hall for seventy children and a separate section had been set-aside for the senior citizens, all thoroughly enjoyed the atmosphere. All children, on leaving, received a gift bag.

Funds that remained were used to take the children to Bristol Zoo or they could go Ice Skating, there was also a coach trip to Weymouth; the trips took place later in the year.

Jubilee Gardens

Local Guides and Brownies about to 'enter the stone picking contest' which had been organised to clear the Jubilee Garden site of all unwanted stones.

In November 1975 a group of local residents met to discuss ways of improving the physical appearance of Highbridge, the outcome was an "Action for Highbridge" Committee. They were to set themselves the task of clearing the land around the Town Clock, part of the site being over the old lock gates that had controlled the original River Brue.

This proved to be a much harder task than first envisaged, part of the land had been used as a coal yard by T.F.Norris and for many years a railway siding had run from the wharf directly to the site. The first job was to clear the site of rubbish, with the aid of local Sea Cadets fifteen large railway sleepers were removed and, as the site became more manageable the Guides and Brownies were able to move in. Originally the intention had been to dig over the ground, but the presence of building rubble and hardcore made this impossible. Funds were then raised to purchase several tons of topsoil, which was spread over the site and then sown with grass seed.

The next stage was to lay paths and a patio area; to prepare the rose beds alongside the clock required the removal of five tons of rubble. The first three months of 1976 were bitterly cold, this was followed by four months of drought and then almost continuous rain the rest of the year; the workers were not to be deterred and during the year they successfully planted trees, shrubs, rose bushes and flowers. Through all the adverse conditions a few people kept their vision alive and through their effort the garden was created.

To mark the official opening of Highbridge Jubilee Gardens on the June Bank Holiday. 1977 the Mayor of Burnham and Highbridge, Councillor C. Willis and Deputy Mayor Councillor C.Booth jointly unveiled a beautiful stone; the engraving read: - "**Jubilee Gardens. These gardens were created and financed by the residents of Highbridge and opened to commemorate the Silver Jubilee of her Majesty Queen Elizabeth II June 1977**"

Mr.P.Wilson, Chairman of the Action for Highbridge Committee said that many people had helped with the project by donating seats, trees, shrubs and plants and gifts of money; also he should mention Councillor Denis Hewings without whom, the gardens would never have been created. "In the bleakest days when we were hit by all sorts of problems Denis would overcome them and keep us all going by describing how beautiful the gardens would look when the work was finished".

The gardens hold a reminder of an earlier era, set in them are the pump and plaque from the original Highbridge Waterworks built in 1880, which was over the Brue Bridge in Huntspill Road, a mains supply came to Highbridge in 1906. In 1990 changes to the town's road layout required part of the garden to be removed and Tyler Way was constructed giving access to Newtown Road and Poplar Estate, Newtown Road became a cul-de-sac.

Jubilee Gardens is a spot where a quiet moment can, perhaps, be found during the bustle of everyday life.

The original Jubilee Gardens in the early days around 1980 a

larger area than it is today, a place where locals and visitors could sit quietly and watch the world go by.

(Photo supplied by Denis Hewings)

That is until a large portion was commandeered to permit the construction of Tyler Way, as shown.

HIGHBRIDGE GUY FAWKES CARNIVAL

In 1945 at the end of the Second World War the first Highbridge Carnival was organised by the Welcome Home Fund for the forces. The first consisted of a carnival procession, a giant bonfire, and a squibbing display on the Town Square. It first lined up in the Huntspill Road going along Church Street to turn in the Old Burnham Road; returning down Church Street, down Market Street to finish at the "Coopers Arms". A few years later this changed, it still lined up on the A38 at Huntspill Road and went through the town to North Avenue, where a twenty minute break was taken to clear the traffic; returning through Highbridge. Carnivals were very different back in the late 1940's; it was a torch light procession that attracted people; and the bonfire in a field by the "Coopers Arms" comprised a pile of thousands of cartons and cartridge cases. In the procession was a well-known car Y99, an 1896 two cylinder Daimler (Fiery Liz) owned by a Burnham man; it caused surprise to some American soldiers who saw it and wanted to take photo's of it send to the folks back home.

In 1946 the total prize money awarded was £61.15s.00d.today that would probably cover fourth prize; it is now above £3,000, including appearance money. The Carnival Committee made a courageous decision in 1948 to revive the Carnival after it being abandoned the previous year. Unfavourable weather in November discouraged entries and it was felt that the public of Burnham and surrounding districts could help by reciprocating the support that Highbridge had given to their Summer Carnival.

Appearance money was started in Highbridge in the mid 1950's to encourage more entries. In the beginning a variety concert was held, with local artists taking part to raise fund in order to provide more money for charities. In 1950 crockery was purchased to enable a Sub Committee of ladies to do the catering at dances and other events. In 1951 the Committee was working well but would welcome residents from Burnham who might wish to join them. In August that year some members from Highbridge hired large carnival heads and entered the Burnham Carnival, which was a summer event. Mrs Jackson's Accordion band from Bridgwater was engaged in 1952 and subsequent years when bigger dances were held.

In January 1953 Phil and Irene Harris plus Pam and Dave Reed joined the Highbridge Committee and, in conjunction with the local Council we helped to organise a Coronation Day ball, which was a very successful and enjoyable evening. During 1954 a series of dances were held to find a Carnival Queen, two Princesses and eleven other girls as attendants. Young ladies were chosen to represent Bleadon, Mark, Watchfield, West Huntspill, East Huntspill, Woolavington, Puriton, Pawlett, Bason Bridge, Brent Knoll, East Brent, Burtle Burnham and Highbridge; a total of fourteen. Gentlemen of the Committee constructed the permanent cart; it had a throne, two seats at the top and an oval seat on which sat the other girls. Two electric fires were mounted on the cart to give warmth to the girls; something that would not be allowed these days; it would not be necessary today because of the heat produced by all the bulbs. In those days they wore long dresses, which enabled them to have a piece of polythene wrapped around their legs and a hot water bottle on their laps.

Carnivals are a lot of hard work, also a lot of fun. For the girls there were laughter and tears, at one Carnival Queen selection ball, two of the girls arrived in identical dresses. One had been bought in Bristol, the other made by a mother, the same pattern, material and colour; thankfully neither of them was in the first three. Nothing was easy in the early days. We would, with helpers, transport a piano to Burtle and return in the early hours with a car and trailer. The lighting consisted of a number of Tilley lamps with admission at 3/-(15p) we always hoped to make about £18.00 after paying all expenses. Not all the venues were successful, but there was never a problem to get the girls to take part; sometimes there would be twenty entries. Whilst the gentlemen were building the Queens float, the ladies made long purple capes for the Queen and two Princesses and short red cloaks for the attendants; it was impossible to obtain velvet and often difficult to get material at all, but after much searching, it was finally obtained. A generator, to light the float was usually the last item to get and after much searching, one was found at Chippenham. Rex Emery and Dave Reed went to collect it, dismantled it and brought it back on a trailer. The price was £42.10.00. It was in need of a good overhaul, this cost 3/-(15p) per hour for a skilled engineer, including parts and labour the total came to £62.10.00. Today generators are very sophisticated produce up to a mega watt of power. The cost is running into thousands, some of the smaller clubs still had their own equipment but the larger clubs hired it for the twelve days of carnival, again at a huge cost. In 1955 W.H. (BILL) Tyler was elected as Life President of Highbridge Carnival. The collection raised just over one hundred pounds. In 1956 the donation to the Spastics Association was £190.00.

The 1958 Highbridge Carnival passing along Church Street

A carnival was not held in 1958 because of reconstruction work on the River Brue Bridge and the Bristol Road Bridge. 1959 firms like Weetabix and John Player were entering the trade class in the procession; the Electricity Board gave permission for the sodium street lighting to be turned off for the duration of the Carnival. In January 1960 the County Carnival Ball was held in Highbridge for the first time and in August there were the rumblings of carnivals being wound up. October found us skittling for a lamb carcass and a basket of fruit; a gentleman complained that the ladies were going to be included and they could win both prizes! By November the collection was down to £71.13.00d. The Burnham and Highbridge District Council asked the Committee if it would give some money toward furniture for Southwell House, it had foreseen this for some time and had put some money away for this purpose. This turned out to be the last Highbridge Carnival.

On January 23rd 1961 at the A.G.M. the Treasurer reported a serious loss on the years workings of £181. The question was: - "Can we hold a carnival in 1961?" The Treasurer said we would need £300 in the bank before one could take place; a special meeting was called on the 20th February 1961 when it was decided that there was an absolute lack of interest in the town. Local apathy and poor finances and with most of the Committee from outside the town, a few members resigned; sadly it was decided that the Committee would cease to function. The President, Chairman and Secretary being made trustees.

It was with much regret to local people that the last Highbridge Carnival was held in 1960

T—Tableau **ORDER OF PROCESSION** F—Feature

No.	Entry	Entrant
1	Chief Marshal	
2	Somerset County Fire Service	
3	Burnham and Highbridge Town Band	
4	The Carnival Queen and her Court	
5	One from Mons	Tom Speed, Highbridge
6	Little Dutch Boy	John Atyeo, Bridgwater
7	Little Bo-Peep	Susan Wigley, North Petherton
8	Pied Piper of Hamelin	Jean Barnett, Cannington
9	The Hunchback of Notre Dame	C. Harding, Burnham-on-Sea
10	Nipped Out for the Carnival	F. J. Horne, Burnham-on-Sea
11	Melody Maid	L. Corbett, Exeter
12	Highbridge Keystone Cops	Kings Arms Club, Bridgwater
13	Where will the Dimple be	J. Tucker, Blackford
14	Clown	B. Robinson, Burnham-on-Sea
15	Jester	N. Butt, Burnham-on-Sea
16	When Black Meets White	Douglas L. Pidgeon, Minehead
17	CARNIVAL REMINISCENCES, Celebrating the 350th Anniversary of the Gunpowder Plot (T)	Wills Club, Bridgwater
18	LONGSHIPS LIGHTHOUSE (T)	The Western National Omnibus Co. Ltd., Exeter
19	GAY PEARLYS (F)	Gremlins Club, Bridgwater
20	THE LEGEND OF THE WILLOW PATTERN (T)	Highbridge Bacon Co. Employees Club
21	Roadsters Annual Conference	Fairford Road Gang
22	CRUSADERS (T)	Willmott Breedon Club, Bridgwater
23	H.M.S. CARNIVAL (F)	Roberts Bros. Club, Bridgwater
24	THE WOODEN HORSE OF TROY (T)	Cryptonian Club, Bridgwater
25	The Three Nit Wits	W. G. Bale, East Huntspill
26	CELEBRATIONS OF THE THREE MUSKETEERS (T)	Top House Club, Highbridge
27	Burtle Silver Band	
28	MARCO POLO (T)	British Flag Club, Bridgwater
29	Bridgwater Young Farmers Open a New Restaurant	Bridgwater Young Farmers
30	Illuminated Electric Lighting Demonstration	Workman Reed & Co. Ltd., Hewish
31	EASTERN FANTASIES (F)	Cardiff Arms Club, Bridgwater
32	THE LEGEND OF THE THREE PRINCES (T)	Kraft Club, Bridgwater
33	THE ANCIENT EGYPTIANS (F)	Golden Lion Club, Bridgwater
34	Heating, Cooking and Lighting	John Tyler, Highbridge, Ltd.
35	CARNIVAL TIME (F)	John Blands Club, Highbridge
36	Mother's Night Out	Queens Head Club, Minehead
37	THE BROKEN CRYSTAL (T)	Starkey's Club, Bridgwater
38	INSIDE INFORMATION (F)	Highbridge Young Farmers Club
39	THE MISSISSIPPI SHOW BOAT (F)	Lime Kiln Club, Bridgwater
40	Decorated Weetabix	Weetabix Ltd., Kettering
41	THE RED DEVILS (F)	Hope Inn Club, Bridgwater
42	NURSERY CORNER (F)	Currypool Mills, Cannington
43	Beauty Parlour	Wells and Glastonbury Young Farmers
44	THE BANJO'S BACK IN TOWN (F)	Vagabonds Club, Bridgwater
45	Du Maurier Demonstration Van	Gallaher Ltd., London

We thank the Proprietors of "DU MAURIER" Cigarettes for placing their Super Loudspeaker Van at our disposal for making announcements

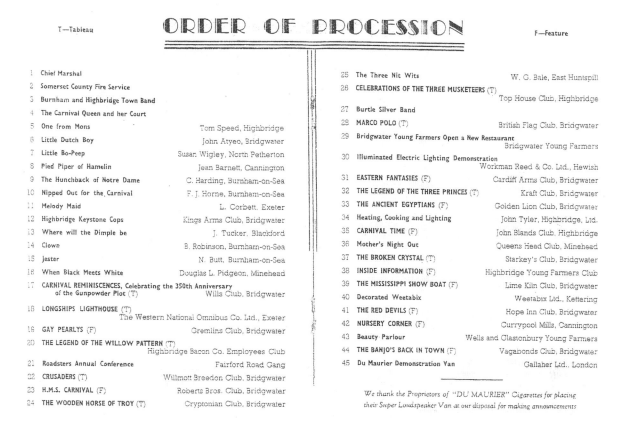

"Order of Procession" for Highbridge Carnival in 1955

Carnival Clubs

The Highbridge Carnivals saw the birth of a number of carnival clubs, following the first procession in 1945. Fairford Road Carnival Club entered their first carnival in 1952. The theme for their float was called "No Workhouse" –(Next Best) Victor House and Bill Puddy came up with the idea of dressing a gang of lads as "Tramps" or "Men of the Road". Vic drove a clapped out "Y" registered Morris car, this towed a trailer carrying the "tramps" who were carrying out various chores – mending socks, alterations to coats/trousers and actually washing! Underclothes.etc. Those not working played cards or drank 'Zummerzet Cider'. Their antics brought laughs and applause from the watching crowds.

Amongst the local Companies entering floats were John Blands, Highbridge Bacon Co., Hicks Bros. (Builders) and the Burnham & Highbridge Council Employees. Some pubs also entered – "The White Hart" "Top House" and the "Globe Inn".

In 1952 the Skrimshire Challenge Cup was, in error, awarded to the" Globe Inn" club (a slight miscalculation of points in the results) instead of the "Top House" club. However, the spirit of sportsmanship prevailed and Mrs. Dinham, the captain of the "Globe" club handed over the cup to Mr. Morey of the "Top House" with her club's congratulations.

In 1953 & 1954 the Fairford Road Gang rested but in 1955 came back having decided to enter all the carnivals in the season, these included: - Bridgwater, Spaxton, North Petherton, Highbridge, Wells, Midsomer Norton and Glastonbury. Their entry was again in the "Comic Mounted Section" and their aim was to win the County Cup. This trophy was awarded to the club gaining the most points from all carnivals.

The gang worked hard throughout the year and the theme was "Roadsters Annual Conference" – Again depicting "tramps" but on this occasion a better 'old banger' a bigger cart and even an ancient wicker invalid chair. The three-wheeled chair had 'Grandad' strapped in and was towed at the rear; unfortunately, when passing through Highbridge and the Town Clock, (which was then in the middle of the road) the wheelchair broke loose, the car and the cart went up Church Street, but 'Grandad' took off down Market Street.

Funds to pay for the equipment are always needed, so in 1956 a Valentines Night party and dance was held at the Highbridge Town Hall. The proceeds would pay for the November carnival entry, and to carry on their 1955 success the party and dance became a "tramps ball" with a competition for the best-dressed tramp. Refreshments offered were cider etc. bread and cheese, the seating comprised of straw bales – music by the "Clubman Dance Band". Over 300 tramps attended, the best-dressed tramps being Arthur Duckett and Jack Saunders. Hangovers were much in evidence the next morning.

The November's Carnival entry was called "Safari" – '(But not too near).' The car used had offset wheels and it towed a cart and a cage; with a warning.

"Stand back ladies and gentlemen, we accept no responsibility for damage inflicted by these terrible

 animals whilst travelling through your streets. We have the greatest team of trackers known to man. No animal too large or small. Name the animal, we will provide it."

The Fairford Road Gang with their 1956 Carnival Entry of "SAFARI" (BUT NOT TOO NEAR)

In 1957 the clubs entry was very different, it was influenced by the news that Russia and the U.S.A. were to travel to outer space. So a tractor was used to tow a large trailer, on which was mounted a rocket – their theme being "Off to seek new pastures"

During the 1950's especially 55 – 56 – 57 the club had achieved tremendous success, winning the County Cup in the Comic Mounted Feature Section for three consecutive years. This was quite a feat and a record, set by the Fairford Road Gang, which has never been equalled or broken to-date.

The founder members of the club were well-known Highbridge men and who, over the years, had an association with carnival. They included: - Vic House, Bill Puddy, Norman Butt, Baden Cann, Ray Davey, Fred Faulks, Doug. French, Ernie Crandon, Alec Dite, Bill Fisher, Dave Brewer, Ray Cross, Bob Millard, Wally Evans, Pete Hale, Archie Dean, Brian Rich, Bob Carnell, and Wally Dudley. Bill Puddy was the club Chairman, Vic House Captain,

Major changes took place in 1958, the gang had always used Vic House's yard, Fairford Road with its limited access and facilities had given the club problems and caused concern when building carnival trailers. Fortunes changed when Jack Gaffney, landlord of the "Cooper's Arms" in Market Street offered the club the use of the car park at the rear of the hotel. The Carnival Queen was at the head of the Carnival and was followed by one of the oldest competitors namely, Tom Speed who was 77 years old, he was dressed as "Admiral Slim" also at the front was a replica vessel manned by 'Jack' Hatcher with his crew of S.Woodberry, C.Haines, L.Cantrill, F.Fisher, B.Williams, H.Norman and R.Whitcombe; Kimber's Boatyard had made the vessel.

The 1958 entry called "Television Mixture" was the last for the Fairford Road Carnival Club; in 1959 it became the Coopers Arms Carnival Club with their entry called Cooper Baby Motors,was based on the Cooper Car.

(*Much of the information covering the Carnivals and Clubs has been provided by Fred Faulks, a member of the Fairford Road gang, and Mrs. Reed*)

Robert Pelham Caswell Millard

Bob was born on November 6th 1927 in Church Street above the Bon-Bon sweet shop, the only child of Pelham and Maude Millard. His parents moved to Springfield Road, known as Gas House Lane in those days, and went to Sexey's Grammar School; upon leaving school he worked as a farm labourer at Watchfield.

This was probably where he took a great liking for cider; this was to have a bearing on the rest of his life. He always kept a 'pike' barrel (sixty gallons) in his old shed at the back of his house. When he first started work on the farm he would drive the horse and cart back home at the end of the day, and this journey always entailed a visit to the Coopers Arms for 'lubrication'. On many occasions Bob would fall asleep in the cart in the car park, only to wake up and find the horse still patiently waiting; this routine was obviously in both their systems.

In 1970 Bob bought a donkey that he named Bambi. Bob was regularly seen walking the donkey to the top of the road and back, locals who would visit the orchard to see it and often fed the donkey. Bambi grew bigger and stronger, becoming quite a handful, often known to kick and bite if you were not too careful. On one occasion Mrs Millard was hanging out some washing in the orchard, bending down to take washing from the basket Bambi seized the opportunity to mount her; luckily a plumber who was working in the house came to her rescue when she screamed.

Bob was a member of the carnival club and a keen local skittler; when visiting a country pub to play skittles Bob was told by a landlord that his language was disgusting, Bob replying 'so is your beer'. Workmen were keen to visit Springfield Road as there was always a warm welcome and a glass or two of beer or cider, Bob would have a friendly chat, probably for a couple of hours. He was sincere, friendly and an old softie at heart with hardly a bad word about anyone, a cheery 'How be on yer' would greet everyone.

He was best remembered for his daisy upright bicycle with a sack over the handlebars, his trilby hat and his pipe full of Condor tobacco, with smoke drifting down the road behind him. In 1985 a funeral business was founded in his name and Bob helped to some degree but was never really cut out for that type of work. He always made it clear that when his time came, he would lie in state in his own front room before heading for the church. Those wishes were carried out to the full when he died on the 27th

February 1988. Many thought he was older than his 70 years. In summary he was a wise man who lived his life to the full, never interfering with anyone; his main philosophy was ' as long as you have a roof over your head and food in your belly, you want for nothing.'

(Article and photo supplied by Andrew Holley)

Clyce Road Carnivals

The Clyce Road in Highbridge, held two carnivals of its own, these were during the summers of 1965 and 1966. In 1965 the Carnival Queen was Diane Lock, who had two princesses in attendance, their names being Jennifer Ladd and Tracy Mitchell.

The second carnival in 1966, Jennifer Ladd was elected as Carnival Queen and her two princesses were Shirley and Erica Lynham. Jennifer's prize as Carnival Queen was a Rupert Annual that she still has.

Most of the residents took part in the events in fancy dress costume. The late Freddie Fay judged both carnivals and Mrs. Johnson who owned a hairdressing salon in Highbridge, presented the children with their prizes. After the fancy dress parade the children and grown ups joined in a lovely tea party in the open air at the top of Clyce Road. All had a great time and have happy memories of our two carnivals.

(Information provided by Mary Ladd)

Highbridge Crysanthemum Society

A show programme from 1943
Gardens were being used to produce food, not only for show purposes, during the war years.
The pencilled numbers indicate the number of entries.

138

The first Highbridge Chrysanthemum Show was held in 1936, when a Society was formed to promote an interest in the growing of chrysanthemums. This brought back an earlier interest in flower growing after the demise of the Highbridge Flower Show. Support for the show was encouraging and once it had settled into the Town Hall, the annual event became very popular with the local community. As the show grew in size and status over the following years it became an event where old friends would meet and enjoy the displays. Held in November, it included many classes apart from those for chrysanthemums, there were vegetable, fruit, honey, and handicraft and pigeon classes. A children's' handicraft section was also encouraged and in 1940 a special class for evacuee children was included as part of the show.

It is interesting to note that for many years the railway workers, who enjoyed the rivalry to win the "Best of the Day" award, supported the show; this rivalry carried the show forward and brought in many successful changes to the shows' programme. Over the years there were further changes, the pigeon classes disappeared in 1956 but a growing interest in floral art was discovered and this section was enlarged to encourage more exhibitors.

In the 1980's the biggest change for the Society took place with the demise of the Town Hall; in 1984 the show moved to King Alfred School on the Burnham Road. Once established there, the Society introduced several new classes to the show including wine, photography and painting.

 Some sixteen successful years followed but gradually the number of chrysanthemum growers declined. Efforts to encourage new members met with little success and with no new blood coming into the Society it was felt that an annual show could no longer be sustained.

This was not just a local problem. The National Society reported that it was countrywide. So the last show was held in 2001, after sixty-five years the Society was dissolved, it was a difficult decision by the current Membership especially after all the years of hard work put in by predecessors. The Society disappearing ended the long association with the town and the community. There are surely many grandparents, parents and children who have enjoyed many happy memories of the show.

The Show and Officials at The Town Hall .1983

HIGHBRIDGE FESTIVAL OF ARTS

In 1948 a former Headmaster of Highbridge V.C. School, Mr A Mason with few teachers and a group of enthusiasts decided to form the Highbridge Music Festival. The object was to encourage the appreciation of music, both vocal and instrumental. The Festival would provide, nor only an opportunity for entrants to receive a professional adjudication, but they would gain experience of performing in front of an audience. This audience would in turn have an opportunity to gain knowledge of the various arts and could relax to enjoy listening to the local artistic talent.

It was therefore in May 1948 that the Festival started, it began as a one-day event; the adjudicator receiving a "Thank You" plus a cup of tea for services rendered. Local residents and visitors to the area were no doubt surprised to find that a small town like Highbridge could organise and support such an Art Festival. Originally classes were for singing and piano, later another day was added for English folk dancing. This theme continued until folk dancing was removed from school activities.

So successful and popular was the festival that classes for adult singing, including choirs and instrumentals were also added. In 1977 the Festival had grown very popular and was extended to cover three weeks, it included over 1,200 entries with classes ranging from music to speech, drama, literacy, dancing and one-act plays. The old Highbridge Town Hall had always been the venue and on choir nights the hall was full to capacity, choirs queuing on the stairs and into the old Council Chamber whilst waiting their turn to sing.

Speech and drama classes and one-act play sessions were held at King Alfred's School, the stage facilities being more appropriate. A dance section was added in 1971 and this too was growing, the stage at Highbridge Town Hall finally became unsuitable so that dance classes had to be held in the Burnham Town Hall. Highbridge Town Hall had always been the ideal venue, the acoustics were second to none; adjudicators were known to remark on this many times. Unfortunately in 1984, within weeks of the Festival, the Highbridge Town Hall was condemned as unsafe. Alternative venues had to be found at short notice, that year St John's Church, the Ritz Cinema and many other places were quickly booked.

The Festival has, for a number of years held its performances at the "Princess Hall" Burnham over a three-week period and it closes with a Festival concert.

Entrants are drawn from a wide area, some from as far a field as Leicester and Scarborough and, up until 2002 the Festival took place each year in May, and there were some functions that were held at other times to publicise the event. However, in 2003 the Festival moved to March in order that pressure was taken from schools thus enabling them to continue to participate.

A Festival of this importance needs the support of the local community both as entrants and audience, long may it continue to produce such notable names for the entertainment world as Rupert Graves, Stephen Daldry, James Gray and others. There are many others who have been encouraged to make a career in the arts of Dance, Drama and Music following their appearances and successes at the "Highbridge Festival of Arts".

(This article compiled from information supplied by Ann Bannister and Joyce Dunbavan)

ASSOCIATIONS/CLUBS/SOCIETIES

Highbridge Young Farmers Club

The club was officially formed in 1935, when four farmers donated £5.00 each, they were Mr. Tom Tripp, Mr. Gilbert Gilling, Mr. Ben Arney and Mr. Jim Tewksbury. The club started as a type of "calf club" where sons and daughters (approx ages 10 – 26 years) of farmers and farm workers could have a 'hands on' type of practical education. This often included rearing a calf or other farm livestock. At that time, most of the milking was done in the lush green fields and all cows were milked by hand. The young farmers motto was "Good Farmers" "Good Countrymen" "Good Citizens"Many of the members went on to run or managed their own family farm. The Young Farmer Movement was also known as the rural country marriage bureau. Highbridge Y.F.C. held their first meetings in the upstairs of a stone barn, reached by an outside stone stairs – with no rail! – (There was no health and safety then), and no record of anyone falling off. The stone barn belonged to Mr Willie Ashford of Bridge Farm, now Highbridge Caravan Centre. Over the years the club has held their meetings in the Adult School, in Church Street.now converted into a house, also in the Council Chamber of the old Town Hall, at the "George Hotel" and at present in the "Cooper's Arms".

The farming industry changed a lot during the second world war, the horse became less practical than the tractor; when the country had to become self-sufficient, to produce enough food to sustain a wartime economy. Mechanisation was the priority and this led farmers into the expansion era of the fifties and sixties.

Highbridge Young Farmers entered a float in the 1960 carnival. A trailer was borrowed from Mr. E.J.

Tucker and construction headquarters were set up in "Southview Farm", the "Watchfield Inn" and the much loved "Railway Hotel". A month was spent dreaming up ideas for a subject to be acted out, and two or three weeks building produced what was called, "Motorway Madness", depicting the construction of the then proposed M5 Motorway. This was the Clubs first very amateurish effort and sadly their last, as the Highbridge carnivals ceased in 1960.

In 2004 the Highbridge Y.F.C. is still going strong with members coming from many of the surrounding villages.

In 2002 Highbridge Y.F.C. progressed to the National Y.F.C. Entertainments Final and came 2nd

Highbridge Y.F.C. has evolved with the times, many of the members are third generation of the original members, they still have speakers at meetings but with more varied subjects, from Falconry – Bomb Disposal – the effect of Drugs and Alcohol etc. Money is raised for charities with carol singing and holding slave auctions; in 2002/3 monies were raised for the Air Ambulance. The club has approximately 35 members, but few members are actively working in agriculture; a sign of the times. The motto is the same but with more emphasis on the "Good Countryman" – "Good Citizen" then "Good Farmer".

(Information supplied by Mrs. Wendy Welland. Field Officer for Y.F.C.'s in the Sedgemoor Area).

Highbridge Social Club - "A Dream Realised"

"Probably a no more generous action has ever been done for the welfare of the town of Highbridge" was a statement made in the "Burnham Gazette"& "Somerset Advertiser" in October 14th 1913. This referred to the erection of a handsome building in Church Street, to be known as the Highbridge Social Club. It is certain that there has never been a more useful one; the construction was carried out at the entire expense of Mrs. John Tyler. This lady was the wife of a local businessman John Tyler who owned the well-known shop on the Cornhill in Highbridge, it sold practically all your household needs – that is the non-edible type.

The splendid building would, at the end of two years be handed over to the people of Highbridge. There being a proviso, that, in the event of the club falling through at any future period, it would pass again into the hands of the donor.

The new social club was built on the site of property owned by a Mr. Hardacre. His family had lived in the house in Church Street from 1897 to 1912 but sold up before relocating in Wales. The buyer was Mr. John Tyler a local ironmonger who purchased the property for the princely sum of £160. The new premises were to be built on the site of workshops that ran parallel to the cottage's garden.

Mrs. Tyler performed a formal opening ceremony with a silver key (jointly subscribed for by the architect and builder) in the presence of a large and representative gathering. During his speech in 1913, the Chairman of Highbridge Urban District Council – Mr. A.E. Fisher – alluded to the fact that two large educational events had recently taken place in the town; the opening of the Council School and of this new club.

The club had been formed several years earlier (probably in 1905) but was dropped owing to the lack of good accommodation and various other reasons. It was hoped that this would not be the fate of this present institution, he emphasised the need to obtain a good roll of members.

The club (institution) was entirely free from religious or political connection, and would not be restricted simply to the reading of papers and the playing of games. Many uses could be found for the building, both from the artistic and scientific point of view, it was hoped that the committee would be able to draw up programmes, which would suit all views. Highbridge had dreamt of having a building such as that now presented to them, but few thought the dream would be realised. Members of the old club had served faithfully and had worked under great disadvantages; but now that there was a new club it could become a centre and an influence for good also prove to be a means of mental and physical recreation. A special point was made that the institute would not only be a club for men, but that ladies would also be admitted to the membership.

When the club was opened in 1913 it was proposed that if it proved to be a success, Mrs. Tyler would hand it over to the town or to a board of trustees for the benefit of Highbridge forever. It was hoped that all would put their "Shoulders to the Wheel" to make it a success. A penny (old money) a week was not a very large sum to pay, this was all that was required to make up the membership fee of four shillings a year (20p). Honorary members could join for five shillings (25p) a year.

The club was a brick construction, practically fireproof, with a reinforced concrete floor and a flat roof. It was artificially lighted by gas, and heated by circulating radiators. There were two large rooms, one on the ground floor and one on the first floor, that on the ground floor being converted into two rooms by means of a collapsible screen, one would be a reading room the other for games. The upper room was for bagatelle and (subsequently) billiards, there were also the usual offices. – (Note - no bar). The architect had been Mr. E. Binding and the builder Mr. F.Hucker.

1915 – Social Club & Institute

On Tuesday September 14th 1915 at a meeting of the Highbridge Urban Council Mr. J. Tyler asked the Council as a representative of the town to accept on behalf of his wife Mrs. Emma Tyler the 'Highbridge Social Club & Institute'. "That excellent and handsomely equipped building in Church Street which, through the generosity and public spirit of that lady, was opened just two years ago. It had since been a highly appreciated rendezvous for the young men who passed many hours at billiards, or in other pastimes, or in the well equipped reading rooms".

This magnificent gift made a splendid addition to the public buildings of the town and was accepted with grateful thanks. Mr. J. Tyler took that opportunity of saying that Mrs. Tyler, the donor, wished to place this Social Club and Institute and all things connected with it, in the hands of the Council.

Two years earlier in late September when the club was opened and placed in the hands of a committee, they were pleased to find that it was a considerable success; the desire had been to appoint trustees for this institution and place the management in their hands. However, after discussions with a solicitor it was found that difficulties could arise and that the best way would be to approach the council, it was the only governing body in the town, there would be no expense to the town. There would be a small governing body elected from the Council and they had accepted this gift; it would be for the benefit of the young people and coming generations of Highbridge.

Sometime during the period 1915 to 1929 proposals had been made that the club committee should comprise six councillors and six members and at the Annual Meeting held on April 24th 1929 the Chairman Mr. W.H.Hatcher remarked on the splendid gathering. It comprised six Councillors: - Messrs.F.Foster, W.J.Keats, G.W.Gulliford, W.H.Pratt, D.C.Murrish and R. Knight; and six Members; - Messrs.E.C.Baker, E. Hicks, C. Marsh, H. Beesley, L. Knight and H. Marsh. At the General Committee Meeting in April a "Caretakers Agreement " was accepted, with the addition that 'whoever it may be' would be responsible for the monies taken in the skittle saloon. During 1933 the question was raised concerning the appointment of new Council Trustees in view of the amalgamation of the Highbridge and Burnham on Sea Urban District Councils It was agreed to defer this until the new Council had been formed. In 1935 following the formation of the new Town Council, the appointment of Club Councillors took place, comprising Councillors and Members. The deeds to the Club had been lost and a new copy was being supplied. Four years later in 1939 the General Committee Meeting revised the rules following the amalgamation of the two councils of Highbridge and Burnham. Subscriptions were raised to six shillings (30p). On 1st January 1945, following the difficult war years it was proposed that the Club start afresh; later that year the it was proposed the subscriptions for 1946 be seven shillings and sixpence for adults and five shillings for juniors under eighteen.

A meeting in October 1945 recommended that the Club apply for a license to sell intoxicating liquors; the proposal was carried on a majority of 17 to 1. On completion of a new bar it was recommended it be opened from 11 a.m. to 2 p.m. and 6 p.m. to 10 p.m. Daily – Christmas Day, Good Friday and Sundays accepted.

Between 1945 and 1970 the Social Club continued as most club's do, with no major upheavals just the usual 'Domestic' problems, which were resolved by the committee. In 1971 there were discussions by the full Council concerning the provision of a 'New Club', in mid 1971 a new site was considered. Discussions continued into 1975 when a suggestion was put forward concerning the possible purchase of London House Motors who had premises next door. There were numerous proposals and counter proposals put forward, but eventually it was decided to demolish the existing club and build a new one on the same site. A cottage next door (No 96, Church Street) was purchased and with the extended site a larger club could be built. There was a grand opening on the 25th April 1981 of the rebuilt club.

At the formal opening the Tyler family's association with the club was continued with Mrs. P. Counsel and Mrs J. Hatcher, carrying out the re-commemoration; both ladies being the granddaughters of John and Emma Tyler who had presented the original club to the town in 1913.

A further wing including a lounge was opened on 9th December 1989. Throughout the following years the club has gone through many phases, having been built in 1913 and given to the community in 1915 it celebrated 80 years 'not out' in 1995 and is looking to 2005 when it will be 90. With another 10 years to go before its centenary, one can only wonder what other changes may occur.

(This article compiled from information supplied by Fred Faulks and Mick Brown)

Town Band

The Burnham and Highbridge Town Band which was originally known as the Burnham and Highbridge Services Band, was first formed in 1945 at the end of the hostilities in Europe. Mr. C.W. King, a local musician undertook the teaching and conducting; he was latterly the Band's President for many years. As a result of the keen interest taken by local businessmen and others, the Band expanded and became a full Brass ensemble. In 1947 it was given official status by the then Urban District Council which made it possible to give public performances and the band has continued to provide music to the people of Burnham and Highbridge up to the present day.

At the end of 1950 Mr. Fred Lewis took over the post of Bandmaster and enthusiastically carried on the efforts of Mr. King's to promote and expand the Band. In 1952 the Band entered its first contest at Exeter gaining fourth place from an entry of 20 bands; from then on the Band climbed through the contest sections and by the 1960's when under the direction of Mr. W.S. (Tommy) Farr, was competing in the South West Championship Section and Nationally in the Second Section. Unfortunately, Mr Farr, after many successful and happy years directing the band, was obliged to retired through ill health. The Band then came under the baton of Mr. E.W. Heath who has remained Musical Director until the present day.

In 1980 the Band was obliged to vacate the practice room at the Clarence Hotel. Burnham, as a result the members built their own Headquarters in Worston Lane, Highbridge. This required a large effort from most of the members, but the principal driving force came from the considerable efforts of Gerry Ham who's planning, organisation and enthusiasm made the project successful. After 2001 the Band gave up Contesting choosing to concentrate on Concert work for the Community.

By the end of the summer season of 2003 the Band had provided 56 continuous years of musical entertainment to the local community.

(Information supplied by Sid Golding)

(Photo supplied by EileenPicton)

**The Burnham & Highbridge Town Band in the Marine Cove Burnham
after winning the West of England Championship in the early 1960's**

Standing Left to Right"
Tom Farr (Bandmaster), Len English, Vic Davies, Ron Rowden, Chris Thomas, Eileen Rowden, Spencer Pritchard,
Mike Jones, George Burrows, Bob Manning, Ralph White, Steve mavin, Mike Sealey, Max Jones,
Air-Marshall Fiddement (Chairman).

Young Musicians:
Robin Tremlett, Ralph Rowden, Terry Tremlett.

Front row:
John Brown (Secretary), Harold Hemmings, Brian Salter, Bryn Burrows, Trevor Slade, Brian Rowden,
Charlie Burrows, Danny Howells.

Scouts

This is an international Organisation formed by Lord Robert Stephenson Smyth Baden-Powell in 1908 (and the Girl Guides in 1910); the aim was to produce good citizenship in the rising generation. As a young Cavalry Officer he had served with distinction in the South African War defending Mafeking. On his return from military service, he saw that young men required incentives in order to provide for themselves a better life. There was a need to help boys of whatever class to become all-round men; the aim was develop good character, to train them in habits of observation, obedience and self-reliance. Also instilling a sense of loyalty and thought for others and to teach them services useful to the public and handicrafts useful to themselves, there was also a need to promote their physical development and hygiene.

The first camp for boys was held on Brownsea Island in 1907; 22 boys were chosen to test the scheme; such was the success that the movement was born.

The Boy Scout Creed, which every boy has to promise, is: -

I promise that I will do my best

To love my God

To serve the Queen and my country,

To help other people

and obey the Scout Law   Their motto is: - *"Be Prepared"*

It is not known when the first local troops were formed but we have found that a troop was present in the area around 1910, scout groups were registered with the 'The Boy Scout Association' in London and evidence shows that the 1st Highbridge Group had the registration number 4227 and the 3rd Burnham number 4228.

The Movement, when formed had certain guide lines, one was an age limit; scouts would be boys aged from 12 to 16. But, younger brothers, who also wanted to join this new organisation, became 'Cubs', starting at 8 years old and moving on into the scouts when they reached 12. To cater for the older boys those over 16, the movement formed the 'Rovers'.

During the Great War (1914-1918) records nationally were sparse, after the war scout troops started to re-form; between the wars a meeting was held on 13th January 1931 in "Flook's Royal Café in Burnham High Street which covered the inauguration of the Burnham and Highbridge District Boy Scouts Association. The first indications of scouting activities in this area are that in the Burnham and Highbridge District Association Directory of 1939 it states "Still only two groups in the area". But it is interesting to note that the 3rd Burnham Troop attained its majority in 1937 and 1st Highbridge Troop celebrated its 21st birthday during 1939". This does indicate that Scouting was present soon after the Great War.

In 1939 Scouting was again affected by hostilities, troops were again 'stood down' as Scout Masters and other officers were called up for active service and mothers, obviously concerned for their son(s) safety, refused to let them attend Scout meetings. Also, with father away at war, mother wanted her family around her; this resulted in a shortage of young men capable of running Scout troops after the war. It must be remembered that during the early days of the last war the Scouts were actively involved in collecting paper and other 'scrap' for the war effort. Also, after the war, do you remember "Bob-a Job" when lads toured the town offering their services to do jobs for local people? This was an attempt to obtain funds for the Boy Scouts Association; the only reward the boy himself got was the satisfaction of knowing he had played his part in keeping the Scout movement out of debt.

From the "Scout Handbook" 1946 it is noted that Miss Bertha Knight was a Scout Mistress, her meetings being held in the Highbridge Town Hall on a Tuesday. Three local groups were active 1st Highbridge, 3rd Burnham and 1st Brent Knoll.

In 1951 Mr, Graham S. Hayter formed the 2nd Highbridge Troop, registration No 28826 it was sponsored by Highbridge V.C. School, this meant it was controlled by the school and was not an independent troop and it was free to operate whcrc it pleased; there were 40 members at the time. During the 1950's the Troop went from strength to strength and collected many awards for its members. Scouts and Cubs attended camps and jamborees all over the country.

(Photo supplied by David Derham)

St George's Day Parade-1960.
From left: John Brown, Arthur Warmington, Chris Hall, Frank Brierly, Frank Howarth, David Derham, Chris Meaden, David Dyer, Terry Yard, Malcolm Yard, David Holmes, Steve Bamsey, Bernard Druce.

The Census forms returned in 1956 the 1st Highbridge had disappeared, (it was assumed it had disbanded.), leaving the 2nd Highbridge which was still (sponsored) by the school. However, on Tuesday 3rd November 1959 the Highbridge Scouts and Guides were devastated to find their headquarters, situated in Coronation Road had been totally destroyed by fire, its contents, which included their records plus treasured trophies and equipment was destroyed; the headquarters had been built in 1948 by the local association and many improvements had been carried out over the years.

Following the fire the troop continued to meet, their aim now being to obtain funds so that the Headquarters could be re-built. Many money-raising events were held the Scout and Guide Associations launching appeals for funds. The Chairman of the Highbridge Scout Group Committee (Mr. M. Bamsey) confirmed at a meeting that an "all out effort" would be made to rebuild the Headquarters as soon as possible. St John's Church had offered the Scouts and Guides use of the church hall as a temporary measure and for this the groups were most grateful.

Funds were being steadily built up from door-to-door collections and in May 1960 the Highbridge Scout and Guide Headquarters Rebuilding Fund presented a variety concert in the Town Hall, with songs from "Carousel" plus sketches by Billy Jacobs and Bob Nicholson. The Silver Stars Rock & Roll Group, a local band, provided lively music for the evening.

Following twelve months hard work by the Scout and Guide Movements, and true to their determination, a new hut was built and officially opened by Lord St.Audries on the 12th November 1960. The final cost of the new hut was £2000 and it offered more facilities to both movements.

The 2nd Highbridge Troop were inspired by their new Headquarters and for the next few years were to win a number of trophies. In June 1960 when competing for the Kodo Horn Competition four members (Geof Tanner, Chris Meaden, David Holmes and Terry Yard) sailed their homemade craft on Apex Park Lake, they had built the raft using timbers from their burnt out H.Q. They were required to spend the night in a tent on the raft; their 'look-out' was David Derham who was to be on hand in case of an emergency. The troop was successful, wresting the trophy from the Berrow Scout Troop that had held it for the past two years.

Unfortunately, during the 1960's interest in the Youth Movement appeared to wain, many organisations had very lean times with memberships declining until only the dedicated few remained. The 2nd Highbridge Troop was no exception, membership fell and in 1963 it is recorded that the remaining officers (Scout Master Malcolm Yard and Assistant Scout Masters David Derham and Frank Brierley) were left in charge of very few scouts. David Derham revived interest and ran the troop as Scoutmaster from 1963. Two Cubs, now older, moved up into the Scouts and Don Mulholland became Assistant Scout Leader. When Dave retired and with more Cubs Scouts moving up into the Scouts, Don became 'Skip'. Colin Hall ('Squire') joined him. Membership was still fluctuating and in order to keep the Scout Movement active and alive locally the 2nd Highbridge amalgamated with the 1st West Huntspill troop to become the 1st Huntspill and Highbridge troop. This took place in 1968 the new registration number being 38955.

At present the Troop meets regularly on a Monday evening at the Headquarters in Coronation Road; the Group Scout Leader is Sue Hunter.

Cubs

During research into the Scout Movement it was found that the "Cubs" have been active in Highbridge since 1915, on 1st October 1919 Miss Bertha Knight registered a Cub pack its number being 6851. The pack was well supported having 18 Cubs, it was called the 1st Highbridge and meetings were held in the home of Miss Knight, 25 Church Street. It later included Scouts and it was noted that 16 boys were in the troop in 1920. The Scout Master was Miss A.M. Wade and meetings were in Southwell House, in 1928 Miss Hilda, became Quarter Master of the Cub pack.

During the 1914/1918 conflicts the Knight sisters served with the V.A.D. Movement in Highbridge. Miss Hilda Knight after the First World War formed a pack of Brownies and later a Guide Company. In 1951/52 Highbridge V.C. School re-formed the local Cub Movement under Miss Megan A. Jones.

The Cub pack continued for some years at Highbridge but unfortunately it was disbanded during the early 1960's. Their headquarters in Coronation Road had been destroyed in a fire on 3rd November 1959 and although efforts were being made to continue with the Cub pack, it did not appear to be successful.

In March 1968 Don Mulholland had restarted the Highbridge Cub pack at the Headquarters in Coronation Road with one Cub from the previous pack and proceeded to recruit members and soon had

23, before long there was actually a waiting list; Don had two assistants, Jim Whitlock and George Davison. George had returned to the area in 1968 and, having two young sons, he encouraged them to joined the Cubs; his own Scouting experiences had been from 1949 – 53 and he became a 'civilian' instructor to the pack but before long received his warrant as an assistant Cub Master and soon became 'Akela' – Cub Master. He ran this pack until 1980 when he retired his warrant after twelve years. Around this time Colin Hall (known as Squire by the cubs) arrived to help, he was a 2nd Highbridge Scout and the team continued to run the Cub pack for three years. It was around this time that the 1st West Huntspill and 2nd Highbridge troops amalgamated.

Don Mulholland retired in 1975 after fifteen years service; in 1976 following an appeal for an assistant Cub leader Mrs. Joyce Beard joined the pack, she had had previous experience with Cub packs in the London area. She took over as leader in 1981 starting the Christmas Charity post and in the early 1980's Joyce started Somerset's' first Beaver Colony (River Brue Colony) boys up to eight years old, this being one of the first in the Country, They were not officially recognised by the Scout Association, they were however, later to be accepted within the Association as a group for younger boys.

Cubs regularly take part in Community Projects such as "Britain in Bloom", Carnival gangs and features. The first local Cub to get the Gold Arrow Award (The highest award at that time) was James Yard, he was obviously following in the footsteps of his parents who were both involved in the Scouts and Guides Movement. In 1984 for her work in the Scout Movement, Joyce Beard received the Scout Medal of Merit; this followed fifteen years of service.

This picture shows the 1st Huntspill and Highbridge Scout Group in 2002 after they had successfully opened their own website in an attempt to recruit new Scouts and Cubs

(The information on both the Scouts and the Cubs was obtained from David Derham, Mrs Bourner-, the Somerset County Scout Archivist-, Don Mulholland and a number of other sources)

Girl Guides Movement

A Miss Hilda Knight around 1918 formed the 1st Highbridge Brownies and Guides; the Brownies were registered at the Movements Headquarters in London in 1919, the Guides being registered three years later in 1922. When first formed the groups were attached to the Girls Friendly Society and, for many years met in Miss Knight's home. With the interest and numbers growing it was decided they should set up their own separate groups and apply for formal registration.

Sir Robert Baden Powell following the success of the Boy Scout Movement founded the Girl Guide

Movement. Girls had felt that they too should be able to have programmes of activities like the boys. The fellowship within the various groups encouraged all to partake in activities so that girls could develop their own personality. The programmes were both enjoyable and character building, physically, mentally and spiritually.

Lady Mave Baden Powell became the Chief Guide.

All girls when accepted into the movement must say the: -

> *I promise that I will do my best*
> *To love my God,*
> *To serve the Queen and my Country,*
> *To help other people,*
> *and to keep the Guide Law.*

Although the Girl Guide Movement has been active in the area for many years details of their history have been difficult to obtain, it is known that the 'Knight Sisters' served in the V.A.D. Movement during the Great War (1914-1918). Miss Hilda Knight formed Brownie and Guide Groups upon the end of hostilities. The local group grew in numbers and as the girls started to get older Miss Knight formed a Ranger Company.

Memories of activities between the two wars is very sparse; we do know that the Guides were in existence in the 1920's because they celebrated their 25th anniversary in 1945 with a concert in the Highbridge Town Hall in the presence of parents and friends. For their 21st anniversary in 1941 the group comprising Brownies, Guides and Rangers, presented York House Children's Home in Burnham with a swing and a trapeze. Alongside the Girl Guide Movement there was, of course, the Boy Scouts, with Cubs and Rovers; the two groups now completely autonomous, each with its own national organisation.

In 1948, in association with the Scouts, a hut in Coronation Road became the combined headquarters. Unfortunately, whilst the hut was being used as a classroom for the St. Johns' school, it was burned to the ground. Equipment and records were regrettably lost in the blaze; these obviously being the reason so many local records have been lost. Following the fire the Brownies met in the Methodist Hall and a room in the Town Hall housed the Guides.

Mrs. Kathleen Incledon joined the Highbridge Guide Company as a Lieutenant with Captain Kathleen Nutter in February 1959 her warrant had been signed by Mrs. Baden Powell. Captain Kathleen Nutter, who was a talented violinist, having won a scholarship to the Guildhall School of Music, when twelve and become the Youth Orchestra Leader in London. During her period as Guide Captain in Highbridge she organised schemes to help the elderly, including chopping bundles of wood for their fires and other schemes to raise money for the Guides. Having erected a tent in Guide Pat Burge's garden, the Guides were sitting in front of it and were asked by Captain Nutter if anyone had a bright idea to raise some money; and received the suggestion "We could rob a bank".

During 1961, after much hard work organising a variety of functions, sufficient money was raised to open their headquarters in the new hut. In 1963 the 1st Highbridge Brownie pack helped to raise more than £300 towards the Highbridge Scout and Guide hut fund. The Deputy Mayor of Burnham & Highbridge, Mr. Denis Hewings made the draw and a clock was presented to the movement by some of the earlier Brownies and Guides, who had had a re-union each year. In 1965 Mr Kimber, a local boat builder, made replicas of the Scout and Guide badges in beaten copper. These were mounted on a wooden base, together with the special tools he had needed to complete the work, and presented to the headquarters as a wall plaque.

In 1969 the Brownies celebrated their fiftieth anniversary, with the Rev. Burton blessing the pennant, which was then proudly carried into church by the Brownies for a special service. The Guides held a thanksgiving service and party, their families and friends attended. Miss Hilda Knight was the guest of honour. During the 1970's there were, throughout Somerset, waiting lists, of young girls wishing to join the Brownies. Due to limited accommodation in some areas, new enrolments were restricted. Highbridge was no exception and a second Brownie Pack was formed in January 1974, this being attached to St John's Church.

Miss Hilda Knight died in January 1975 and in the December Brownies and Guides donated a flower vase to St. John's Church in the memory of their friend and leader. Flowers are arranged in the vase as often as is possible. Also during the 1970's, Mrs Pat Burge received her warrant as an Assistant Brownie Guider in May 1974, her warrant being served by the Chief Guide Mrs. Mave Baden Powell and the warrant for Brownie Guider in April 1978, resigning her warrant six years later in November 1984. A Jubilana was held in 1985 at Cheddar. This was a 75th Anniversary Camp where over 1000 guides from over fourteen countries worldwide attended the celebration. A wide range of activities had been organised for the girls including Canoeing, Hiking, Horse Riding, Dinghy Sailing, Fencing and Swimming; plus some crafts such as leather work, crochet and hand bell ringing.

The Highbridge Brownies were always ready to raise money for a just cause and it is recorded that they raised £640 for a "Blue Peter" Cambodian appeal, receiving congratulations from the Mendip Division of Guides to which they belonged.

When the Brownies and Girl Guide movement were formed over 80 years ago, many local young girls joined and we have had views from two such 'girls'. Mrs Hilda Lismore remembers joining the Highbridge Brownie pack round about 1934, when she was "just a slip of a girl". They had their meetings in an anti-room at the Town Hall, their storeroom, a sort of loft space, was reached by a small flight of stairs, which presented the youngsters with problems if they needed equipment.

Miss Hilda Knight their leader; she was also a teacher at the Highbridge Infants School. Hilda says the Miss Knights used to make lovely homemade sweets at their house in Church Street. Another lady who deserves a mention is Hilda King who was in the movement for 81 years. Hilda was Captain in the Guides from 1967 to 1980. She says they went camping every year and undertook a lot of tests in order to get the proficiency badges, all being thoroughly enjoyed. She had three girls who obtained 1st Class badges and were chosen from this district to attend the Lady Baden Powell celebration at Windsor. One of Hilda's 'young girls' became a District Commissioner.

The Highbridge Guides and Brownies held their meetings in the Scout Hut in Coronation Road up until 1992; meetings are now held in the St John's Church Hall, on Friday evenings.
(The information on both the Guides and the Brownies was obtained from Mrs J. Garton, Mrs P.Burge and a number of other sources)

St John Ambulance- Highbridge & Burnham Division

The Ambulance Division was first registered on 24th June 1932 as Highbridge & Burnham Division, single sex Divisions only were operated - Ambulance for men, Nursing for ladies and corresponding for Cadets. Today there are combinations of Quadrilateral - one Division with all members- men, women, boys and girls; in 1932 there was a very definite segregation of the members. The Highbridge and Burnham Division were formed mostly with men who worked on the S & D Railway and had trained in first aid. Early paperwork indicates that the Division met in the Council Chamber of the Highbridge Town Hall; Mr. F. Hayes was the Superintendent, Dr. Jack Burns as the Surgeon and 30 members.

Ladies soon followed into the Service and were first registered on 20th August 1938 under the leadership of Mrs. Lumber. It is interesting to note that in those days she was referred to as "The Lady Superintendent"; Dr. Burns's wife, Phyllis (also a Doctor) became the Nursing Division's Surgeon. On Sunday 10th December 1939 the first ambulance was dedicated at the Bristol Blue Bus Garage, which later became part of Woodberry Bros.& Haines Ltd near the Bristol Bridge. The first patient to be conveyed to hospital in the new ambulance was their Superintendent Mr. Hayes who, regrettably, died just six days after the dedication; he was succeeded as Superintendent by Mr. W Young who remained in office until his death in 1947.

A new Headquarters was opened on Sunday 25th June 1943 at the Constitutional Club in Highbridge this was a building between the Railway Hotel and the Town Hall in Market Street. Also, during 1943 two Cadet Divisions were formed - the ambulance cadets under the leadership of Mr. Fred Webb, this was registered on 5th October. The Nursing Cadets were formed with Mrs Hansford as Superintendent this started on 20th December. On VE Day 1945 a newly acquired American Ambulance was involved, tragically, involved in a fatal accident in which Mrs Lumber the Lady Superintendent of the Nursing Division lost her life. A window in West Huntspill Church is dedicated to her memory. In May 1950 Dr Jack Burns the Division's first surgeon died and a very well known local GP Dr Gerald Clayton was appointed to take his place, Mrs Edith Clayton became Nursing Officer of the Nursing Division. The Doctor and Mrs Clayton were stalwart supporters of the Division for many years. At that time Mr Harry Miller was Superintendent having been a founder member of the Division.

The first recorded AGM of the Nursing Cadets refers to the resignation of Mrs. Hansford in 1955. In 1956 Miss Muriel Cox of Mark was appointed Superintendent. To celebrate their Silver Jubilee in 1957 the members held a week of social events. By now all four Divisions were flourishing, there was over 100 members in all. The members were carrying out hundred of hours of duties; not only at events as they do today, but in those days they were covering the ambulance service in the district. This was still run on a voluntary basis, the Division did receive payment for fuel, equipment etc but the were not paid for the 24 hour cover that they operated on with the rosta system.

At the Highbridge and Burnham St John Ambulance Division A.G.M. in May 1959 it was reported that Ambulances had travelled over 16,600 miles during the year and dealt with 983 removals and 62 accidents. Praised was also levelled at the cadets for their service to the general public especially when so much is reported on juveniles causing trouble. The local Division continued to operate the County Ambulance Service on a voluntary basis through the 1960's until intervention by the unions in the early 1970's; the service was then prevented from continuing. Sadly when this work was lost membership dropped, but the Divisions continued to cover all the events in an extensive area, these included Brean, Biddisham, Mark, East Huntspill, Pawlett and of course Burnham and Highbridge.

The first "paid" staff were those stationed at Highbridge on 24th May 1963. Two Divisional members— Mr Les Copper, a paid driver on the 'sitting' ambulance and Private Joe Haines, part of the front line emergency crew. The Highbridge St John Ambulance radio call sign was also the first on the new system and was BASE 1. In June 1964 Superintendent Harry Miller retired, he had been admitted to the Order of St John in 1954 and promoted to Officer Brother in 1963 for his services to the Brigade. Many Officers from the local Divisions have been honoured in this way. A brand new ambulance was dedicated in November 1964 it cost £1,584.11s.3d. The vehicle was sold privately a few years ago to a local person who has maintained it as a "Classic Vehicle". Over the years a number of vehicles have been purchased, usually from the County Ambulance Service; two ambulances are at present owned by the Division.

Upon Harry Miller's retirement Mr. Ken Walker took over the Ambulance Division, followed by Mr. John Brewer in 1977. Subsequent Superintendents have been Joe Skinner, Terry Major-during whose time the two adult Divisions combined, and Phil Thorne took over from Terry Major when he retired due to ill health. The person currently in charge of the combined Adult Division is Keith Gough. The Ambulance Cadet Superintendent Mr. Webb was promoted to the Area Staff and subsequent leaders include Cyril Gowan, Mike Facey, Gordon Howe and David Drinkwater, until, due to lack of numbers, they combined with the Nursing Cadets.

During this time Mrs P. Vowles was Superintendent of the Nursing Division until her retirement. Miss Muriel Cox ran the Nursing Cadet Division from the late 1950's until her promotion to Area Staff Officer Cadets in 1965, then Mrs Pat Comer took charge of the Nursing and Nursing Cadet Divisions until her promotion to Area Superintendent in 1971. Mrs Lyn Thomas took over the Nursing Division and remained in post during the change to a Combined Adult Division, working with Mr. Major. Mrs. Pat Masterman took over the running of the Cadets until 1987 when Mrs. Valerie Young took charge. Mrs. Masterman was appointed to the newly introduced role of County Badger Leader. Following a long career of Area Staff Officer Cadets, Miss Cox became County Staff Officer Cadets until her retirement in 1993. Mrs Masterman followed in her footsteps in Area and County Staff Youth appointments. The Division is currently under the leadership of Mrs. Sarah Westlake and as our picture shows has a considerable membership, together with the Badger Sett led by Miss Julia Gibson.

(Photo supplied by Mrs Sarah Westlake)

All members of the Cadet Division and Badger Sett taken in March 2004

Mrs. Comer went on to become Deputy Commissioner, then County Commissioner for Somerset and is now Deputy Commander. In recognition of her Service to the Organisation she was honoured by being promoted to a Commander in the Order of St John.

All four Divisions independently celebrated their Golden Jubilee prior to combining their membership.

As mentioned earlier, the first H.Q. was at the Constitutional Club on the Town Hall Square with the garages and duty room underneath the Town Hall. Early in 1970 the Railway Hotel was pulled down so that the new Medical Centre could be built and with it the sheltered housing. The Division was homeless for some time but true to the traditions of the Knights of St John we kept going. The Cadets used the old Railway Hut opposite where Kwik Save Supermarket now is and the ladies met in the homes of members. The men! Yes you've guessed—in the Coopers Arms; the closest to the garages and duty room.

In 1976 it was decided that it was essential we needed our own permanent Headquarters and a major fund raising campaign was launched. The Council leased to us an area under the Town Hall and work was started to convert this for our use. It was an ideal location, adjacent to the garages and within a year we had completed a lecture room, kitchen and other facilities; at last we were settled and plans were made to renovate the rest of the premises under the Town Hall. But fate had conspired against us, history was to repeat itself-the main Town Hall had been condemned as unsafe and we were forced to leave. A second major campaign was launched to build a replacement building. Thanks to the generosity of the Sedgemoor District Council giving us land adjacent to Bank Street Car Park plus substantial grants from them and Somerset County Council; together with support from many organisations and members of the community our new premises opened in April 1985. One point of interest is that we moved back to our roots, this current, and hopefully permanent building, has taken St John Ambulance in Highbridge back to property once owned by the Somerset and Dorset Joint Railway.

St John Ambulance continues to give service to the community in many ways:-

First aid cover at events, whether by ambulance, fully trained crew or a person with first aid kit and knowledge.

A youth organisation catering for boys and girls from six to eighteen years of age.

A venue for the community to use for functions, meetings etc. Social services frequently use the HQ

Training courses in first aid, ranged from basic skills, to a full certificate by our fully qualified instructors, for all types of organisation.

(Article supplied by Mrs. P.Masterman and Mrs. P.Comer)

In 2004 Thomas Hancocks, a 15-year-old cadet, from Burnham Road, received Royal recognition at Buckingham Palace, when the Princess Royal presented him with the Grand Prior Award; this is the highest recognition a cadet can achieve.

Footnote - *One of the founder members of the Highbridge and Burnham Division was a Mr. Ronald (Chummy) Andrews, he also served in the St. John (Railway) Ambulance Association for 37 years. He was employed by the S. & D. Railway for 50 years, retiring in 1964 as a driver-in-charge, he was employed straight from school at 14, working in the paint shop, as a call boy, then cleaner, moving on to be a fireman and a driver. Interviewed by a local newspaper in 1988 he gave details of his early life in Highbridge, how he remembered the town as a busy port with many coastal vessels plying between South Wales and the Continent, the many cargoes of timber, coal, bricks, tiles and foodstuffs. "Chummy" as a young man was a keen swimmer and won many prizes, including a gold medal for the Steart Island Swim.*

Air Training Corp.

The Air Training Corp has been in Highbridge and Burnham since 1940 the current headquarters being just off the Highbridge Road. The Army Cadet Force and Sea Cadets had been in existence for some years and upon the outbreak of hostilities in 1939 cadets from these units were naturally drafted, when old enough, into the Army and Royal Navy. The Royal Air Force being a relatively young organisation did not have such a cadet force in which to train future airmen.

With Air Training Corps units being formed around the country Highbridge/Burnham felt that they too would encourage recruitment and a flight was formed in 1940. Flight Commander A. White and the new cadets met at the Adult School in Church Street, Highbridge – meetings were held twice weekly on Tuesdays and Thursdays. Originally the unit was a detached flight of the 65 Bridgwater Squadron. In the early days the instructors included Deputy Pilot Officer J. Freeman and Superintendent H. Miller of the St John Ambulance Brigade and Mr. Hawkins. Towards the end of the war Mr. Brabner ran the Flight in the Territorial Army Drill Hall that was on Burnham Road, Highbridge. At the end of the war F/O V. Ruskin took over the running of the Flight. The membership increased and in 1955 the unit gained Squadron status becoming the 2302 Highbridge/Burnham Squadron under F/Lt Ruskin. In 1958 F/Lt Ruskin joined Wing H.Q staff and F/Lt Hoey took over with F/O A. Lismore, F/O C. Stell and P/O V. Drew.

The Army decided it no longer needed the Drill Hall and it was sold. The Squadron moved into temporary premises at the rear of Church Street, Highbridge, until the present Headquarters were built off Highbridge Road. The Squadron did rifle shooting at R.N.A.S. Yeovilton and R.A.F. Watchet, glider training at R.A.F. Locking and spent a week at a R.A.F. station every year where the cadets flew in non-operational aircraft. They also had regular flying experience in Chipmunks at R.A.F. Filton. Three cadets, P. Hoey, P. Chidzey and R. Stell gained the Duke of Edinburgh gold award. Many cadets left to make a career in the R.A.F. In the late 1960's F/Lt Hoey transferred to Wing staff and F/Lt A. Lismore took over Command. Following Flt. Lt. Arthur Lismore came Flt. Lt. Viv Drew who commanded the unit from the late 1960's until 1982, when he decided to retire from the R.A.F.V.R (T) and Flt. Lt. Paul Upham assumed command of the detached flight. Cadet numbers in the 2302 Sqdn. had steadily dwindled and it became increasingly difficult to retain cadets for a long period of time, eventually, in about 1982 the squadron was downgraded to the detached flight status becoming a detached flight of (Weston-super-Mare) Squadron.

Flt. Lt. Paul Upham joined Squadron 2302 as a cadet in April 1970, in those days the unit met weekly on Monday and Wednesday evenings. In the summer months formal lessons on the theories of flying were kept to a minimum and the light evenings were used to take on the Army and Sea Cadets at cricket or football. There were also outdoor projects such as constructing and flying model aircraft. In the early 1970's the cadet's uniform still comprised the World War II pattern, called "Hairy Mary's" battle dress. Life as a cadet in the unit changed very little during the decade. Opportunities did arise twice a year to go to Filton and fly in Chipmunks and there was gliding at Weston Airport, again twice a year. Some cadets including Paul went on a complete gliding course and ultimately, he stayed at the Gliding School as an instructor, a position held for 18 years. In the early 1980's the 2302 unit did not have direct access to its own rifle range, but every Monday evening two/three members of staff drove cadets out to R.A.F. Locking to use the indoor range. There was regular shooting with 303 rifles at Yoxter on the Mendips and at Langport. The unit won several R.A.F. Wing competitions and Paul represented the Somerset Wing at the Bisley Championships.

Cadets were given the opportunity to attend a weeks-training camp held on a R.A.F. Station somewhere in the U.K. Some were lucky being selected to attend camps overseas, such as Germany or Malta. During these training camps cadets had

(Photo supplied by P.Derham)

the opportunity to visit various sections on the R.A.F. bases, if it was a "flying" one, meaning there were aircraft on the base, cadets had the opportunity to 'crawl' all over the aircraft that had been stripped down for maintenance. This gave them the chance to put into practice what their theory lessons had taught them and to see, first hand, how an aircraft was constructed and how systems worked. In 1978 Cadet Paul Upham was successful in getting a commission in the Royal Air Force Volunteer Reserves –Training Branch and was posted to 2302 as a staff member. It became increasingly difficult to retain cadet numbers for long periods and in 1982 the Squadron was down graded as mentioned earlier.

Fortunes changed and the A.T.C. across the country was about to make a huge step forward in its role as a premier youth organisation. A handful of units, in each county, had for a few years been allowed to recruit girls, this was, however, under very strict rules. The number of girls had to be no more than 10% of the total strength; obviously there were some activities in which the girls could not take part. Trials had, however, been a success and the green light was given to 2302 unit to recruit girls. This change in policy produced quick results, within a few years three female A.T.C. Cadets were recruited and with females joining, boys suddenly became interested again. Both sexes took part in identical activities, with the exception of sport. Boys played football of rugby and the girls netball and hockey. There was quite a shock for boys when girls beat them when participating on equal terms.

Numbers slowly increased and in the late 1980's the unit was once again granted Squadron status, being given it original Squadron Number 2302. During the mid-1980's transport had improved and the unit began to participate in adventure training activities, Duke of Edinburgh Awards. Cadets regularly took part in exercises on Dartmoor, Lake District and North Wales. These additional activities created renewed interest in the A.T.C. and brought new recruits. A number of cadets gained awards, but with the whole country falling into a well-forecast "Demographic Trough" numbers of eligible teenagers reduced and numbers again fell. In 1993 a week's adventure training trip to the Isle Arran off the Scottish coast was organised. Several cadets units from Somerset participated and the whole event was a huge success and continued on an annual basis until 2001. The foot and mouth disease that year caused the cancellation just weeks before the trip was to take place. Later in that year the owners of the premises on the Island sold the buildings and future visits ceased.

(Information supplied by Sqdn Ldr P. Upham and Flt. H.H.Hoey)

British Legion - Women's Section

Formed in September 1929 it covered Highbridge, East and West Huntspill, Watchfield, Mark and Burtle; the agreed subscription being 1s. 00d per year. The first general meeting was held on 21st November 1929 with 96 members being present. Total membership was 123 ordinary and 8 honorary, this increased to 168 ordinary and 10 honorary by January 1930.

A Legion standard was purchased and a sewing guild and thrift club were established, Mrs. Wade was the Chairman and Poppy Organiser the total collected that year being £71 11s. 01d. during the years 1940/41 only the Annual General Meeting and committee meetings were held due to the hostilities. The sewing club closed down and the members joined the Red Cross depot, branch meetings restarting, in July 1943. After the war (1939-45) Mark and other villages formed their own branches, the Highbridge membership dropping to 60. At their Jubilee Conference in 1971, Queen Elizabeth II conferred on the Legion the honour of being the Royal British Legion. Another memorable occasion was when, in October 1973, the Women's section of the new Royal British Legion's standard was dedicated at St. John's Church, Highbridge. Standard bearers and representatives from other branches joined the service for the laying up of the old standard and the dedication of the new standard.

The Burtle Silver Band attended and a Company of over one hundred were in the church hall afterwards for a celebration tea. Branch membership was 44 in 1973, but it had dropped to 20 by 1985. Social activities were many, picnics, whist drives, film shows and coach trips were organised, together with raffles, jumble sales, coffee mornings and fund-raising events, between 1963 and 1995.

In 1997, the officers and committee members decided it was becoming increasingly difficult to keep the branch functioning properly, with just a few active members, therefore the officers officially and very reluctantly closed the branch in 1997. To mark the closure of the Highbridge branch a service was held in St. John's church in July 1998 to cover the laying up of the standard, this was followed by tea in the church hall. The local branch was honoured in that one of their members, Mrs. Greener, paid homage in Westminster Hall in 1957 to the late King George VI.

British Legion Headquarters (Near the Coopers Arms)

(Information supplied by Nadine Northcombe)

British Legion - Men's Section

We regret that, although we believe a Men's Section was formed in 1925 and was very active within the town, we were unable to confirm any details covering its activities.

Burnham Area Youth Club (B.A.Y. Club)

The B.A.Y. club was built in 1966 on the playing fields next to the King Alfred School at a cost of £10,000. The local community raised 25% of the money. The floor area was 5000 sq. ft. with a hyper para'boloid roof, designed to reflect the maritime nature of the area. A voluntary Committee managed the Club and their first leader was Ken Hindle. Prior to the building of this new club members met in a variety of places: -"The Hall" on Berrow Road, the Community Centre and on one occasion the home of the local brewers, the Holt Family.

The B.A.Y.Club inCassius Close

The intention was to form a club for the benefit of young people between the ages of 14 - 21 years; the average membership at any given time being about 100. The variety of activities on offer was wide and varied; these included sailing, swimming, rugby, football, cricket, motorcycle maintenance and events for mini car owners. This was the era of Mods. and Rockers, so in addition to motorcycles there were also scooters. The Club was open six nights a week; a well-known Highbridge resident Miss Vera Moxey often staffed a coffee bar. Dances were held once a month on a Friday night, these were very popular, with groups from Bristol often appearing.

On one occasion there was great excitement, when the Bomb Disposal Unit took over the club because an unexploded bomb had been found in the Apex Ponds.

(Information and photograph supplied by Ken Hindle)

Stroke Club

This club meets every Tuesday at Morland Hall, Highbridge where everyone is made welcome. The club is independent, self-supporting and is run by a committee of volunteers and club members.

Aims of the club are, to relieve and support persons, who have suffered a stroke and, as a result are disabled; to provide and assist in the provision of facilities for recreation and leisure activities. The object is to improve the quality of life of sufferers and their carers. At the meetings everyone enjoys the social atmosphere, the chatter, games and handicrafts; the latter being within their capabilities. Refreshments are provided. Occasionally guest speakers attend to give talks on topical and practical subjects. Transport is provided to and from the club meeting if it is required.

In July 2003 the Highbridge Stroke Club Committee Members attended a Garden Party at Buckingham Palace, to receive from the Queen a **Golden Jubilee Award** for their dedication to the cause, they had been chosen from the 22 Somerset charities to be so honoured.

(Information supplied by Lyn Parkinson)

The Visually Impaired (V.I.) Club

Can you imagine, suddenly to be plunged into a world of not being able to see to do the little things you enjoyed doing, or being able to go out on your own. Blindness can make a person feel very lonely and vulnerable.

In January 1986 this Club was formed in order that blind people could go out again and enjoy, as far as it was possible, a social life; to also enjoy, with a sighted person as a guide, some of the every day activities. The Club meets every Friday morning at St. Johns' Church Hall.

We have coach trips throughout the summer months with a lunch or tea to finish. At Christmas there is a Fish and Chip lunch and at New Year we go to a hotel for a dinner. During the year we usually go away for a few days on a Tinsel and Turkey Holiday; Coffee Mornings are held to raise funds.

There are Craft sessions, including Knitting, Crocheting and Basketwork and members enjoy playing skittles. Some Fridays we play a special type of Bingo, not like the usual way, but with dominoes so that we can feel the raised dots when a number is called. Some members are very good at the quizzes we hold; occasionally we have some very interesting speakers.

We have 40 members who enjoy coming out every Friday morning, so that they can be with the friends they have made. Without this Club some people would not leave their homes.

(Information supplied by Audrey Lomax)

U.3.A. of Highbridge

The U3A of Highbridge is 5 years old in the town and is one of over 500 within the United Kingdom; its full title is the "University of the Third Age".

The idea originated in France around 1972, the idea being to have an organisation that would provide to retired persons the opportunity for additional learning. Although people may have retired from full time employment many wish to occupy their leisure/free time with some worthwhile activity. The idea was taken up in England in 1982, quickly spreading throughout the country. It has now spread worldwide and it is understood that there are about 20,000 U.3.A.'s in China.

The Third Age Trust, to which the majority of clubs are affiliated, recognises that there is an immense resource of skills, experience and enthusiasm possessed by people who are no longer in full time employment. The emphasis is on the value of doing something to keep active, of meeting people who have like interests and, together you can acquire and improve skills in a relaxed and friendly environment. Members are free to undertake to learn and help others to learn whatever they wish, no previous experience is needed – just enthusiasm and an interest in taking part.

The local club meets on a Wednesday morning from 10.00 a.m. to 12 noon at the Highbridge Social Club. It is self financing and it has groups which cover many subjects, art, swimming, social, travel, theatre and keep fit and is continually aiming to provide more facilities for the people of Highbridge.

Footnote - A majority of the Highbridge History Project team responsible for the research and production of this book are U.3.A of Highbridge members.

CHARITABLE ASSOCIATIONS

National Blind Children's Society

This Society was originally called "Help the Blind" being set up in 1995 by Rod Carne. It then became a Charitable Organisation and the charity was renamed "The National Blind Children's Society".

Its prime focus is to provide the resources and equipment needed by blind and partially sighted children to give them access to the social opportunities usually taken for granted by their sighted peers. The N.B.C.S. was, in line with the 1981 Education Act, prompted to supply computer equipment and other items to visually impaired children so that they could work independently on their school projects whilst at home. The state had made no provision for this equipment to be available to these children.

The Charity has increased its age limit to so that it can support young people up to 25 years of age whilst in full time education. N.B.C.S. moved its Headquarters to Market Street, Highbridge, after being at several locations in Burnham and Bridgwater. The Charity's "Mission" is to enable blind and partially sighted children and young people to achieve their educational and recreational potentials. Their "Vision" is a world where blind and partially sighted children have equal opportunities in education, an education which is adequately supported with the provision of sources of information in a suitable format for their needs and that there should be no barriers in sport or recreational activities.

The Charity's aims are to have honesty and integrity in all it does, to be a client focused outward looking organisation and be dedicated to deliver a quality service to all its clients. It is committed to have regular communication with its employees, clients, organisations and supports of N.B.C.S., to believe in trusting and empowering employees and to get things right –first time – every time.

During 2001 the N.B.C.S. was able to help over 500 families who had visually impaired children and aims to help many more. Donations help fund recreational activities and equipment, supply computers and I.T. equipment for home use, provide activity holidays and respite care.

"Custom Eyes" books, with large print, are provided in fiction and non-fiction or as curriculum textbooks. Also professional advice and liaison with Local Education Authorities and other such bodies are provided.

The National Blind Children's Society can be contacted on 01278 764764 or www.nbcs.org.uk

(Information provided by permission of Carolyn Fullard-Chief Executive)

Age Concern - Somerset

As a member of a federation of many Age Concern organisations, which are active in this country and across the world, Age Concern Somerset is a non-profit making charity which gets financial support from local institutions, to solely help older people in Somerset. Eight services now exist to help older people maintain an independent lifestyle and two of these services are tucked away in a small office in the UK-Online centre, at the rear of Alpha House in Market Street Highbridge.

'Ageing Well' operates throughout Sedgemoor and West Somerset and aims to promote a healthier lifestyle and outlook, by the provision of gentle exercising and activity in a variety of centres.

In just over two years of operation, **'Safe and Secure'** has helped over a thousand older people feel more secure and safe, by installing or replacing locks and providing help and assistance to reduce the risk of accidents in their homes across the county.

In order to operate successfully, Age Concern Somerset are reliant on their remarkable volunteers and are always looking for the men and women to join them who are willing to give some of their free time to help older people.

For more information about services or becoming a volunteer, contact Rachel on 01278 785921

Primary Care Trust

Under the auspices of the Primary Care Trust, two Groups have been set up in the town; these are concerned with catering for the elderly and people who have mobility problems. Many elderly people, especially if suffering from rheumatism or a similar problem, suffer falls and the resulting hospitalisation and aftercare that follows is very costly to the National Health Service. In an attempt to reduce the instances of 'falling' one Group has undertaken the task of trying to encourage the elderly to be a little more careful when moving around both their homes or when out side, shopping or whatever.

The second Group has been set up to help people who experience mobility problems, depression or bereavement. It is intended that once a week they will meet at the Bay Centre, enjoy a cup of tea and a cake, make a few friends and have a social gathering. They would be with people who have similar problems to them and can, hopefully, get their worries off their chest by seeking friendship and advise. Outings are to be arranged and meetings will include games e.g. cards, beetle drives, quizzes; also speakers will be invited to talk about everyday events.

Contact Dae Morris on 01278. 785424 if interested.

Contoc Christmas Concert

There is a service called "Sounds and Voices" that provides cassette tapes to blind and visually impaired people in order that they may be kept up to date with both local and international news.

Another service that provides cassette tapes to the blind and visually impaired moved to Highbridge from Burnham (where it originated) in 1998 and, as the name implies, is available at Christmas. H.Sydney Cox, a local man, thought up and launched this service to entertain its listeners.

In January 1969, Sydney Cox was a resident in 6, Market Cottages, he moved to Bridgwater for a brief period, then Burnham, and in 1998 he moved into General Higgins House.

Sydney was introduced to C.B. (Citizen Band) Radio in 1983 and, in 1986 whilst on holiday in Scotland, switched on his set and started talking to other 'breakers'. One, a lady, he kept in contact with and started to 'tapespond' – 'corresponding' but sending your voice (and chat) by cassette tape. This continued and when the lady announced she had become a grandmother, Sydney sent the usual congratulatory words. Thinking about the forthcoming festive season he decided to send a Christmas fun tape to his friend and to others who had joined their 'circle'. The tape comprised seven minutes of 'nonsense' about a man coming down the chimney; this was for the benefit of the friend's granddaughter and was intended to a 'one off'. However, it was so well received and appreciated by his friends that it became the start of "Tapespondent's Christmas Concert.

As a youngster Sydney had been fascinated by the wireless and had longed to be a 'voice' on the radio. Years passed and at the age of twenty-two he was presenting live entertainment in hospitals etc. also becoming the leader of a children's theatre. In 1954 he was awarded 96 marks for his singing ability at a Music Festival, where the adjudicator was Anthony Hopkins. In 1971 ill health caused the termination of his live charity concert work, but he was determined to carry on entertaining and the Christmas tapes, which had, become his pleasure, started in 1987. During 1988 he included on his tapes interviews with well-known personalities from T.V. and radio, this he did with some trepidation. Some interviews were live, Sydney meeting and personally chatting to the celebrities. At first the entertainment was for ninety minutes but in 1990 it became two and a half-hours, then three hours, where it remains. The tapes include music, comedy, sketches, poetry and interviews etc.

When writing the scripts for his tapes. Sydney found that the civilian loss of life during the war was not recorded and he turned to Charlie Chester whose radio programme "Sunday Soapbox" asked his listeners for information. Charlie responded by writing and recording his poem "Blow the Bugle Softly" for Sydney's tape. Charlie Chester was a regular contributor to the "Tapespondent" service until his death in 1997. Others who contributed to the tapes included Sir Harry Secombe, Moira Kerr the Scottish singer/songwriter and operatic contralto Shirley Eddy. If a 'live' interview was not possible the celebrities recorded answers on a tape to written questions, Sydney would then add the questions himself on to a master tape and 'dub' the answers. A method he used when doing a sketch with Stanley Unwin. In 1999 ITV invited viewers to make a promise for the year 2000 and a pledge was made to make tapes available to more blind people. It was felt that the name "Tapespondent Christmas Concert" was inappropriate; 'outsiders' now outnumbered the tapespondents. Initially 'Contact' seemed to be apt but it developed into ContoC. The two C's capitals embracing the tape spools on the front of a compact cassette, - this became the logo

Sydney has received many awards for his work; a 'Blue Peter' badge in 1996, acknowledging his work for the blind. At the end of 2000 a certificate was awarded by the Dark Horse Venture for work with the blind and visually impaired. In 2002 three awards came his way, the first, a Millennium Award in which £2,150 of Lottery Cash was made available for his 16th edition. He had to give 100 volunteer hours, including recycling issues, take tuition in Presentation and Script- writing and fulfil the project within twelve months. He gave 266 hours, 10% of all the tape referred to recycling, completed the tuition, all done for less than £1,500. He also received a Golden Jubilee Commemoration Award (a certificate and medal) from Somerset County Council in recognition of his Christmas tapes, and another Dark Horse Venture certificate recognising his training in Presentation and Script-writing. It is estimated that the 16th edition in 2002 was available to 1432 folk, 91% of whom were blind. He is now aiming for an audience of 2,000.

(Article supplied by Sydney H. Cox)

Alstone Wildlife Park

This comprises a 50 acre site about 400 yards from the town of Highbridge where can be found a collection of 40 red deer, two llamas, assorted wallabies, emus and other birds, pigs, ponies plus horses, three bullocks and a camel.

The Park is owned and run by Arthur and Helen Duckett. The Park was started about ten years ago when Mr Duckett, a former bull dealer, became a full time animal technician. Mrs Duckett had a collection of ducks plus a hand reared badger and these had proved to be popular with their neighbours; so they decided to turn their farm into a wildlife park. Their collection of animals grew and, Mr Duckett who had always liked breeding animals added a bullock to the menagerie. This particular beast, Mr Duckett felt, had the potential to become really big, these has since proved to be the case because in 2003 the 'Colonel' as the bullock was known was a 'giant'

Both the regional television and national newspapers covered the story concerning its stature and a competition was held, proceeds for charity, to guess the weight of the 'Colonel', which was 1,660 Kg.

Chapter 7

HIGHBRIDGE AND WORLD WARS

THE GREAT WAR 1914 to 1918

It was obviously a traumatic time for the people of Britain with this conflict arising so soon after the Boer War; the country was, at that time, also undergoing many changes in its political and social lives. There was obviously much activity in and around the town, many men left to fight in the war, as the War Memorials bear witness. Troop movements through the town were fairly regular; a photograph of the troops assembling on the Town Square highlights this:

(Photo supplied by Mrs Pam Lyes)

**In 1915 troops assembled on the Town Square with their tracked vehicles
prior to leaving for Avonmouth for shipment to France**

The people 'at home' did their bit for the troops, many Clubs and associations organised activities to produce home comforts, these were sent to France and other overseas areas where British Troops were stationed, jumble sales and similar functions raised monies for the war effort.

In 1916 the town presented at the Town Hall, a Musical WAR Masque, this was entitled "The Empires Honour" and, as will be seen from the photograph and programme, this must have involved a lot of organising. The programme makes for very interesting reading and from the 'Dramatis Personae' it appears that a lot of the participants were business people and local persons of note. Miss Hilda Knight who was a School Teacher and many of the cast had business interests in the town; Major, Dudderidge, Kimber, Sparks, Cooks, Gass, Marsh, Hurley and others.

(Photo supplied by John Lancastle)

Above, the assembled company and below the programme.

"The Empire's Honour."

"The Empire's Honour" presents in allegorical form the fundamental issues of the war. Scene I represents the outbreak of war in 1914. Britannia is seen upon her throne in perfect peace. She is startled by the noise of battle, and a Herald enters to report that the Hun has declared war on France and Russia, and is invading Belgium, while urging Britannia to disregard her obligations to protect the latter.

A silent figure, symbolizing The Empire's Honour, appears beside Britannia at the first sound of danger showing her indignation and anxiety, until Britannia commands the Herald to announce her refusal to the Hun. Honour then disappears to rally the Daughter-Queens, while Scotland, Wales, and Ireland, introduced by national songs, arrive, and join Britannia. Led by Honour, the Dominions, singing the "Song of the Daughter-Queens," arrive one by one, each kneeling before Britannia and offering the symbol of her gift to the Empire. Honour withdraws satisfied, while Britannia replies to them.

Scene II represents 1916. The Herald recounts to Britannia and the sister kingdoms the deeds of the Army and the Fleet, and announces that the Allies desire to approach and bear their messages of gratitude.

Britannia summons the "Daughter-Queens," together with figures personifying the Warriors, i.e., the Army, Navy, Aviation Corps, and Army Service Corps; the Healers, i.e., Chaplains, Medical and Nursing Staff; the Industrial Workers, i.e., Munitions, Mining, Agriculture, Railways, and Factories.

The Allies then arrive one by one, each proclaimed by the Herald—France, Italy, Russia, and Japan— who salute Britannia. The music changes to a funeral march, and Belgium (veiled in black) and Serbia and Montenegro enter, bowed down by affliction. Britannia crowns each with laurels, and all join in the "Song of Belgium's Sorrow."

Britannia comforts each in turn, and then encourages the other Allies, while all reply to her in the song, "God of the Nations, hear!"

The Allies offer their thanks to the Warriors, Workers, and Healers, and finally Britannia addresses the "Bravest of Women," the mothers and wives of the warriors. The Empire's Honour reappears bringing in Peace and Freedom, and the scene closes with the "Hymn of Peace," in which the audience should join standing.

Dramatis Personæ

Britannia,	Miss Hilda Knight	A Herald,	Harold Doughty
England,	Kathleen G. King	Lord Kitchener,	Harry Major
Scotland,	Violet Hurley	A Soldier,	Edgar Hicks
Wales,	Ethel Gass	A Naval Officer,	Harold Marsh
Ireland,	Hilda Highnam	A Seaman,	Frederick Lancastle
Newfoundland,	Mary Lovell	An Airman,	Charles King
India,	Gladys Toseano	A Scout,	John Slocombe
Canada,	May Kimber	Doctor,	Albert Hobday
Australia,	May Cook	Chaplain,	Harold Lockyer
New Zealand,	Lilian Vincent	Red Cross Nurse,	Mabel Gass
South Africa,	Iris Toseano	A Miner,	Walter Duddridge
Egypt,	Nettie Meader	A Shell-Maker,	Clifford Besley
Rhodesia,	Lilian Amesbury	A Land-Worker,	Alfred Biffin
France,	Cecilia Bigglestone	A Railway-Man,	Hubert Marsh
Italy,	Dorothy Slocombe	A Factory-Girl,	Elsie Lake
Russia,	Florence Saunders	The Empire's Honour.	
Japan,	Kathleen King		Miss Ruth Hobart
Belgium,	Louise Bigglestone	Freedom,	Nora Sparks
Serbia,	Freda Evans	Peace,	Jessie Major
Montenegro,	Dorothy Chiek	British Mother,	Miss Phyllis Bicknell

Tenor Soloist : Mr. F. H. Baker

Soprano Soloist : Miss Phyllis Bicknell

By kind permission of COL. A. GILBEY, V.D., the following members of the 3/1st Bucks Battalion will assist :

Band-Sergt.	Smith	Drum-Corpl.	Cohen
Bandsman	Kirby	Drummer	Stephenson
,,	Brill	Bugle-Corpl.	Silvey
,,	Bristow	Bugler	Rundle

ORCHESTRA (Conductor : Victor Dyer).

Pianoforte, Miss Backway	T. Parsons	Flute—D. Ward
1st Violins—	T. Austin	Horn—W. D. Luxon
A. C. Harris (Leader)	Viola—M. Broad	Euphonium—Pte. Kirby
Miss Pople	Violoncello—	Cornets—
T. W. Petherick	Mrs Lemon, A. MUS.T.C.L	Band Sergt. Smith
C. Ward	B. Belby	R. Marsh
2nd Violins	Bass—G. Stone	Trombones—
Mrs. T. Austin	Clarinets—	C. H. Dyer
Miss C. Needs	W. Pratt	Pte. Brill
	Pte. Bristow	Drums—Pte. Stephenson

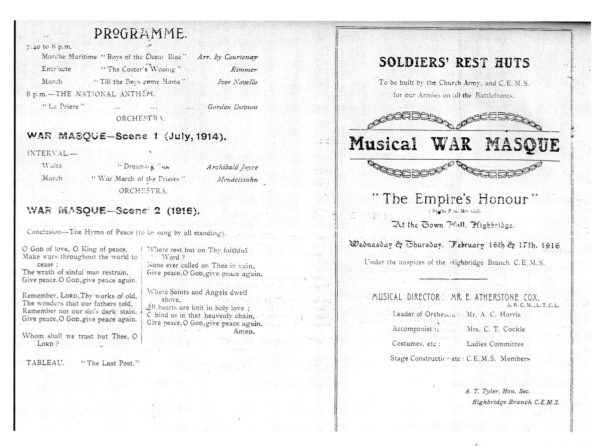

(Programme supplied by Ken Dyer)

Memorial to Railway Employees

The Memorial to commemorate the Somerset & Dorset Joint Railway Staff who served in the First World War was originally erected at the Locomotive Works at Walrow. The Service of Dedication for this was a solemn occasion in Highbridge and was marked by a special service.

The Memorial erected at the end of a Locomotive Workshop, was designed by a S & D Apprentice, made in the workshops and subscribed for by the staff of the Locomotive, Carriage and Wagon Depts. The Memorial was later moved to the Station buildings and was later moved to Southwell Memorial Gardens.

UNVEILING OF THE MEMORIAL

In the memory of the Staff who left the Locomotive,
Carriage & Wagon Departments of the Somerset &
Dorset Joint Railway to serve with the Forces
During the Great War
By
Sir Alan Garrett Anderson K.B.E.
(Director, Midland Railway and Somerset & Dorset Joint Railway)
At
Locomotive Works, Highbridge.
On
Monday May 8th 1922 at 3 pm.
Names of Railway of the Locomotive, Carriage and
Wagon Department who died in the Service of their
Country during the War
1914-1918
"Our Glorious Dead"

William Burton	Arthur Henry Lane
Walter Charles Bullock	Alfred Henry Lock
Harold Edward Clarke	Francis Charles Maggs
Ernest Dicker	Sidney Edward Rabbit
Richard William Gale	Charles Herbert Sealey
Albert John Hill	Fred Talbot Thompson
	Reginald Webb

Highbridge War Memorial

War Memorial dedicated in 1921

The Highbridge War Memorial was erected at the junction of Church Street and Burnham Road, on it has been engraved the names of the local men who gave their lives, for their King and Country in the Great War.1914-1918.

When research into the History of Highbridge was first proposed in 2002 a member of the team undertook to find out more about the men who had died during active service. All the names were copied from the plaques and upon completion of the list the details checked against the Internet; it was found that the Naval & Military Press Ltd. had a comprehensive listing of all those who had died during active service.

(Photo supplied by Chris Brown)

166

The following is a reproduction of the listings: -

Soldiers Died in the Great War

Naval & Military Press

Printed from Soldiers Died in the Great War CD Rom by the Naval & Military Press Ltd. Innovators in the field of military publishing

Place of Residence was Beginning with highbridge

Sort Order : Surname, Christian Name(s)

SURNAME, Christian Names(s), Born, Enlisted, Residence, Number, RANK, Cause, Place, Date of Death, ADDITIONAL TEXT

AMESBURY, Edwin Frank, b. Kingston, Somerset, e. Chichester, r. Highbridge, Somerset, 75952, GUNNER, Killed in action, Salonika, 23/04/17.

BRIMSON, William Thomas, b. Highbridge, Somerset, e. Weston-Super-Mare, r. Highbridge, Somerset, 17422, L/CPL, Killed in action, France & Flanders, 01/07/16.

BURROWS, George, b. Burnham-on-Sea, Somerset, e. Taunton, r. Highbridge, Somerset, 9477, PRIVATE, Killed in action, France & Flanders, 26/08/14.

CARPENTER, Raymond, b. Cheltenham, Glos, e. Weston-Super-Mare, Somerset, r. Highbridge, Somerset, 45535, PRIVATE, Died of wounds, France & Flanders, 26/03/18, FORMERLY 226653, R.F.A..

CHARMAN, Edgar Charles, b. Walcot, Bath, e. Bristol, r. Highbridge, Somerset, 9925, PRIVATE, France & Flanders, 01/05/17.

DAY, Hugh, b. Highbridge, Somerset, e. Taunton, r. Highbridge, Somerset, 9677, PRIVATE, Died, France & Flanders, 17/03/16.

DAY, Reginald, b. Highbridge, Somerset, e. Weston-Super-Mare, r. Highbridge, Somerset, 26525, L/CPL, Died of wounds, France & Flanders, 03/09/18.

DOWDEN, William, b. Mark, Highbridge, Somerset, e. Burnham-on-Sea, Somerset, r. Highbridge, Somerset, 7756, PRIVATE, Killed in action, France & Flanders, 06/07/15.

DYER, Arthur George, b. Barry, Glam., e. Weston-Super-Mare, r. Highbridge, Somerset, 34197, PRIVATE, Killed in action, Egypt, 06/11/17, FORMERLY 1836, NORTH SOMERSET YEOMANRY..

GILBERT, George, b. Leeds, e. Maesteg, Bridgend, r. Highbridge, Som., 18384, L/CPL, Died of wounds, France & Flanders, 12/07/16.

HALE, Richard, b. Highbridge, Somerset, e. Taunton, r. Highbridge, 37679, CPL., Killed in action, France & Flanders, 13/11/16.

HAM, Frederick Charles, b. East Brent, Somerset, e. Blaenavon, Mon,, r. Highbridge, Somerset, 1735, PRIVATE, Killed in action, France & Flanders, 01/07/16.

HEAL, William Thomas Turner, b. Highbridge, Somerset, e. Cheltenham, r. Highbridge, 17266, PRIVATE, Killed in action, France & Flanders, 18/11/16.

HOLDER, Mark, b. Huntspill, Somerset, e. Burnham-on-Sea, Somerset, r. Highbridge, Somerset, 27626, PRIVATE, Killed in action, France & Flanders, 31/07/17, FORMERLY 2031, WEST SOMERSET YEOMANRY..

HUNT, Frank, b. Bason Bridge, Somerset, e. Weston-Super-Mare, r. Highbridge, Somerset, 242422, PRIVATE, Killed in action, France & Flanders, 24/04/18, FORMERLY 8176, CAMBS REGT..

HUTSON, William, e. Bath, r. Highbridge, 1392, PRIVATE, Killed in action, France & Flanders, 13/05/15.

MILTON, Arthur Frank, b. Wimborne, Dorset, e. Bridgwater, r. Highbridge, Somerset, M2/078802, PRIVATE, Died of wounds, France & Flanders, 09/04/18.

NICHOLLS, Reginald, b. Bridgwater, Som., e. Weston-Super-Mare, r. Highbridge, 36305, PRIVATE, Died of wounds, France & Flanders, 03/10/18, FORMERLY 21318, SOM. L.I..

NORMAN, Fred, b. Brent Knoll, Highbridge, Somerset, e. Cardiff, r. Highbridge, 10446, SERGT., Killed in action, France & Flanders, 07/11/14.

PARSONS, Percival James, e. Weston-Super-Mare, Somerset, r. Highbridge, Somerset, 212866, GUNNER, Died, Home, 28/03/17.

PUDDY, John, b. Mark, Somerset, e. Taunton, r. Highbridge, Somerset, 17373, PRIVATE, Killed in action, France & Flanders, 08/08/16.

PUGSLEY, Horace, e. Taunton, r. Highbridge, Som., 156248, SHOEING SMITH, Died of wounds, France & Flanders, 27/06/17.

The Naval & Military Press Ltd. PO Box 61. Dallington. Heathfield. East Sussex. TN21 9JS. England. Tel: 01435 830111. Fax: 01435 830623 email: order.dept@naval-military-press.co.uk. http://www.naval-military-press.co.uk and http://www.great-war-casualties.com

Printed from Soldiers Died in the Great War CD Rom by the Naval & Military Press Ltd. Innovators in the field of military publishi

Place of Residence was Beginning with highbridge

Sort Order : Surname, Christian Name(s)

SURNAME, Christian Names(s), Born, Enlisted, Residence, Number, RANK, Cause, Place, Date of Death, ADDITIONAL TEXT

RABBITT, Sidney Edward, b. Iluntspill, Som., e. Bristol, r. Highbridge, Som., WR/271339, SPR., Died, France & Flanders, 17/07/18, (1ST L.R.O. COY.)..

RICHARDS, Archibald, b. Exeter, e. Highbridge, r. Highbridge, 466, PRIVATE, Killed in action, France & Flanders 08/01/16.

RICHARDS, Edward Eli, b. Chard, Som., e. Taunton, Som., r. Highbridge, Som., A/205000, RIFLEMAN, Killed i action, France & Flanders, 01/04/18.

ROWDEN, Mansel, e. Taunton, r. Highbridge, Somerset, 2891, PRIVATE, Died, India, 26/05/16.

SHIER, Wilfred Fowler, b. South Molton, Devon, e. Taunton, r. Highbridge, Somerset, 27208, PRIVATE, Killed i action, France & Flanders, 22/09/17.

STEVENS, Albert Edward, b. Ashcott, Somerset, e. Weston-Super-Mare, r. Highbridge, Somerset, 26480, PRIVATE Killed in action, France & Flanders, 22/08/17.

TIDBALL, Harry James, b. Evercreech, Som., e. Weston-Super-Mare, Som, r. Highbridge, Som., 20748, PRIVATE Killed in action, France & Flanders, 27/08/18.

TOOMER, Albert, e. Weston-Super-Mare, Som., r. Highbridge, Som., 105409, PRIVATE, Died, Home, 08/11/18 FORMERLY 59866, DEVON REGT..

WASHER, Henry James, e. Keynsham, Somerset, r. Highbridge, Somerset, 184357, GUNNER, Died of wounds France & Flanders, 24/12/17, FORMERLY R/4/139551, R.A.S.C..

WASHER, William, b. Bridgwater, Somerset, e. Taunton, Somerset, r. Highbridge, Somerset, 1078, PRIVATE, Die of wounds, France & Flanders, 24/05/15, FORMERLY SOMERSET L.I..

WEBBER, Alfred George, b. Highbridge, Somerset, e. Taunton, r. Highbridge, 3/8315, PRIVATE, Killed in action France & Flanders, 01/07/16.

WEBSTER, Herbert Henry, b. Highbridge, Som., e. Weston-Super-Mare, r. Highbridge, 291292, GUNNER, Died o wounds, France & Flanders, 14/09/18, FORMERLY 240, 127TH BRISTOL HVY. BTY. R.G.A..

WELLS, Henry Arthur, b. Highbridge, Somerset, e. Taunton, r. Highbridge, Somerset, 3/7749, PRIVATE, Killed i action, France & Flanders, 08/01/16.

WEST, Fred, b. Chedderton, e. Keynsham, r. Highbridge, Somerset, R4/139552, PRIVATE, Killed in action, France & Flanders, 10/10/17.

WILLIAMS, Frederick James, e. Taunton, Somerset, r. Highbridge, 59017, A/BDR., Killed in action, France & Flanders, 16/05/16.

WILLIAMS, Henry, e. Weston-Super-Mare, Somerset, r. Highbridge, Somerset, 1025, SPR., Died of wounds Salonika, 26/12/16, (2ND WESSEX FIELD COY., R.E.)..

YOUNG, Robert, b. Highbridge, Som., e. Taunton, Som., r. Highbridge, Som., 25867, DVR., Killed in action, France & Flanders, 28/04/18, (6TH DIV. SIGNAL COY., R.E.)..

The Naval & Military Press Ltd. PO Box 61. Dallington. Heathfield. East Sussex. TN21 9JS. England. Tel: 01435 830111. Fax: 01435 83062 email: order dept@naval-military-press.co.uk. http://www.naval-military-press.co.uk and http://www.great-war-casualties.com

WORLD WAR 1939-1945

With the probable approach of hostilities in the late 1930's and of possible landings by the German Army preparations had been made around the area in readiness. Pillboxes appeared along the lines of the railway, river and canal, these stretched eastwards from Highbridge into Wiltshire, the 'Green' line began at the mouth of the River Brue; it then continued north towards Bristol. Some of these defences remain as a reminder of the fears that existed all those years ago and looking at their robust constructions today, one may wonder how successful they would have been if the enemy had landed. There is still a pillbox by Highbridge station and many others along the banks of the Rivers Brue and Parrett.

'Forts' appeared on arable land, these were disguised as straw stacks, the straw being cleverly woven into a frame of wire netting; flaps over the gun firing apertures were detachable and the railway was provided with 'dragons' teeth' of steel rails and concrete posts, these formed an outer defensive screen.

On September 3rd 1939 Britain war was declared and we were again at war with Germany and those who survived until 1945; and the six years of upheaval, sadness and stress that it caused by the continuous uncertainty, found that their lives had changed. Lives had to be rebuilt, men and women coming home from the war would require jobs and a new sense of belonging, a belonging to families who had also survived, but without them.

What of Highbridge? -What happened in or to the town? Our near neighbour-Weston-super-Mare received a fair share of bombing; many high explosive bombs and incendiaries had been dropped on the town and over 800 buildings were damaged or destroyed.

At the outbreak of hostilities the reservists from the Territorial Army, Royal Navy and Royal Air Force were immediately called up, closely followed by men who volunteered their services.

Men who were not eligible for active service, due to a variety of reasons, joined the Air Raid Wardens, Auxiliary Fire Service or Local Defence Volunteers, (later to become the Home Guard); not forgetting the Observer Corp.

It is not too well known that Highbridge had a Parachute Factory; it was situated at the far end of Newtown Road; about where there is now a block of flats and where the cycle/footpath goes through to Apex Park. Parachutes were made for star shell bombs. The factory was, presumably, built at the start of the war. It employed about 40 people; amongst the employees were, Peggy Hicks, Betty Atkins and R.Pitman

Joan Fackrell and Mrs Broadstock were conscripted from the milk factory at Bason Bridge as 'compulsory labour'

(At the end of the war the factory changed from manufacturing parachutes to the making jewellery.)

With their husbands, sons or brothers doing their bit for the war effort the ladies of Highbridge also rallied round and became organised. They formed themselves into clubs or groups so that they could provide a service to the town, utilising their abilities and interests so that everyone benefited.

One such organisation was the Women's' Voluntary Service, later to add "Royal" to its title in recognition of the service it gave to the nation.

The local service was formed in 1941, initially the membership numbered forty and over the next two or three years its numbers grew to about seventy. Within the service were a number of groups that dealt with specific duties, "Housewives Service" had sixty members, with nine canteen workers, there were three "Rest Centres" in the town, at the Adult School, Methodist Schoolrooms and the Salvation Army Hall. The Centres worked on a three shift system, 6.00 a.m. to 2.00 p.m. - 2.00 p.m. – 10.00 p.m. and 10.00 p.m. - 6.00 a.m. Each had a "Centre Leader" plus a Deputy, a "Registrar" "Checker" and canteen staff plus an "Information Officer".

The First Aid post list comprised nine ladies, and the Clothing Depot had a staff of six in 1944. To look after transport needs, there was a list of fifteen car drivers and messengers. With strict petrol rationing it is not known how they managed to get petrol, unless, of course, they used "Service Vehicles". As always, there was paperwork and three typists were available to cope with this.

"Saving for Victory" had a staff of eleven, presumably to collect the money and there were "Knitting Groups" these were made up of twenty-six members. The service was kept quite busy and the groups did sterling work in maintaining and giving a sense of duty "To the Town" and helped Highbridge fulfil its wartime role. Later into the war ladies also became involved in a more active role, joining the newly formed sections of the Armed Force, plus Nursing organisations and the Land army.

Action around Highbridge was varied, comprising a number of incidents: -

In 1942 a large balloon hangar was built at Pawlett, this was to house a Barrage balloon that was to be used for research purposes. Both sides used barrage balloons to deter bombers; they effectively prevented planes getting too close and thus upset accurate bomb aiming. To counteract this we tried various methods, one being a cutting device attached to the leading edge of a bombers' wing. They did however, need to be tested and this was where Pawlett and Pawlett Hams came in, the flat open country between the village and Bridgwater. It was during a test flight on 21st March 1942 a Hampden bomber fitted with a cutting device and on an experimental run, crashed at Watchfield killing the crew of four, its wing had been badly damaged causing a loss of control.

Early in the war work started on the Royal Ordnance Factory at Puriton and instructions were issued to ensure it was well camouflaged. It worked, because in September of that year 14 H.E. bombs fell in the area between the plant and Highbridge and the buildings were unscathed. Troops passed through the station at all hours of the day and night, either going home on leave or returning to their units in the South West. As the war progressed Highbridge became a sort of "Crewe" for the South West. In 1943, on the 4th April, a Whitley bomber crashed, east of Highbridge (presumably the Watchfield area). It is understood the plane carried personnel from an officer's training unit, luckily only two were injured. Also in 1943, when nearing Highbridge, on the night of 17th/18th May, a freight train from Exeter to Cardiff was machine-gunned; it was not damaged. A lady from Highbridge who worked at Puriton saw the bomber and upon hearing the machine gunning dived for cover in the canteen. During 1943 the American forces started to arrive in Somerset and Highbridge station became a staging post. Their troops were all around the area and it was said that at times they almost outnumbered the locals; they were housed under canvas or in camps comprising mainly wooden huts.

The county was practically bursting at the seams. At Walrow, where the industrial estate now stands, the Americans had a vast store, the old Somerset and Dorset Joint Railway workshops were utilised and additional sidings were provided to facilitate the loading and unloading of equipment. Apparently there was a vast fuel dump on the site, this being constantly under a very tight guard. There was much speculation of what else was there, but it is doubtful if many people knew and if they did, they were not saying. With D.Day approaching fighting materials and the troops to use it, poured into the County and dumps sprang up everywhere, stores of all types: - ammunition, fuel, guns, tanks etc. appeared at the roadsides, if there was room for it, it was stored/stacked.

Following D.Day it was to be replaced by the movement of transport ferrying injured troops to hospital around the County. During this time plans had been drawn up for reception centres to be provided to receive Home Guard and American Army casualties in the event of an attack following D-Day. Thankfully these centres at camps/barracks around Somerset were not needed.

On the night of 27th/28th March 1944, the target for a raid was Bristol, but the anti-aircraft batteries around West-super-Mare caused some bombers to scatter and as they turned for home, bombs were jettisoned and many fell between Weston and Highbridge. These caused numerous fires in such places as Cannington, Bleadon, Edingworth, Weare and with incendiaries falling at Bridgwater, Burnham, East Huntspill, and Taunton the county had a night full of activity.

An incendiary bomb dropped on "Chubb's" cheese factory in Highbridge, the late Jack Major recalled:

After leaving school and keen to 'do my bit' I joined the National Fire Service as a messenger, being too young to be a fireman. This involved night duty at the Fire Station below the old Town Hall on a rota basis. One night whilst on duty, reports came of incendiary bombs falling in the area. Those on duty split into groups and toured the town. A fireman and myself went into Church Street and saw that Chubbs Cheese Store next to the "George Hotel" was alight. My companion and myself, and by now many onlookers, found some buckets and collected water from the static water tank, that was sited behind the barbers shop just opposite. We tackled the blaze with great enthusiasm but very little success. Fortunately a fire tender soon arrived and rendered professional help, but it was a scene of desolation the following morning, the only casualty as far as I can recall of the Highbridge Blitz.

Rationing continued for some time after the war and, (into the 1950's) in order to help families cope with the post-war problems, Groups and National Organisations were set up to provide help. Some families were setting up homes again after being demobbed; some had lost their homes and were re-starting. Everyone needed help from some quarter. This is where the W.R.V.S. and similar organisations were again able to provide a service. Food, especially that which came from abroad, was slowly appearing in the shops again. The Ministry of Food published many leaflets, posters, etc. Dispensing advice, recipes and information on which vitamins helped build your strength. A leaflet issued in January/February 1946 is re-produced and it gives you some idea what circumstances were like in the post-war period.

Ministry of Food Information

(Circulated through the W.V.S. in January 1946)

SUPPLY POSITION

Pitted Dates	Supply position easy.
Unseeded Raisins	Satisfactory.
Sultanas	Easy, ample supplies.
Figs	Unobtainable.
Currants	Not obtainable in early part of the month, but should begin to be more plentiful towards the latter part of the Month
Peaches and Apricots	Practically non-existent
Pears	Unobtainable.
Dried Vegetables	Threshed homegrown peas in plentiful supply.
	Split peas -in reasonable supply; fairly plentiful in the London area.
Custard Powder	Production is slightly over 100% pre-war but demand is very strong.
Baking Powder	Supplies adequate for demand.
Soya flour	Supplies adequate for demand.
Semolina	Supply equals demand.

Rice, Sago and Tapioca	none available.
Oatmeal	Production is increasing satisfactorily although there may be instances of local shortages.
Pearl Barley	Supplies adequate
Pepper	In normal times the source of supply is Java. Supplies being received from India are not sufficient to meet demands and shortages will remain until Java supplies are resumed.
Mustard	Position now satisfactory.
Vinegar	There is no shortage of vinegar either malt or synthetic but a dearth of bottles is making the distribution difficult.
Salt	Position is still difficult but slow and steady improvement continues.

D.B. 2571-2 1500 D/d 372 1/46 R P

During the war the Americans learned of the problems experienced by the British War Brides in finding enough 'clothes coupons' from their clothes ration to be able to buy a wedding dress; or perhaps material in order to make a dress. The outcome was a scheme devised by President Roosevelt's wife Eleanor whereby service personnel could borrow a wedding dress for their big day. There were several designs to choose from and the one used for the Highbridge Wedding arrived in a large box packed with tissue paper to protect it during its long trip. The outfit consisted of a wedding gown, veil, and underwear and white stockings.

The only condition was that the outfit be dry cleaned before its return. The Highbridge was reported as follows: -

The Wedding of

MISS V. BIGGS to CPL. E. DIFFORD

at

ST. JOHN'S CHURCH - HIGHBRIDGE

On October 1st 1945

The bride wore a

ROOSEVELT'S WEDDING DRESS

(Information and photograph supplied by Mrs Difford)

Post War:

Memorial Gardens at Southwell House

The original Southwell House and surrounding land' that included the "Home Field" (now the recreation field) was purchased in 1903 by Dr. Reginald Wade (Surgeon). Prior to this it is understood that the property and surrounding land on which St. Nectan (now Wade House), 'The Grange', 'San Raphael' and also Grange Avenue now stand was in the ownership of the Cox family. They were proprietors of Cox's Brickyard and operated from land at the rear of Church Street. Dr. Reginald Wade had a practice at Southwell House, Highbridge up until 1932. His son Arthur continued the practice until 1944 from his own home St. Nectan, which he had had built. The house was situated at the corner of Church Street and Grange Avenue.

Dr Egerton who took over the surgery in 1956, was followed by Dr. Creamer until 1979 when the surgery was re-located to Alpha House in Market Street, it became a joint practice. Dr Creamer continued to live in St. Nectan until his retirement in 1989. This house was subsequently demolished and Wade House was built and opened in 1995. Prior to 1903 it is believed Southwell House had been the home of a Mr.P. Estlin who, had connections with the brickyard on the Walrow side of the G.W.R. line, opposite the end of Grange Avenue.

In 1932 Mr Gilbert Valentine Sheppard, a local builder bought the property. It is believed that during the Second World War the premises were rented to families who had been evacuated from, in particular, London.

A group of Highbridge residents, many of them councillors, (they were to become the First Trustees) put forward a proposal to buy the land and set up a **Memorial Garden,** tennis courts, a reading room and a general recreation area. The land to be purchased by public subscription in memory of Highbridge people who had given their lives in World War II. On August 31st 1949 Southwell House was purchased from Mr Sheppard for the sum of £750 and a Trust was set up to look after the new venture. **The Memorial Garden Trust** was subsequently registered with the Charity Commissioners and the property became a Registered Charity. In 1952 the First Trustees transferred the trusteeship to the Burnham Urban District Council.

It is not clear what took place between 1952 and the early 1960's, except that the land became overgrown and the house derelict and as a result it was eventually demolished.

The Highbridge Town Football Club was relocated to the grounds in 1952 and set up a Clubhouse.

In 1960/1 the remainder of the land was cleared and the present building, tennis courts and **Memorial Garden** was set up and opened to the public.

The present garden of remembrance includes a large **Memorial Plaque** dedicated to the railway workers from the Somerset and Dorset Locomotive Depot who left to join the services for duty in the 1914 – 1918 war. The **Memorial** was originally erected at the Locomotive, Carriage and Wagon Works; later it was removed to the north end of the booking office on the Somerset and Dorset Railway Station. Probably around the mid-sixties it was re-located to its present position in the **Southwell House Memorial Gardens**

In the garden there is also a plaque unveiled in **Memory of American Troops** which reads:

"In Memory

Of the Americans who were privileged to have served in Highbridge and Burnham-on-Sea during World War II. They were responsible for the operation of a large petrol depot located east of the Great Western Railway and served by the Somerset and Dorset Railway. Petrol from the site played a major role in the invasion of the French coast on the 6th June 1944 and in support of Allied advances on the continent. These Americans came as strangers to your shores and were taken into your homes, extended hospitality, food, shelter and understanding, for this they will be forever grateful.

Inasmuch as ye have done unto one of the least of these my brethren ye have done it unto me".

(Photo supplied by Collin Moore)

Sited below the **Railway Memorial** is a plaque in honour of Major Frank Foley "The spy who saved the lives of more than 10,000 Jews from the Holocaust". Born 23rd November 1884 at 7, Walrow Terrace, Highbridge. Died 8th May 1958. This plaque was unveiled on the 7th May 2000 by Sabine Comberti, whose father Mr. Meyer-Michael was saved by Frank Foley and is mentioned in Michael Smith's book about Foley.

The present situation:

As previously mentioned in 1952 the Burnham U.D.C. became the Trustees of the Charity, but when Sedgemoor District Council came into being in 1974 they managed the property as Trustees although in fact they never should have done so. Because it is stated in the original Trust deed that the property should be managed by … "the Burnham District Council or by a Local Authority having from time to time powers most nearly corresponding thereto in respect of the Highbridge area"… and so the property was handed over to the present Burnham and Highbridge Town Council to manage in 1996. By this time the property was in a sorry state and running at a loss of £3.500 per annum and the Council were not interested in running it. Soon after this time a group of people expressed their interest in running the property and in 1999 the Council set up a Management Committee run by volunteers who managed to turn the Charity's fortunes enabling the Charity to pay for itself.

On the 10th December 2002 the Charity Commissioners drew up a new scheme whereby the Charity was transferred to the Management Committee, who became the new trustees thereby releasing the Council from any involvement whatsoever – **the property was handed back to the people of Highbridge!**

(Much of the foregoing information supplied by Mrs Pam Lyes)

From a local newspaper on 29th July 1944

RECEIVED ARMY FOOD & EQUIPMENT

Highbridge Mother in Court

A Highbridge mother of five children was charged with receiving War Department Property. When she appeared at Burnham Police Court on Monday she was place on probation by the magistrates for a period of twelve months and ordered to pay 4 gns. Advocate's fee and 4/- court fees.

She had received from her husband, a soldier in Glasgow, 1 Army cook's apron, 1 pair grey worsted socks, 1 forage cap, 1 Army clothes brush, 1 pair braces, 5 spoons, 1 pair webbing anklets, 2 new anti-gas capes, 14 Army blankets, 4 tins of corned beef, 2 lbs. Margarine, and 3 tins of condensed milk; valued at £9. 2s. 6d. She pleaded guilty:

The prosecution said that an Inspector and a P.C. had kept watch on the lady's house. A post woman delivered a registered parcel and another person billeted with the lady in question accepted this. The officers later interviewed the lady and inspected the parcel, it was found to contain some of the goods already mentioned. The defendant admitted having received another registered parcel some time before, it contained corned beef and margarine. She produced two-? lb, packets of margarine; she had used the corned beef, which was all she ever had. The P. C. was not satisfied and asked further questions; further articles were then produced. Some of the blankets had been made into garments for herself and the children. The prosecuting council pointed out to the Bench that this was a serious offence, it was contrary to section 156 of the Army Act of 1881 and under the ruling the defendant was liable to a punishment of up to three months imprisonment or a fine.

The Probation Officer described the mother's circumstances and said she kept her house very well and was a good mother. After a short retirement, the Chairman said it was a **very serious offence**. These things came from your husband, if it had been anybody else you would have gone to prison.

The mother was ordered to pay the Advocates and court fees at the rate of 5/- per week

Major Frank Foley

Francis Edward Foley was born at 7, Walrow Terrace in Highbridge on 23rd November 1884. His father, Andrew Wood Foley, had come to the town a couple of years earlier with his wife Isabella and two sons,

Andrew and Arthur to work as a fitter at the railway locomotive works. Isabella was a devout Catholic, so although when they first started school all three boys went to the National School next to St Johns Church in Church Street, Highbridge. As soon as the French Nuns opened a Catholic School in Burnham, the three brothers transferred to the new school in Oxford Street.

According to the Highbridge School records (there are none for the Catholic School) Frank started school on 11th June 1888 so he was little more than three and a half years old! An entry in the school record book states "Sept. 12th 1890 "The three Foley (Catholics) have left for the school just opened at Burnham. Their father came to thank me (the headmaster) for the trouble taken with them". However when their younger brother, George, was ready for school – all four boys went to St Johns and according to the record book – "1st July 1892, the Foleys have been re-admitted this week". Their actual date of return and George's starting date was 27th June 1892. Whether it was the long journey or the boys were unhappy, it is not known why their time at St Joseph's was less than two years. Their sister, Margaret went with her brothers to the Highbridge School and later she became a Nun.

Frank had ambitions to become a priest and he went to a Jesuit school in Lancashire when he left St John's National school to pursue his career. He then went to the continent to study French and became fluent in French and German. At the outbreak of the First World War, Frank went into the Army and from then on world events changed the course of his life completely. Frank became part of the diplomatic life in Germany when the war ended and lived in Berlin with his wife and daughter, as head of the Passport Office. However, this was an innocent "front" for his more dangerous and important work for MI 6.

His exploits can be read in Michael Smith's biography "Foley – the Spy who saved 10,000 Jews". Highbridge is indebted to Michael for researching the story of Frank's life and letting us know through Mr. Pascoe (an earlier headmaster) that his humble beginnings started in Highbridge at the local school where we now hope that all the pupils will aspire to great things.

Frank died on May 8th 1958. He is reputed to be one of the best intelligence officers ever to serve with MI 6 and also with MI 5

Since the launch of Michael's book many other stories about Frank have come to light and children and grandchildren of the Jews whose lives he saved have come forward to record their "Thanks" to this English Gentleman. Israel had been asked to honour a British spy who helped at least 10,000 Jews to flee Nazi Germany and escape the holocaust. The call to recognise the forgotten hero Frank Foley was made by the British Holocaust Educational Trust, following the book by Michael Smith.

Foley helped to rescue more Jews than Oscar Schindler. Whilst being head of the British M.I.6. Intelligence station in Berlin during the 1930's he controlled visas to Britain and having no diplomatic immunity himself could have been arrested at any time. Foley fluted strict British immigration rules to get visas for Jews and had some of them staying in his own home, hiding from the Gestapo and helped them to get false passports.

The story of Frank Foley's exploits stayed buried because his work in Berlin was still to remain secret and although some aid workers wished to honour him the British Government blocked its publicity. Probably, it was because, at the time, diplomatic relations with Israel was not too good.

Sabine Comberti, whose family received a precious visa, said "He saved our lives, if anyone deserves a place in Yad Vashem he does, he was a wonderful man". This lady came to Highbridge to unveil a plaque to Major Frank Foley, which is in "Southwell Gardens of Rememberance" on 7th May 2000. In June 1959 a small group of men and women gathered in a grove, on the edge of a windswept forest just outside Jerusalem where over 2000 pine trees had been planted to commemorate the memory of a remarkable Englishman.

In The 25th February 1999 the Israeli Holocaust Memorial Centre Yad Vashem named Frank "Righteous Among the Nations", this is the highest honour that the Jewish Nation can give a gentile.

An annual Foley weekend is held in Highbridge at the beginning of May to keep his memory alive. A plaque has been out in the Gardens of Remembrance in Southwell Gardens – this is fittingly beneath the large bronze memorial there, which was made by the railway apprentices to commemorate the men from Highbridge killed in the First World War.

Mrs. Phyllis Walsh, a resident of the Clyce, has written a book entitled "The Three Local Pioneers" which covers the lives of Major Frank Foley. General Edward Higgins and Richard Locke.

Chapter 8

MEMORIES OF HIGHBRIDGE PEOPLE

MEMORIES

When this project was first discussed it was agreed that people who had lived and worked in Highbridge most of their lives were part of the 'history' of the town. We therefore set out to discover what these residents had to say about their early days; where and when they were born, school days, where they worked, when did they start work, what did they do, memories of their lives in Highbridge.

It was appreciated that some residents may have be reluctant to divulge details of their early years; but we were fortunate in finding that a few of the residents at Frith House in Burnham-on Sea, would be willing to be interviewed. A number of visits were made to Frith House in order to talk to the residents that were happy to provide details of their 'life' stories.

The residents vetted all the interviews and each gave their permission for the details to be published.

(Interviewed by Fay and Ken Burston.)

Residents of Highbridge

Harold Foxley

Harold was born in 1908 at a house in Walrow, but at the age of six months his parents moved to East Huntspill, where he lived until the age of 21 years. He started work at John Blands on the wharf when he was 14 years old and stayed there for 41 years.

His first job was collecting shavings for the boilers, he had to pick up the shavings and put them in a basket, which was taller than himself, for this he was paid 9/-(45p) per week. After doing this job for eighteen months, he got a rise of 6d(2½p) per week. When asking for this rise, (he was encouraged by a senior worker) he watched the foreman and his habits, he then waylaid him one morning and said "Good Morning, Sir" the foreman replied "Good Morning, Lad – What can I do for you?" Harold replied, "I have been here for eighteen months, Sir and I would like to know if I can have a rise?" "So we are talking money are we?" replied the foreman. "Well, leave it to me and I will see what I can do"

Later he changed jobs and moved to a cutting saw, slicing planks at 15/-(75p) per week, as a further advancement he moved to a moulding machine where he had to make, shape and sharpen, his own tools. Tools were made to details from a book of designs. Later on, he progressed to more complicated machines and eventually picked up £23.00 per week.

Four Senior Managers, each with 50 years service were awarded £10.00 only, when they retired. When John Bland's finished, Harold was asked if he was interested in taking charge, he would get a pension-but nothing transpired!!

Harold has a daughter, who works locally, also one granddaughter and one grandson, plus two great granddaughters.

Mrs. Kath Morgan (nee Crandon)

Mrs Morgan lived in a council house, in Love Lane, Burnham, it is still there. It contained a scullery, kitchen and living room on the ground floor and three bedrooms upstairs.

She went to the Princess School in Burnham and recalls wearing Hobnail boots. In the Senior School, the Headmaster was Mr. Holly, who was not averse to giving the cane to the pupils, when he thought it was necessary. She remembered Miss Lavacore as a domestic science teacher in Technical Street (five other residents of Frith House, also remembered her) they had to wash the teacher's clothes, also learnt cooking and domestic work. There was also a Mrs. Roberts she was the sewing teacher.

Another of her childhood memories is "Freddie Fay's Follies" on the beach at Burnham; he came from Highbridge and his daughter Erin, used to do acrobatics.

Win Fear

Win was born in Glastonbury at 12, Northload Street on 6th May 1912; the house is no longer there. At the time of Win's childhood, the house had a best room, live-in kitchen and an outside scullery, upstairs were two bedrooms, one for her parents and one for Win. Bath time, was a tub in front of the fire in the live-in kitchen.

Win left school at fourteen and worked at the "Ring of Bells" public house, looking after four children. Later in life she met and married Robert Wilfren Whiting Fear, a pupil from the "Blue" school in Wells. His father was the Relieving Officer, Attendance Officer for schools, also Social Worker in Burnham. They lived at 8, Worston Road. Highbridge.

At one time Win worked at the Bacon Factory in Highbridge where she earned 11d per hour, running out sausages, she was sometimes in trouble for making them either too thick or too thin. On one occasion Mr. Cobb from Harris's came to the Bacon Factory and told the staff "No music, you can't work and sing". Incidentally, the same sausage meat went into both Harris's and the Highbridge Bacon Factory sausages. Win mentioned the cheese market in Highbridge where she can remember seeing cheeses weighing 50 lbs. each.

Childhood memories of meals, by the standards of those days, these must have been very good, as she can recall having egg, bacon and fried bread for breakfast. Most mid-day meals consisted of meat and two veg. Mondays and Tuesdays were fry-up days, she can't remember tea times very much, and so can't think they were very exciting. The main item for special occasions was beef. As a child she was never allowed to speak at mealtimes.

Joyce (surname withheld)

Joyce was born in Bristol; her first job was in a toy factory. After the war in 1946 she visited Bridgwater fair, met her future husband and six weeks later, on the 2nd November 1946 they were married. Clifford and Joyce moved into her mother and father-in-laws home at 16, Bristol Road, Poples Bow. Her father–in-law worked at Cox's brickworks, Bristol Bridge, which was in Highbridge. The house is still standing and at the time Joyce is talking about, it had an outside scullery and a toilet down the yard, plus a kitchen and best room. Upstairs there were three bedrooms, one bedroom for the in-laws, one for Clifford and Joyce and later one for their first son. Heating was supplied by a coal fire, but only cold running water. The back garden was large enough to grow vegetables, also room for hens to supply enough eggs and also to keep a pig. The house also had a back yard and a very narrow front garden adjacent to the A38.

Normal meals were: -

Breakfast	Eggs & Bacon (Chickens + Pig in back garden)
Mid-day	Meat & two veg.
Tea	Bread & Dripping plus cocoa
For special occasions either beef or chicken	

Later they moved to East Brent where they had another five sons, she currently has fifteen grandchildren and five great grandchildren. Joyce and Clifford were married for 54 years.

Joyce has been abroad to Germany once to see her oldest son, an ex British Squash champion, and he now owns a sports business in Germany.

Eileen Clapp

Eileen is in her eighties and was born in Walrow, Highbridge, her family later moved to West Huntspill and when she was five years old she went to West Huntspill School. There were about forty in her class, they did the usual 3R's but her favourite lesson was geography, she also had an opportunity to play tennis and hockey. She stayed at school for the school dinners, which at that time were very nourishing, she recalls having milk during the morning break. At that time West Huntspill School was also a senior school, so she stayed there until she was fourteen years old. Eileen cannot remember the first job she had upon leaving school. Later when she was about seventeen or eighteen she worked for the railway and during the war was involved in the transportation of the troops, including the Americans, issuing rail warrants etc. Later in life, she worked for "Orchards" the chemist in Market Street for many years.

The house she lived in with her parents was one of the first Council houses in the Withy Road area of West Huntspill. It contained three bedrooms, kitchen and also a bathroom; it had gas lighting, coal fire and cold running water that had to be heated in the wash boiler for baths.

Eileen was one of the luckiest children, as she also had a cooked meal in the evening when her father came home from work.

Grace Dyer

Grace was born in Street, at the age of seven she moved with her parents to Burnham. She worked at the Creamery in Highbridge from the age of 16 – 21. The pay was very poor, she can recall her best pay packet at the time, which was £1.19.00(£1.90); for that she had to work all week, from 8 00a.m. to 5.30p.m.and 7.30p.m. once a week.

She met Cyril at a dance; they were courting for twelve months and in 1939 were married, moving to a new semi-detached house in Highbridge, (it is still there). It comprised of three bedrooms, a living room, best room with open fire, the house was lit by electricity and at that time, cold running water only. Two sons were born there; later Grace had another son, born in Burnham.

These days it seems strange that houses were built with cold running water, no hot water but that was normal in pre-war times. They had quite a large front garden and vegetables were grown in the back garden.

Mealtimes, when Grace had her family were as follows: -

> Breakfast - Porridge
>
> Mid-day - Meat & two veg.
>
> Teatime - Bread & Jam, Cake

On special occasions i.e. Christmas, Chicken but when the children were older, they had a small turkey. Grace and her husband allowed the children to speak at mealtimes, she felt it was the only time they had chance to catch up with the family news. As she suffers from travel sickness, she has never been abroad.

Frith House Residents

Left to Right: Mrs Joyce Adams, Mrs Phyllis Redman, Jim Kempson, Mrs Eileen Clapp, Harold Foxley, Mrs Wyn Fear, Mrs Grace Dyer, Mrs Kath Morgan

At the rear: Jo Phillips, Activities Co-ordinator
(We regret that since the photograph was taken both Mrs Redman and Mrs Fear have died)

The following have been compiled, from interviews with the persons concerned or members of their families and reflect their life in and around Highbridge, also their own feelings about this small Market Town.

Hugh Frederick Berryman was born at Johns Terrace Highbridge, on the 25th June 1896 and baptised in Highbridge Church on the 13th August 1896. His mother, Emily Clapp was born in Highbridge in 1865, his father John Edward Berryman was also born in Highbridge in1867.

Hugh joined the Somerset and Dorset Railway on the 9th September 1914 and worked as a porter at Burnham-on-Sea station. His starting rate of pay was 12/- per week, and this rose to 14/- per week on the 25th June 1915.

He enlisted in the army on the 2nd February 1916, joining, it is believed, the 1st Battalion of the Somerset Light Infantry for his basic training, service number 6268. The medal roll records at the Public Records Office in London show that Hugh was then drafted to the 24th Battalion of The London Regiment. (The Queen's). He was on active service with the 24th from the 16th June to the 21st September 1916 during this period part of the 47th Division serving on the Western Front in France. The Battalion then moved to the Angres sector and were involved in various diversions and raids, also burying cables and tunnelling in order to place large mines under the German trenches. Relieved by the 1st Battalion Royal Marine Light Infantry on the 14th July 1916 moving south away from the front line on 1st August 1916 for rest, recuperation and additional training.

The Battalion moved into a forward area on the 10th September, arriving at Becourt Wood;the following day they relieved the Northampton's, and held the line. On the morning of the 15th September began the battle of High Wood, the 24th and 21st London's attacked together advancing in open order meeting with such heavy fire that they could not get forward and dug themselves in. Tanks were used here for the first time. The Battalion was relieved the men being very exhausted and covered in mud, unable to eat their rations due to the mud and a scarcity of drinking water. He was then on active service with the 3rd Battalion, London Regiment from 4th August 1917, (service number 275199) until the Battalion was marched away from their billets to the railway station at Watten where they boarded a train for Belgium, and marched to a position a few miles southwest of Ypres. From the 12th August the 3rd Battalion London Regiment were on the front line right through until some time in September. It is understood that Hugh Berryman was taken prisoner by the Germans and spent some time as a prisoner of war. Hugh married Mabel Annie Dean at Christ church, Henton, Somerset on the 22nd June 1922, when he was twenty-six years old he was living at 1, Cuthbert Street, Highbridge they later moved to 17, Council Houses, Love Lane, Burnham-on-Sea. During World War One, Mabel was in the Women's Land Army, working on farms in the Highbridge area.

Somerset & Dorset records show that Hugh returned to work at Burnham-on-Sea on the 31st January 1919 at a rate of 18/- per week. The Register records of the Somerset & Dorset show that on the 12th February 1923, he was seen by the Superintendent and severely reprimanded for causing a wagon to be derailed and damaging the Goods shed during a shunting operation at Burnham; he was suspended for one day with loss of pay. However, on the 26th March 1923, Hugh was made up to a Grade 1 Porter.

One of Hugh's pastimes was working on his allotment at the side of the railway, keeping his family in fresh vegetables. In Burnham, he was well known for his homemade rhubarb wine. Another hobby was repairing wirelesses, Joan his daughter remembers one particular day when he had to go to a farm near Edington Burtle station to return a radio he had repaired, she went along for the ride on the branch line. Unfortunately there had been a couple of days of heavy rain and as a result the Somerset levels were flooded, they had to use a rowing boat to get out to the farm. Joan didn't like the water, so was not anxious to go again.

It was generally accepted on the railway in those days, that if you wanted promotion you had to move where and when the railway wanted. So in 1937, Hugh, Mabel and his daughter Joan, moved away to the coalfields of Radstock, where Hugh became a shunter, working on the little Sentinel engines, they worked in and out of the many coal pits in the area, moving the coal wagons. The family moved into some newly built houses in the small village of Haydon, near Radstock. After five years the family moved again, this time to Templecombe, Hugh was by now a goods guard; it was very difficult to find a house in Templecombe. However, there was, at the same time, a vacancy at Park Lane Crossing for a crossing keeper, which included a cottage for the keeper, so Mabel took the job in order to get the cottage.

Joan remembers she was working in Bath at the time her parents moved to Templecombe, and recalls her father meeting her at the station and saying it was a nice little cottage. When she awoke the next morning, she had a culture shock, one she had not expected, no electricity, only candle lights, paraffin lamps and a well for water. She stayed with her parents at the cottage until her marriage in 1952. Hugh was a member of the Home Guard at Templecombe during the Second World War and being a very keen swimmer, was involved in both the Highbridge Swimming Club and the Burnham Amateur Swimming Club, and was a member of the water polo team. He was the first person to win a gold medal for the annual swim across to Steart Island. The Highbridge club used to meet at the "Cooper's Arms" in Highbridge where they had built a diving board beside the River Brue, just behind the pub. Hugh died in 1955, his wife Mabel in 1967 at Highbridge.

(Information supplied by Mrs. Fisher (nee Joan Berryman))

Ada Hooper

Ada Hooper (nee Richards) wife of Arthur was the only Highbridge mother, on record, to give birth to twins and triplets, bringing her total children born to 13. Ada is pictured in about 1915 with 6 of her children, Bob, Jim, Ted, Jack, Gladys and Dolly. Sadly, one of the twins and two of the triplets did not survive, the youngest child, Lennie died at the age of 5. The surviving 9 children, those in the photograph plus Phyllis, Betty and Bill, lived with their parents in a 3-bedroom house in Worston Road, where Betty the surviving triplet, still lives. Ted, aged 92, has also lived in Highbridge all his life.

Before their marriage Arthur, a member of Highbridge Harriers Running Club, ran approximately 10 miles to Morland to meet Ada, this was part of his training.

(Information and Photo supplied by Mary Draper)

Gordon May

Mr May, you were born in the Clyce in the 1930's, what was life like in the Clyce?

Well, it was a good place to live, everybody was friendly, they helped each other and everyone knew each other as well. I started school at the junior infants school in Highbridge, in 1934, later I went to West Huntspill school until I was fourteen. I left school and got an apprenticeship at Mr. Kimber's, this was at the top of the Clyce in the boatyard. I did an apprenticeship for seven years; it was the later end of the war. "How many people did Mr Kimber employ at that time"? There was John Parrish, we always used to call him the senior apprentice, in fact he was the last paying apprentice, his mother paid for him to go there. Then there was Dave Blake, Ivor Cook, who are no longer with us, Wilfie Foster, myself and John Meader..

We were building wooden lifeboats, which went on to drifters or trawlers, in the fishing fleet. When the war ceased, that work fell off, we then started doing repair work and building the new boats. Then Mr Kimber got the contract from the Royal Lifeboat Institute, to service the Barry, Minehead and Weston boats and we would be on call. If either of those two boats, Weston and Minehead were damaged, we would have to go down and be on site to repair them and get them back into service again.

After I did my apprenticeship, I went and did my two years National Service in the R.A.F. Nothing exciting there, out of two years I was only in camp for sixteen weeks. I came back and re- joined Mr. Kimber for a period of a couple of years, I then went out on the building site for a couple of years. In the meanwhile I met a guy called Mike Salisbury who was building a boat, he had a radio and television shop in Burnham, him and Cliff Brent; they talked me into starting up and building boats again. Which we first of all started in Coronation Road, Highbridge, from here we went down to the old locomotive works where the buildings were still up, we took a building over down there and also where the present Arian Printers are, we bought that and we were getting on, quite successfully.

Then the decision was made to build the factory on the Worston Road site, which was known as

"Brensal Plastics". We went to the Boat Show, quite successful, building a seventeen-foot motor cruiser in plywood, from then it was decided to go into glass fibre and we started to make glass fibre boats. Then the Directors decided to sell the Company to the H.A.T. Group, then in the 1960's when we went into the building industry, building glass fibre/concrete form work and cladding for many big contracts, actually two of the biggest which were done in this country. At one time we were employing about eighty people, we were lucky to get guys from the old "Colthurst & Symons" brickyard who were used to working in moulds on piecework. They adapted very quickly to our requirements in glass fibre.

(From an interview with Gordon May by Jo Osmond)

W.T. Pepperall *(always known as Tom)*

Tom was born in Brittania Buildings, Highbridge on 11th June 1899. (Ref. Map dated 1902 this shows the Brittania Brickworks was behind Victoria Place, the clay pit is now the pond by Morlands Estate, so presumably this is the location of Brittania Buildings). His parents later moved to Church Street, where they ran a retail shoe shop. He was a member of the St Johns Church choir and was heard to say, he had climbed the church steeple when he was a lad. (The steeple was demolished in 1911).

A keen footballer and cricketer he played for Highbridge, in later years he served on the Highbridge Town Committee.

His worked as a sawyer at John Bland & Co. Newtown and joined the army in the First World War, after which he returned to Highbridge. In later years he worked as a Saw Doctor at Wake & Dean, Yatton.

In December 1923 he married Rose, together they devoted their lives to the community. Rose started a swimming club on the River Brue (by Highbridge station). This was an area roped off, so that she could teach people to swim, many activities were undertaken, such as a greasy pole competition. Unfortunately this was closed down during the 1930's.

Rose became a post woman. Tom and Rose did voluntary work for Weston-super-Mare hospital, and collected eggs from local people in Highbridge, to help feed the patients. From 1931 –7 a total of 21,993 eggs were collected; the Newtown Road area although considered a poor district was renowned for being the most generous part of town. They also ran a Concert Party that toured the villages; this was to aid Weston Hospital each member of the party paid a weekly sum to cover the cost of costumes and transport, Mr Herring from Burnham, used to drive them. After expenses all the profits went to the hospital.

Another interest was teaching dancing at St Johns School, this was for children over twelve years of age, and called the "Gay Nineties Dance Club" everyone paid 6d per week. Tom and Rose never took any money from the proceeds but instead paid for six coaches to take the members of the Gay Nineties Dance Club to Weymouth for the day and provided them with lunch and tea. The trips stopped during the war but continued afterwards, and carried on for many more years. Nadene Slade (Mrs.Bob Northcombe) was the pianist for the dancers and about once a month a dance was held in the Town Hall with Alf Read and his band.

Tom was a special constable during World War II. He was a member of Burnham Council from 1953 – 1959 and again from 1961 until he died in 1969. He was secretary of the "Globe Inn" Pigeon Club and secretary of the Oddfellows (Highbridge) Branch. Subsequently he became Grand Master of Bridgwater District Independent Order of Oddfellows. Manchester Union.

He together with his son-in-law (Arthur Lismore) started a shoe retail and repair service and both were founder members of the Highbridge & District Chamber of Trade and Commerce. Arthur was secretary for many years. Tom also served as a Manager of Highbridge V.C. School and was a member of the Civilian Committee of the Air Training Corps.

Pepperall Road was named after Tom and the residents of the Resources Centre also wanted it called after him.

Rose meanwhile was a member of the Highbridge Tennis Club and the Keep-Fit Club, both these ceased at the commencement of the Second World War. She was awarded a Poppy Brooch for her services to the British Legion. Woman's Section and was their standard bearer in Highbridge for many years.

(Information supplied by Hilda Lismore.)

First Impressions of Somerset

Until 1968 I lived in Luton. Bedfordshire; we lived in a typical pre-war three bedroom semi-detached house, my husband and I had spent seven years renovating it and we had reached a stage when we felt all the work was completed. Then out of the blue, my husband announces," let's move". After long discussions, including planning the children's schooling we decided to either move then, or wait for several years until their schooling was completed. The decision was made; we would try to move now and to Somerset. Why? Because, neither of us had ever been to Somerset. What better reason?

We wrote to various Estate Agents and got a wonderful response, all the houses appeared to be within the price range we had requested. This was about £4,000.00 for a minimum of three bedrooms, we selected ten houses we thought would be worth looking at, made arrangements to view the first five on a Saturday. Plans made, we proceeded as follows:

The children Carol, aged ten and Mark, aged five, had a day off from school, my husband being a self-employed glazier, took the day off work and we all bundled into the car at 6.30 a.m. on the Friday to travel to Somerset. The first stop was outside Oxford for a picnic breakfast of egg and bacon sandwiches at about 8.00 a.m. then on to Kingswood. Bristol (our first visit to Bristol). We stopped at a sub-post office got the Local Yellow Pages and my husband rang local glazing firms to apply for a job interview. The second one had a vacancy and it was arranged that he could have an interview at 12.00 noon. It was now 11.15am, which meant it was a case of getting directions and going straight there. I remember we had to pass a big yellow glass building on the right hand side, but because of the one-way system could not get the building onto the right hand side, eventually we made it. We arrived on time and found employment, this would start when we had found a house and moved to Somerset, providing it was within three months. I think the pay was around £19.00 per week, quite a reasonable rate of pay at the time.

The next stage was to find somewhere to have our picnic lunch, this we would not do until we got into Somerset, so the moment we crossed the border, we stopped immediately as the children were starving. In those days we could not afford to eat out very often, if we did, it was for a special treat, certainly not when about to try and move house. We decided to carry on driving until we saw the first Estate Agent on the A38; there was no motorway, (still to be built) in 1973. This whole journey was without hold-ups, how times have changed. The first Estate Agents we found was in Highbridge, at that time Abbott and Frost had an office in Church Street, about the same position as Mike Applegates' is today. Then to find a car park in order to pay a visit, we had not written to this agent, for details of houses.

Here we had to wait in Highbridge as road works were going on, the men were in the process of taking up some railway track from a level crossing. Of course we did not realise just how significant this was, in fact quite an important date for Highbridge, this was on the **21st June 1968.**

The Agent who took us around four houses, the fourth, in West Huntspill, was to be where we lived for nine years; it was in fact our first choice of all the houses. It was a three/four bedrooms chalet bungalow with garage, just a year old; I believe we paid £4,100.00. On that Friday and Saturday we had managed to get employment for my husband in Bristol, buy a house West Huntspill and arranged a mortgage; we also measured for the curtains. It was too far to come back just to measure for curtains.

We eventually moved to Somerset on Friday the 7th November 1968 the weekend before the carnival, again this was something we could not understand, everyone kept referring to the carnival on Monday, so what! We had seen a carnival before! Not! however a Somerset Carnival, that's a different kettle of fish.

The greetings we received from local people and the traders, was something I had never before experienced, neighbours were so helpful. The school accepted my children on the following Monday, parents spoke to me on my first day taking them to school, school dinners were marvellous, with second helpings if you wanted them, I was told by my children. Within the first week representatives from the local traders had called giving us samples of their wares i.e. a duster from "Tylers" the ironmongers, an electric light bulb from "Shepherd and Sparks" these are just two I can recall. Within a couple of weeks, we as a family, felt very welcome in the area. Later we moved into Highbridge' where we lived for seventeen years, both my husband and daughter having businesses in Highbridge.

This was all a very long time ago. Since then my husband and daughter have both died of cancer. My son bought a house locally and is very happy there, he moved away from the area for a few years, but somehow was drawn back. Myself, I re-married two years ago and I now live in Burnham. Someday soon, I may be considered a local, you never know! However, Somerset is where I will stay for the rest of my life, more than half my life has been here now. This all goes to show just how much life has changed in thirty-six years. I don't think you would be able to travel to another area of the country and, within two days find new employment, buy a house and arranged the mortgage all without any pre-planning.

(Account supplied by Fay Burston).

My Memories of Highbridge

My father was born at 17, Market Street, Highbridge. his father was a Baker/Confectioner, and had a restaurant. My mother lived at 11 Walrow Terrace for a time, her father was on the Somerset and Dorset Railway he had started when a boy as a fireman and worked himself up to engine driver, but in order to get more money they had to move to where the railway said. They spent quite a while in Evercreech, and then came back to Highbridge. Unfortunately the Locomotive Works closed and the workers had to go to Derby, Birmingham or Bath and we ended up in Bath where I was born and lived for 12 years. My first memories of Highbridge, as a little girl, were entering Highbridge Station by train with my parents and Grandmother.

The thing that impressed me most about Highbridge was the comparison between the dirty grey Bath stone and the lovely red bricks; these came from several brickyards in Highbridge. We used to travel on the G.W.R. because my Grandfather, as an engine driver, used to get a concession.

My earliest recollection was getting off the train and walking up through Market Street. The friendly atmosphere of the people struck me, presumably because my maternal Grandmother was a Highbridge person and everyone seemed to know her. This was certainly different to the way we lived in Bath.

In the early 1950's when things began to improve after the War my father wanted to move back to Highbridge and in 1953, when I was twelve we moved back and lived in Burnham. I attended Burnham

County Secondary School, which had its main building in Technical Street; various other classes were dotted around. The Headmaster was a Mr Edge, Mr Strickland was also there; I believe he had started at the school in 1948 and stayed there until he retired. I left school and spent a year at the Commercial School in Weston- Super- Mare to learn shorthand and typing and my first job took me back to my Grandparent's old shop in 17, Market Street, which was then an Estate Agents. Whilst I was there, I found out that No 3 Bertha Terrace was on the market, so my Grandparents bought it staying there until they died. Hence that is how I came to live at No 3 Bertha Terrace because my Grandmother left the house to me.

Highbridge Station in those days was very busy. I remember a Mr Fowler and another postal worker going from Highbridge Post Office (6 Market Street) with their basket cart to collect the mail. I recall when a lorry knocked down the old Highbridge Town Clock it had been bought by public subscription to commemorate Queen Victoria's Diamond Jubilee in 1897. During the turn of the Century, Highbridge was a very important place; the first Somerset County Council meeting was held in 1894 in the Old Town Hall, it also had its own Magistrates Court and Police Station. My Grandfather was a Magistrate I remember that cyclists would be fined if they didn't have a rear light. My Grandfather was fined for this misdemeanour, others were fined 5 shillings, but my Grandfather was fined 10 shillings, and he was extremely annoyed. He was told that as a Magistrate he should have set a better example.

Highbridge always had its own market, there was a Tuesday Market when the farmer's wives used to come in on the train with their produce, the chickens were carried in big baskets; these were ready plucked and dressed. The Highbridge Guy Fawkes Carnival started at the Royal Artillery Arms went down through Church Street into the Burnham Road finishing outside the Morlands Factory

 My great aunt who was born in 1896 told me that she could remember when the A38 from Church Street through West Huntspill to Bridgwater was a dirt track. She remembered a Circus travelling through with a man leading the elephants.

The main industry in Highbridge was the Somerset and Dorset Railway and the Great Western Railway. There were two brickyards and of course work on the wharf unloading the timber boats. There were lots of shops, I can remember at least three grocer's shops, a fish shop, a shoe shop, three butcher's, two bakers, a Milliners, a Dress shop; even a Music shop. We had a Bacon Factory shop and the Creamery on Huntspill Road, and Buncombe Steamrollers.

Over the past thirty or so years, there have been numerous changes; the Railway Hotel was knocked down and made way for Alpha House, which is now the home of the Library and Sedgmoor District Council Housing office. Stanley Stone the Builders were where Kwik Save now stands. The builders' merchant Tylers (which eventually became Jewsons) was on the site next to the Coopers Arms, Barratts built a new estate there. The GWR station buildings were demolished, as was the S and D station and part of the bridge that led to it. In Market Street, the old Town Hall was demolished; this made way for the new Community Hall and the Town Green; next to that was Lloyds Bank, now taken over by a Charity. Where the railway line went through to Burnham has been built on, Regal Court has replaced the Cinema. The Jubilee Gardens site was originally a coal yard, next to it was the Corn Store, all made way for the new housing development of Ladd Close; the line gates were always a landmark. John Burnett lived in Island House, his family imported wines and the bonded warehouse is still there. A hostel for the homeless called "Wade House" now stands where the original house" stood. Dr Wade lived in Southwell House, that has now been demolished and replaced by the Reading Room and Memorial Gardens financed by public subscription in memory of the Highbridge men and women who lost their lives during World War II.

(From an interview with Mrs Pam Lyes)

John Meader

I left West Huntspill School and started a six-year apprenticeship on the December 27th 1949 with Kimber's boatyard we did repair work for the Admiralty, Ministry of Transport, Lloyds and the Royal National Lifeboat Institution, and including private yachts. With Mr Harold John Kimber, there were just two apprentices, another lad, and I, but four or five other boat builders working there, Gordon May, Dave Blake, John Parrish, and Des Higgins. It was a small family owned business that did varied work, it was all timber and woodcraft in those days, there was no fibreglass. "Fresh Breeze" was one of the largest yachts we built, it was an Uffa Fox design, and it was built for a man by the name of Morrell who lived at Porlock Weir, it was the largest one built. A Nelson Baker lived up the Clyce he was a painter; he was also a wood carver. He painted watercolours; he was always sitting around, painting different scenes. The watercolours I have, are basically of the wharf, and boat building, this would have been in the early 1930's. At Southwell House in Highbridge there is a Memorial from the old S & D Station; Nelson Baker carved the pattern for the casting. There was a big grey building; we used to call it, "The Winkle Works" why I don't know; I think originally they were anthracite works. It was an American Forces Depot, during the war.

(From an interview with John Meader by Jo Osmond)

An Appreciation

As a researcher I would like to thank the many people who shared their memories, happy, sad, but always proud, of their community.

I have learned so much that it leaves me with a large place in my heart for the 'not so little town' where I was born, and its people — HIGHBRIDGE.   *Pearl Rawles.*

I am sure this is the sentiment of all who worked on this book, we all spent a lot of time asking, what must have seemed silly questions, but we wanted to know about Highbridge. So, as they say; if you don't know—ASK.!!

There are a few old buildings in Highbridge that warrant recognition as "Listed", those that are included are given:

ISLEPORT FARMHOUSE – Isleport Road. East Side
Grade II Listed Building Number 13245
Farmhouse. Early 19th century. Flemish Bond brickwork.

HIGHBRIDGE INN – West side of Huntspill Road
Grade II Listed Building No LB 13244
This building is mentioned in Kelly Directory 1848
1889 the proprietor was Albert Withycombe
Inn, Probably late 18th Century, mid 19th century alterations, some painted brickwork.

81, Church Street, Highbridge (West side)
Grade II Listed Building No LB 13237
House. Late 18th century, Painted Flemish bond brickwork.

82, Church Street, Highbridge (West side)
Grade II Listed Building No LB 13238
House, Early 19th century, Painted brick, hipped slate roof, brick stack.

82 Church Street Highbridge (West side) –Stable adjacent
Grade II listed Buildings 13239
Stable and Coachhouse. Painted brickwork.

HUISH – Old Burnhan Road (South Side) Highbridge
Grade II Listed Building Number 13246

House once divided into two, now a single house. Mid-eighteenth century. Flemish bond brickwork.Postulated as the Manor House of the small local parish of Huish

1670 Parish of Huish juxta Highbridge

According to Mr Wrigley's account of Huish in his history of Burnham-on-Sea & Highbridge – "It is clear the Huish House, Old Burnham Road is of considerable antiquity. In fact S.G. Nash who lived there, found pieces of pottery showing Roman and Medieval occupation. Parts of the present house are probably 17th century. Mr Nash also found evidence of existence of the "Lamb" in 1831.

Richard Locke previously of Pillsmouth Farm Burnham, came to live at Huish – he was responsible for draining the levels and was an eminent engineer.

There is mention of a Huish in the Doomsday Book.

There has been much speculation about Huish House as it is now known. The first house on this site was built about 1650, but there is documentary evidence, together with various 'finds,' that there was some sort of building on the site as early as the fourteenth century. The current owner Mr. Orledge has researched the history of the property. However over the years it has also been referred to as Highbridge Cottage and Sandyway Farm.

Apparently when the last 'appurtenant' to 'Huish' or Highbridge Cottage or 'Sandyway Farm' was sold in 1979 all deeds passed to the Hatcher family, who then gave them to the current owner. (2000). The ten deeds were dated 1762,1814,1833,1882, (two) 1886, (two) 1887, (two) and 1891. The earliest contained reference to 1756 and to Francis Jeune, (Bishop of Peterborough)

Mr. Samuel Nash once owned 'Sandyway Farm' which he bought for its antiquarian features and he researched the area over many years. He was disappointed because he feared that nearby 'modern building' would destroy the 'Old World' atmosphere.

Another previous resident of Huish/ Highbridge Cottage/Sandyway Farm was a **Richard Locke** (1737-1806).

Richard Locke is credited as the person with first thought of an 'Old Age Pension'; he founded a Benefit Society called the Burnham Society, in 1774. He was born on 6th June 1737 at Pillsmouth Farm. Burnham. (An area that now includes Frith House, Burnham Holiday Village and the Steart area). He was the son of Richard and Hannah Locke; his maternal grandfather was John Dodd who owned the farm. Upon his grandfathers death, Richard was willed 10 acres of land and gradually added to this and by 1760 had purchased a further 81 acres of land in the area.

In 1758 at the age of twenty-one he became Chief Constable of the Court Leet of Bemstone Hundred, the court being held in the Highbridge Inn since time immemorial. In 1760 he married Elizabeth Lovibond and was, by now, one of the largest landowners in the area.

The Burnham Society was founded in 1772 and by 1792 he was Lord of the Manor of Huish Juxta Highbridge and one of the richest men in the immediate area. He was living in "Highbridge House" in 1792 then at "Highbridge Cottage" after 1801; he died on 31st October 1806.aged 69 years. In his will he directed his son Richard, as executor, to cover his vault in St. Andrew's Church, Burnham with a large stone on which should be engraved "Never to be Removed".

Richard Locke, although born outside Highbridge, was brought into the history of the town because he lived here for much of his life and was prominently associated with its affairs.

Benefit Society

Strange rules were associated with the eighteenth century benefit society started in the Highbridge locality by **Richard Locke**, who made a fortune by trying out advanced ideas on land improvement, and who was a local historian and public benefactor. He was credited with a scheme to affect the drainage of the levels.

His benefit society, started in 1774, must have been one of the earliest in the country to make provision for old age pensions. **The "Burnham Society"** as it was called, had its origin in the fact that Locke and several other members of the gentry in the locality used to meet and organise collections to help the aged and sick, also lend small sums of money without charging interest. There was "a public feast" when the "Burnham Society" was formed, Officers were appointed, and the rules adopted stated:

"In this room there is fixed to the floor a strong box made secure with iron, which has on it, five different locks, and a key adapted to each. In this box there are deposited twenty pounds, for the purpose of lending to any of the society; which is never to be diminished, but may be increased as shall be after agreed upon."

Members were to meet annually on the anniversary of the formation of the club for a feast. Each member was expected to pay a shilling (5p) towards the cost, and a minister of the Gospel was invited to give an address free of cost. Membership was open to people in Burnham, Highbridge, Huntspill, East Brent, Brent Knoll and Mark. Every member who lived within two miles of the room was expected to attend a meeting once a month on a Friday night or send a deputy. After "Singing and prayer" members were required to put eight pence (3p) in the box. Members living further away were excused personal attendance provided they sent their contributions. For failure to pay there was a fine of two pence (1p). In addition there were quarterly meetings at which all the members were required to be present if they lived within a radius of ten miles of the room. Failure to do so meant the forfeit of a shilling. (5p). Two members were appointed as sick visitors.

After a year's subscription every member was entitled to six shillings (30p) a week during sickness providing he was "confined to his bed and cannot help himself, but if he can sit up, walk about, or can do without a nurse," the benefit was reduced to three shillings (15p). It was also stipulated that "every impostor shall be laid under such forfeiture as the officers should think fit".

Another rule was: "If any member happens to be maimed or crippled, so that he cannot get his bread, he shall receive three shillings (15p) a week for life, provided his malady is incurable. But no advantage is to be extended to persons those folly or wickedness was the cause of their misfortunes".

Every member over seventy was to be given three shillings (15p), a week for life, even though he might still be able to work. On the death of a member the widow or next of kin could demand forty shillings (£2.00) out of the box and was expected to invite all members living within five miles radius to attend the funeral. Every member who attended had to give the widow or next of kin sixpence (2 1/2p) and all who were invited to attend and but did not do so were to pay 1s. 6d.(7 1/2p).

Even those who lived outside the five-mile limit were expected to pay 1/-(5p) whether they attended the funeral or not for neglect, to be fines five shillings (25p).

Another law was: "Every member who behaves disorderly in meeting, or is guilty of any vice punishable by the laws of England, at any place, or time, shall for every offence forfeit sixpence (2 1/2p)"

The five locks were put on the club's strongbox to make sure it could not be opened unless the five key-keepers were present. The officials were expected to be punctual. If they were half-an-hour late on being summoned to the room, they were to forfeit three pence. The fine for not turning up at all was two and sixpence (121/2p). For not being present, even if they sent their keys, the fine was sixpence.

At one time the society had a membership of 500, and the trustees built eight separate tenements for their officers with a large room to be used as a library or lounging room, and a Sunday school supervised by the Rector of Burnham.

It appears not only to have been a benefit society but a debating society, for it was at one time known as the Religious Disputing Club, and invited members to borrow books from its extensive library. Some of these books were evidently very heavy going.

Mrs. Phyllis Walsh resident of the Clyce, written a book entitled "The Three Local Pioneers"; this covers the lives of Richard Locke, Frank Foley and General Edward Higgins.

A view of Huish House from the Old Burnham Road, a view more well known than that shown earlier.

Another prominent resident of the premises, then called 'Sandyway Farm' was **Mr.W.H.Hatcher**

A familiar figure in the Highbridge district for almost fifty years was Mr. Hatcher, who was born at Brent Knoll in 1879; he commenced his career as an orchid grower. This occupation took him to Lincolnshire and Ireland. As a lover of flowers and a keen horticulturist, he was for many years, Chairman of the Highbridge Chrysanthemum Show. This was an interest to which he devoted many hours, especially in the preparation for the Annual Show, he had presided over a meeting of the Show Committee just a few weeks before his sudden death aged 69.Mr. Hatcher had been a familiar figure in the Highbridge District for almost half a century both as a butcher and farmer. During the past 35 years he had been closely connected with public life, having served on the old Highbridge Urban District Council and the Burnham-on-Sea Urban District Council for a number of years with the exception of two brief breaks in service. Mr Hatcher came to Highbridge and some years later took over the butcher's business from his father. After residing over the shop for some time he left those premises after 27 years, when he acquired Sandyway Farm. As a farmer he was an authority on cattle and although never a breeder he showed a number of fine specimens on several occasions and secured several prizes, he was also a member of the National Farmers Union.

(Details from the Gazette and Express Oct 1948)

LOCAL DISASTERS

The area around Highbridge has not been without its disasters, in 1606 the sea banks at Burnham broke and it was reported that many people in the district lost their lives; 28 in Huntspill parish. A book describing the great floods of 1606 states" A true reporte of certaine wonderfulle overflowing of waters nowe lately in Somersetshire, Norfolk and other places in England, destroying many thousands of women, and children and overflowing and bearing downe whole townes and villages and drowning infinite numbers of sheepe and cattle" The account tells that through the breaking of the Burnham sea banks some thirty villages were inundated and their cattle destroyed "women and children besides". Without warning the county for twenty miles around by five was flooded to a depth of eleven or twelve feet right up to Glastonbury, The deepest part was at Kingston Seymour where a board commemorates the flood.

On Sunday December 13th 1981. Three Hundred and Seventy-five Years after an earlier great flood the area was again devastated when snow fell steadily all afternoon, building to a blizzard followed by heavy rain that prompted a quick thaw. By teatime winds had increased to gale force. At 9 p.m. there was an appeal on the television for all local small boat owners to report to the Royal Hospital in Weston. This was quickly followed by a report that the sea wall at Burnham had been breached. The wind following the high tide did untold damage along the Bristol Channel coast. Locally the extent of the damage unfolded the following day. The sea wall had breached in 12 places. Houses and flats on the seafront and all the main streets were flooded. Hugh pieces of concrete from the promenade were ripped up. The sea wall was also broken on the Huntspill side and Alstone Road and Church Road, West Huntspill were flooded for several days. The main road from the Artillery Arms to Pawlett, were under varying depths of water. A farmer in Stretcholt lost some 700 pigs. Lasting damage was done to pastures from Huntspill to Pawlett Hams. The damage to the sea wall was estimated at £500,000.

Many volunteer organisations were involved in helping to bring food to the elderly and in the clearing up process. Carpet drying centres were set up at various sites including the bottom floor of Highbridge Town Hall. A flood relief fund was also established. Although is was the worst storm in 80 years and there was much damage done to property and resulting hardship, unlike the flood of 1606 thankfully there was no serious injuries of loss of life.

Chapter 9

A STROLL THROUGH THE TOWN

Since the arrival of the Somerset & Dorset Railway to the town 150 years ago there have been many changes, so we invite you to take a stroll through, so that a brief history of the Commercial Businesses can be covered. The Shops, what they sold and who owned them, of the Banks and Public Houses, of all the places that catered for the inhabitants of this Market Town. We will start from the north on the A38 and leave to the east on the B3139; upon entering Highbridge from the roundabout near the Isleport Business Park, on the right is the Highbridge Caravan Centre, this is one of the largest caravan and camping retailers in the South West.

Upon reaching **The Bristol Bridge Inn,** at one time there were 12, possibly 13, hostelries in the town however, majority of these hostelries have long disappeared. **Mr David Williams of Knowle End, Woolavington** has provided us with a brief history of those in the town; and we are indebted to him for allowing us to make use of his research. Mr.Williams produced a list of inns and other drinking establishments utilising information from Kellys Directory, newspapers plus local knowledge and these are given, together with a selection of some of the landlords from the1930's, 40's, 60's and 70's.

"Years ago Highbridge had numerous fairs, plus cattle and cheese markets; a thriving brickyard, timber yards and saw mills. Also, auctions were held every week for cattle, sheep and pigs. The attendance at the latter would have been enormous, market days were where the locals, farmers and folk from miles around met to buy and sell produce and gossip with friends The inns, beer houses and hotels played a vital role in the town; who knows how many farmers sold their surplus wares over a pint or two of beer or cider."

The Bristol Bridge Inn. First landlord was William Vincent in 1866 and from 1956 to 1971 it was a Robert Henry Swale.

The Coopers Arms is in Market Street, where a Mr. Card was mine host in 1863; in 1897 an advert stated that it was a 'Free trade and posting house'. in 1939, when Mr. John Rowe was the landlord, a report in the local paper stated: "At the 'Coopers Arms', which stands almost opposite the 'Railway Hotel' a window had been forced, the bar searched and about 8/-(40p) in coppers was taken.

A dog on the premises was not disturbed and did not give any alarm; it is thought the dog may have been doped, as on the Sunday morning it was unwell. A piece of bread had been found nearby the dog, this had not been given to the dog by anyone on the premises."

The George Inn (later Hotel) in Church Street, George Hooper was the first named landlord in 1840, from 1923 to possibly 1939; Mrs. Mary Stokes was mine host. Dennis Bagshaw and Ronald Ballentine were landlords in 1966 and '77.

The Globe Inn is the last of the three public houses that were once in Newtown Road; these being frequented by the crews and workers from the wharf, which was nearby. During the Jubilee Year of 2002 the Globe was a blaze of red, white and blue, flags adorned the building and the appropriate coloured flowers had been planted along its frontage.

The Highbridge Inn or Hotel has been either an inn or hotel many times during the roughly 200 years plus, it has stood in the Huntspill Road.

It is probably an 18th Century building, having served many purposes: a Lodge for the early Freemasons in the area and as the headquarters of numerous Clubs/Associations.

A Miss Stevens put the Inn up for sale in 1837 and in 1840 Thomas Rogers was a licensee, many followed, but one who is still remembered by the 'older' inhabitants, is 'Bette Smith' or to give her full name Beatrice Caroline Smith. She was in charge (we believe 'in charge' was correct), from 1966 to 1983. This picture is from around the 1930's. An interesting

point about the Inn is, that it was originally in Huntspill, but when parish boundaries were altered in 1806 following the digging of the new Clyce, changing the course of the River Brue to the other side of the Inn put it in Highbridge.

The Lamb Inn in Church Street (now the Hong Kong Takeaway) was an inn around the 1850's and

James Davis was the landlord (David Williams has a copy of the man's Will). It was originally a beer-drinking establishment, its full licence was granted in 1960; in 2000 it was also a café. This old photograph shows the start of a charabanc trip by the 'men' of the town, not a very comfortable ride on those solid wheels, but no doubt thoroughly enjoyed.

(Photo Supplied by Trevor Dinham)

The remainder of the Inns, Hotels, and Drinking establishments in Highbridge have all been demolished for various reasons, usually redevelopment, but their details are given purely for interest. The last to go was:

The White Hart Hotel in Church Street., it was demolished in 2003. In 1883 it was a 'Beer Retailer' then various other people ran it until, during the tenure of Charles Frederick Morgan and his wife Mabel a Wine Licence was granted in 1950. It closed as a licensed establishment in 2002 and was demolished in 2003; the gap it left soon became overgrown and was an eyesore for many months.

A well known landmark and meeting place in Highbridge was **The Railway Hotel,** this Hotel in its time was also called the "Central Somerset Railway Inn" and the "Somerset Arms"; it stood on the Town Square in Market Street. "Alpha House" now dominates the position. John M. Anning was the man in charge in 1848, then in the 1930's Vivian McGuffie Stevenson was the landlord, and it is said, he was a friend of Lawrence of Arabia who frequently visited the hotel on his way to or from his regiment. (*A rumour has it that Lawrence was returning from a visit to the hotel when he had his fatal accident.*) The premises were finally sold in 1969.

Another snippet from a local paper in 1939 that refers to a spate of robberies states:
"The Railway Hotel suffered a great loss when a thief made a detour round by the G.W.R. goods entrance and climbed a fence into the paddock at the rear of the hotel; the window of the lounge was forced, also a locked door, considerable force was used. On entering the bar, some 10/- in coppers was taken from the till; also a glass containing 100 three-penny pieces were stolen. Various drawers were rummaged through, but nothing of further value was found so it was thought. Late, after further investigation it was discovered that £40 worth of whisky, brandy and rum had been taken from the shelves. It appears that the intruder was then disturbed.

Another public house in Market Street, across the road from the Square, was **"The Rose and Crown"**. This is now Yeung's Fish Bar. In 1859 a W.B.Johnson put it up for sale and Mr. Withers leased it, in1918 Ernest George Ham an ex. Soldier ran it until his death in 1921, from 1922 to 1960 C.J.Ham was landlord; its owners, Holt Bros. the local brewery; were taken over by Starkey, Knight and Ford, the pub closed but then ran as a snack bar until sold again in the 1970's.This pub is on the corner of an unusual street, one side of which is called Market Terrace; the other side as Bertha Terrace.

Of the remaining pubs not too much is known, Mr.Williams has provided some detail on these:

Jessie and Janet Stephens ran the **"Railway Vaults"** (Market Street) in 1937; this was just off the Town Square.

The **"Somerset"** public house was known by locals as the, **"Somerset Vaults"** or **"Top House"** or **"Somerset Spirit Stores"** this was in Newtown Road, it is no longer in existence; in 1889 William Paddon was a landlord, in 1965/70 Gweneth Lillian May Butcher is named and in 1971/82, Geoffrey Phillips. Newtown Road being close to the busy wharf contained many premises selling beer, the **Anchor Inn** was probably one these. A photograph from those days shows roughly where it was; today there are private houses built in this area.

In Highbridge there were many 'beer retailers' who also ran other businesses, such as: -

Amos Withers (Baker),
Charles Tiley (Baker).
Samuel Hodge (Shopkeeper)
John Channon (Coal Merchant)
David Baker (Haulier) and
John Burnett these are just a sample.

An extract from the Bridgwater Mercury of 1880 reports: 'Temporary transfer (Licence refused)' this is from the newspaper, "At the Axbridge Petty Sessions last week an application was made by a prospective landlord of Highbridge for a temporary licence preliminary to a transfer to carry on business of the **Ship Beer house (**location unknown**)** at Highbridge, Supt Gillbanks objected that defendant was not a proper person having been convicted under licensing laws, whilst holding a licence in another division. The application was refused. There appears to be no other mention of this Inn in any of the Directories.

Mr. David Williams states: "This concludes my brief list of inns, tippling houses and hotels of Highbridge, I hope the reader might recognise some former friends, perhaps even a relative, who once ran these houses. It seems a shame that the houses, where as a young man of eighteen I used to meet my friends in the 1950's, have a game of darts or listen to the piano, are now all closed down or been made into private houses. Of those that are left, I wish the patrons and landlords/ladies the very best of luck".

Mr Williams has published a book detailing the "The History of Bridgwater Inns, Past and Present"

Continuing our stroll; if, when arriving at the railway bridge, you had looked back from whence you had come this would have been the view of the Brent Road, as it was then known, pedestrians were the only hazard to contend with. The road was considerably narrower and traffic comprised horse drawn carriages or the occasional pony and trap and, possibly

cattle being driven to the market.

This is a view of the town in about 1906, taken from the bridge when looking south, St John's Church can be seen extreme right. The bridge and road were first widened and straightened in 1958. Worston Road is on the right, below the railings.

The next building on the left at the bottom of the bridge was the **Bus Depot for the Bristol Omnibus Co.,** previously the Bristol Tramways; in the 1920's there was a service to the town. In the early days buses were garaged at the rear of the Highbridge Hotel.

This garage was built in 1935, but is now being demolished to make room for a housing development.

The picture shows a group of the Bus Company employees in the 1960's

(Photo supplied by P Derham)

The War Memorial was erected where the signpost stands. (circa 1919).

The houses that now occupy the 'triangle' replaced the cottage; the white house on the left is the old school's reading room, this is next to the original school and St John's Church.

This is the view looking from the **Burnham Road** toward the A38. The previous vicarage can be seen through the bushes on the right; the 'new' road through to the main road was still to be made. (circa 1918)

Church Street

(circa 1905), this view is from near the Adult School.

Coronation Road is nearly opposite, on the corner of which were once a shops and a café, these were eventually replaced by 'The Jade Garden'.

On the right in Church Street was Norman's Cash & Carry Stores, it was opened in 1980 on the site of London Motors a company that sold Land Rovers. Norman's employed 120 staff and had 23 stores; they eventually sold out to Plymco. Highbridge was the last store to carry the name Norman"; this site is now awaiting development.

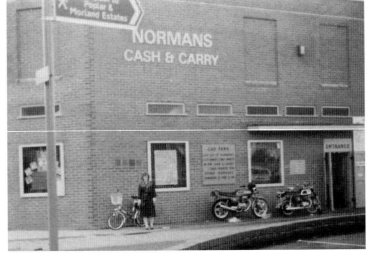

HIGHBRIDGE FROM THE AIR

This Aerial Photograph shows the 'lower' half of Church Street. The Gas Works is top right; the dark patches are the old clay pits from the former brickworks; Grange Avenue is bottom right. Top left is Burnham Road and the Infants School; to the bottom left is Daunton Field (now Poplar Estate) and bottom centre, the old Social Club alongside Church Street. The aerial shot was taken in 1930 and illustrates the many changes to the town.

This was the shop of "F. Foster" who sold poultry, fruit and vegetables and it occupied the premises now known as "Rob's Fish Bar".

These shops are opposite Norman's, their frontage was modified to now include two retail premises.

The corner shop was once the premise of a 'Tailor & Outfitters' owned by a Mr. Herbert Smith, believed to be one of the oldest working shopkeepers in the country; he was still trading well into his 90's.

Opposite the Tailor's Shop was the first Social Club, built in 1913 for the young men of Highbridge; the Club was subsequently rebuilt on its present site in 1981.

On the opposite corner of Grange Avenue was the home and surgery of Dr. Wade, it remained a doctors' surgery until Dr. Creamer moved out to the Medical Centre in Alpha House. The present Wade House was opened in 1995 to provide accommodations for homeless families.

Buildings on the other side of the road have changed quite a bit over the years. Next to the Social Club is 'Skidmarx' the cycle shop, for many years known as 'Stan's Bikes'. Alongside was 'Arien Products Ltd', now moved to premises out of town.

However, in 1911 the 'Somerset Motor & Cycle Depot' owned the buildings and in the 1950's the 'Somerset Motor Depot' was prominent.

By 2003/4 Church Street has seen many changes, businesses have come and gone, one major shock was the demolition of The White Hart Hotel. In 2002 it closed and in 2003 it became a pile of bricks. It was once the home of the Boxing Club and it had many good sporting connections.

Moore's Fish & Chip Shop is in the next block; it is one of the oldest businesses in the town and is next to the Baptist Church. There is a bit of history attached to Moore's Shop, after the first war (1914/18), Florence Moore came to the town with two young sons George and Horace, she met and married Jack Saunders, a former local river pilot and merchant. Florence and Jack opened the first Chip shop in Highbridge in 1926, exactly where it is today. Florence became known as 'Nanny Saunders' and, working full time with Jack built up a very successful business. In 1926 fish and chips were 3d, Nanny made her own faggots that were very much in demand, these sold for 1d. They ran the business for 18 years until Jack's death in 1944. George and Mabel Moore Took over the running of the shop, Nanny continued to help for about 6 years, she died in 1960. George had his own dance band in the 1920's called Moores Melody Makers with his younger brother Horace and four local musicians.

George was one of the founder members of the Highbridge Boxing association and was also secretary of the Highbridge Social Club for many years plus choirmaster, over 30 members, at St Johns Church. Regardless of food rationing during the war George and Mabel ran the fish and chip business successfully and it brought many American Servicemen to the shop often with queues reaching some way down the street. George died suddenly in 1963 and his youngest son Dennis took over the business at 18 years old and, with the help of his mother continued until she died in 1970. He then met and married Thelma and they have run the shop for over 41 years, their hope to continue for a few more years in order to celebrate the shops 80th anniversary in 2006.

(Article and photo supplied by Dennis Moore)

View of Church Street 2004

The Garage was Tuckers Engineering and Motor Works. Mr.Tucker was an enthusiastic cyclist and captain of the local cycling club. He also manufactured cycles; one of his original old time models was still around a few years ago. With the introduction of the motorcar he bought a 31/2 h.p. De Dion Bouton and became

Church Street (circa 1913)

the first in Highbridge to own a petrol driven motorcar and, having an "engineering mind", soon understood the new fangled machine, building up a thriving repair and servicing business. The garage was actively associated with all phases of motorcar development and took part in races at Brooklands race circuit in Surrey, winning many prizes. Car agencies for Austin, Morris and Rover cars and Morris Commercial for vans were handled, but all of these have now disappeared

The appearance of Church Street has changed drastically; most of the buildings in the photograph have been demolished from the Bridgwater Industrial Co-operative Society, (this was the first Co-op in town) up to just beyond the cart in the centre. The area is now occupied by the Post Office and lock up shops.

Cinema

On the corner of Newtown Road is where Highbridge once had a Cinema, called the Picture House, later the "Regent". The Picture House was built in 1920, before this, films were shown at the Town Hall, which was known as the "Electric Theatre" where films could be enjoyed for 1d, it was a popular venue.

An interesting comment from a school magazine (1951) is given below: -

'An Interesting Building'

Perhaps the only interesting building in "Pons Altus" and the most popular to young and old was the cinema. More often known as "The Bug House". It was unfortunately situated near to what used to be called the "Somerset & Dorset Railway". Every time an engine passed by, the building shook, as if in the grip of an earth tremor. When this happened the screen rocked most violently and the sound track was completely drowned by the noise of the engine without.

The most interesting time to visit this "sinkhole" of iniquity was on a Saturday afternoon when one could see hordes of screaming filmgoers armed with an assortment of implements, peashooters, catapults etc.

Once inside, the interior turned into a battlefield. When the film had started the masses made war on someone who was innocently watching the film. Every few minutes, when the excitement rose, like a tidal wave, the Manageress would descend to the "Sevenpennies" picking up other assistants en route to extract, by the scruff of the neck (usually a dirty one) the felons who were the instigators of the mutinous mob. After the main film and during the interval, ice cream used to be served, but due to the curses of the unfortunate victims crushed in the mad rush for them, this enterprise had to be abandoned. During the supporting films, more warmongers were ejected and more peashooters confiscated, until some semblance of order was restored. However, by this time the performance would be over and the mad rush, this time for light and fresh air (Closely resembling the Calgary Stampede) began again.

This was when peace and quiet returned to this "Temple to the Movie Stars" that the Manageress and her wearied assistants sat down and drank a well-earned cup of tea.

Anon. December 1951

After many successful years, the Cinema closed and in the 1960's the building became the "Regal Club". Later, after final closure it was demolished to make way for a residential development.

A Cinema programme from 1939

Church Street showing the Cinema and level crossing; the crossing was removed in June 1968.

Newtown Road once joined Church Street at this point but became a cul-de-sac in 1990, pedestrian access from the main road was still possible. A Telephone Exchange was opened in Newtown Road in 1905, it closed in 1960 when the national system was modernised.

Church Street

The Lamb Inn is on the left. On the right are the Level Crossing gates and the footbridge, when these were removed a new building was erected and this is now the Highbridge Cash and Carry, previously Latifs'; but built initially as a Fine Fare Supermarket.

(Photo supplied by John Channon)

The Regent Cinema and Tuckers' Garage brought back many memories to a local lady, Mary Chalker recalls the cinema not being the best of places to go, but you did not really have much choice. It was dark and known as the fleapit, you had to be careful when you went in, because seats were missing, you could finish up sitting on the floor. A visit to Tuckers' Garage when she was a child brought a surprise. " My grandfather drove his car into the garage and I thought he was going to get some petrol; he said 'Come on then, get out!' I thought 'what have I got to go in the garage for?' Anyway, we did not go in, we went through to the shop. He spoke to Mr.Tucker, who wheeled out a bicycle and grandfather said 'Well sit on it then, is it all right for you? I said "Oh yes" he said 'Right off you go home then, I will catch you up later' grandfather had just bought me my first bike".

Cooks in Highbridge since 1890's

The Cook's arrived in Highbridge in the 1890's and rented the old shops on what was then known as the Cornhill. This is the area to the right of the roundabout; a road called Tyler Way stands on this spot today. George Cook and his wife came from Bridgwater, for the first six months he walked to and from Bridgwater every day to work and back! They did not closed until 10 p.m.! His eldest son Fred joined him when he was fourteen years old as a lather boy, in those days shaving was the main source of income there were no safety razors only cut'throat razors. A shave cost one old penny (less than half a new penny). They soon rented a cottage in South Terrace, which is behind the National Westminster bank in Huntspill Road, where two more children were born. May the only daughter and Ray, my father, I am Alan the third generation. George carried on until his death in 1942

When the 1914 – 1918 war started the young men were called up and came in for a haircut before joining up. George told them "Don't forget to send me a postcard". I still have all the cards from all over the world, young men telling George what it was like (some of it being censored by the military).

The Corn Hill around 1904, 'Sea View Terrace' or 'Bugs Hole Alley' as it was known, was just beyond the building on the right.

The next step was to acquire the premises grandfather was renting as the barbers shop. It also included a shop that supplied the locals and farmers who came to the cattle market, sailors from ships in the wharf, my grandmother ran this and later her daughter May, until they retired in 1958. At this point my parents and I moved in above the shops, I was still at school. It was at this time that I put a message in a bottle and dropped it off the bridge at the bottom of Clyce Road, on my way to my grandmother's who now lived in Clyce Road, the bottle made its way to Lydney. Glos. Mother ran the corner shop, which became a greengrocer in the 1970's; mother ran it until she retired in 1979, when my wife Jenny ran it until she too retired in 1999. By this time we were in new premises, a hundred metres down the road on the opposite side.

Ray (my father and his brother Fred ran the business until the 1939 – 1945 war. They were known as the flying barbers, as they raced pigeons. Fred was too old for service and ran the barbers through the war years. Ray worked in a factory at Bristol making aircraft engines until the end of the war. Highbridge was bombed in the 1939 – 1945 war, one bomb fell on the Cheese Store (now the launderette), father was in the pigeon loft at the time about 25 metres away. It ruffled a few feathers, so I am told. After the war they ran the shop until their retirement in 1962

I did a hairdressing apprenticeship in Bridgwater for three years and became the West of England Junior Hairdressing Champion in 1962. I then came back to Highbridge and ran the business at the old shop until 1985, when we sold the site to Sedgemoor. Jenny and I then bought the three shops we are in now, from Mervyn Knight who was retiring. Jenny and I have two sons, Mark the eldest and Matthew. Jenny continued running the new greengrocers shop until she retired. Mark joined me in the hairdressers in 1990, we worked together until I retired in 1998, when Matthew joined Mark, his wife Abi now runs the ladies salon next door, they have a son Ellis. That's the story of one hundred plus, of one family in Highbridge.

(Article supplied by Alan Cook)

The photographs on the previous page show roughly the same views; the Corn Hill (1904) on one or High Street (1909) on the other, confusing wasn't it.

This view taken in 2004 from nearly the same positions.

Church Street - Reconstruction

Some people in Highbridge may not be aware that the main street through the town was dug up in the winter of 1974/5. A portion of Market Street was also reconstructed in the summer/autumn of 1974.

There was a good reason for this major undertaking? Church Street (A38) was the main north/south route through Highbridge to the South West and had been treated as such for hundreds of years.

The A38 (T.) 'T' for trunk road, had not been constructed for this purpose and as time went by vehicles began to get longer and heavier. The tracks formed by the wheels of carts, wagons, stagecoaches, lorries, coaches and buses, all had an impact on the surface. Before the road was treated with macadam in the early twentieth century it had been virtually a track, sometimes a very muddy track. The road was obviously in constant use, but repairs had to be done, all had been previously carried out on a "make do and mend" principle with rocks and waste, in later days with fast setting concrete. This proved to be inadequate just to take even local traffic and after a very short time started to break up again, causing severe vibrations to adjacent buildings. Earlier repairs to the road had also resulted in the surface levels rising, which prevented further overlays if adjacent properties were to be secure from flooding, this could be from the road/pavement surfaces.

Something had to be done and the opportunity came following the opening of the M.5. The new highway took traffic away from Highbridge, and the Somerset County Council was now able to divert the traffic away from the town. Also, the M5 was now the major route for all traffic and this meant that very soon the Department of Transport would 'de-trunk' the A38 ie remove its 'trunk route' rating. This move would have left the local ratepayers with a hefty bill to cover the reconstruction of the principal route.

Before work could commence on this major project a lot of preparation was necessary, designs/plans had to be discussed with all the Statutory Undertakers to ensure gas, electric, water and telephones services were not disrupted. All the providers had to be assembled and consulted to ensure that there was the minimum of disruption; many of the services had to be completely repositioned and this would, inevitably, create problems.

Gas and water, because of their nature did make life difficult for the providers. Electricity and telephone services would be easier to relocate but these needed to be carried out with the minimum of inconvenience to businesses and householders alike. Another very important side to the project was the need to liase with the shopkeepers and householders along the affected routes. Church Street was going to be closed to traffic for 5/6 months. The organisation and execution of the work would have to be strictly controlled to minimise disruption, but it was essential work. The work was carried out in phases, so that life would continue as normal as possible in Highbridge.

The widening of Market Street was necessary up to and over the railway bridge. Embankments on both sides of the bridge were widened to take two lanes of H.G.V.'s, this included building up the embankment on the North West side of the road. In 1970 the Business Park and its access road did not exist, Isleport Lane was extremely narrow and the work included piping a section of rhyne and traffic signing in an attempt to restrict the lane to car and light van use only. The maximum permitted width was 5ft 6ins, but some drivers 'to short cut' ignored the signs, the Police often checked vehicle widths. It should also be noted that the first rural application of 'variable direction flows' was used in peak hours.

The agreed route for H.G.V.'s from the A38 to Walrow Industrial Estate was via Burnham Moor Lane, numerous bends were widened and kerbed, rhynes piped and some of the road was resurfaced; signing was again extensive.

In Church Street Gas and Water mains, together with services to the properties, were rebuilt at lower levels to allow for the construction of the new road, which was to be set lower than the original road; some Electricity and Telephone services were also lowered. Whilst the Statutory Undertakers were doing their preparatory work no roadwork was carried out.

Lowering and Reconstruction of Church Street This was carried out under the full closure of the A38 to minimise inconvenience, certain designated sections were done at a time. From the bridge to Bank Street car park entrance, then from Newtown Road and so on up to the War Memorial. This was achieved by agreeing the individual lengths of each section of full width construction, with the householders and business people, before carrying out the work.

Somerset County Council then built the concrete base of each kerb line, including all drainage and then the kerbs and gullies before excavating the full width of pavements and road adjacent to these new sections of kerb etc. One completed section up to the base course was then followed by the next and so on up the whole length of road.

Major problems were few but the removal of old concrete road repairs, the foundations of the former Somerset and Dorset level crossing and the Coronation Street culvert did cause difficulty at the time.

The schedule required that work should be carried out for 12 hours each day, 7 days a week for at least 6 weeks. The maximum labour force was 40+. The Statutory Undertaking phase, together with the full width construction, lasted over 2 months of 1974 and into the first 10 weeks of 1975. The approximate cost of £220,000 was considered to be good value at that time.

One Way Working North and South of the Full Closure This was essentially the same form of construction as for the main re-construction, but with traffic control rather than a full road closure. With the end of all phases, a new wearing course was laid and this is the surface that, in most parts, still survives until the present.

The foregoing is based on the recollections of Mr Alan Lovell, Assistant Divisional Surveyor, North Somerset Division 1974-1976 and we are indebted to Mr Lovell for kindly providing us with all the relevant details and photographs.

The lists given here show the variety and differences in trades over the years.

Church Street

Trades and Shops, available at the end of the 1940's into the 1950's. (a selection).

London Drapery	Smith (tailor-gents outfitters)	Somerset Motor Depot (Garage)
S.W.E.B.Shop (Retail)	Chappell (Baker)	Forsey (Butcher)
Swift (Wool Shop)	Gloynes (Grocer)	Foster (Greengrocer)
Welland (Blacksmith)	Griffen (Fishmonger)	Weall (Confectioner)
Moores (Fish/Chip)	Brown (Corn merchant)	Cox & Cox (Furniture Store)
Steers (Garage)	Toots (Baker)	Robertson (Watch/Clock Repairs)
Pouncey & Hydon	Cooks (Mens' Hairdresser)	Bacon Co Shop (Factory Shop)
Cooks (Greengrocer)		

Church Street

Trades and Shops available during 2004(a Selection)

Jade Garden (Chinese Takeaway)	Quick Sign (Signmaker)	Robs Fish Bar (Fish/Chip)
Chedzey (Upholstery)	Brandon Hire (Tool Hire)	Skidmarx Cycle Shop)
Jones (T.V.Engineer)	Tandori (Indian Restaurant)	Moores (Fish/Chip)
London Connection (Ladies H/Dr)	Movie Mania (Video Hire)	Parkes (Car Accessories)
Clements (Carpet Retail)	Sandra (Ladies H/Dr)	Rikkis (Café)
Whitehouse (Solicitor)	Applegate (Estate Agent)	Post Office (Spar Retail)
Snippers (Mens H/dr)	Cooks (Ladies H/Dr)	Highbridge Upholster
Highbridge (Cash & Carry)	H.K.Takeaway (Chinese)	M.A.G. (Computers)
D.C.Computers	Baywash (Laundrette)	Highbridge News (News/Agent)
Veals (Fishing Tackle)		

Banks

There is just one bank remaining in Highbridge, the National Westminster Bank in Huntspill Road. This was originally, Stuckey's Banking Co. that was formed in 1826 and their site was the first bank in the town opening on 18th October 1876. (The Stuckey Banking Co. was probably the first bank to use printed cheques). The National Provincial Bank Co. had a branch next to the National Westminster Bank; it opened in 1912, closing in 1931

Barclays Bank was the only bank not to change its name during the time it was in Highbridge, it opened for business to the public in October 1922. The Bank having purchased a property known as Highbridge House, Cornhill, in June of that year for the sum of £1200. These premises remained open until 11th June 1993 the last Bank Manager there was Mr. M.J.P. Baker he had been at the Highbridge Branch for six years. The Lower Brue Drainage Board now occupies the building.

Lower Brue District Drainage Board The Lower Brue District Drainage Board, in common with other Boards in Somerset, does not own the watercourses it controls under the powers contained in the Somerset Drainage Act 1877 and the Land Drainage Act 1991. The board has official Byelaws approved by the Ministry of Agriculture, Fisheries and Food, breach of which can be penalised by penalties imposed by a Magistrates Court. The Boards function is to improve and maintain the rhyne system without which the whole of the area would be subject to flooding, the land, generally, being below high tide water mark. It also contributes towards the cost of the upkeep of the sea walls and of the rivers into which the rhynes flow. *(The Board whose address is 1 Church Street, Highbridge, Somerset TA9 3AE supplied this information)*

The **Wilts & Dorset Banking Co**. opened a branch in the town in 1892. In 1914 over 100 branches were taken over by Lloyds Bank. The premises of the Wilts & Dorset Banking Co. were built on the corner of Quiet Street (Bank Street) and Market Street. Lloyds Bank closed this branch on the 31st December 1999, the building stood empty for a while; it is now occupied by the National Blind Children's Society.

(Information covering the Banks was obtained from the Archivists at Barclays, Lloyds and National Westminster Banks)

Earlier in the book there are views of Jubilee Gardens from the past, this is a view taken in 2004 and it illustrates the size of the Garden after the development of the road junction.

The 'One Star' Town.

In 1996 Highbridge received not only National acclaim but also International notice for its Christmas Decorations. The Council had provided just £90.00 toward the purchase of decorations for the town, just five stars mounted on a spindly frame to hang from the Clock (only three of the four bulbs worked) in Jubilee Gardens. Obviously there were comments from all and sundry, the news reached the national newspapers and, eventually expatriates in Australia picked up the news. There was much 'buck' passing, who was responsible? The Town Council, or District Council. There were many red faces around that year, but it did have an affect on the consciences of all who were responsible for decorating the streets of Highbridge at the Festive Season. Since that unfortunate occurrence Highbridge has 'out shone' many towns, not a million miles away and residents can now be proud of the efforts made to decorate their town.

The Clyce Bridge marks the southern limit of the town, on the right, as you prepare to leave is the Clyce Road at the top end of which is the old **Lock Keepers' Cottage.**

Behind the cottage can be seen the old wharf, where, for many years ships tied up to unload or load, cargos of coal, timber, bricks, tiles and assorted other wares

(Photo supplied by Mr & Mrs Carpenter)

Returning to the town, on the right is **John Tyler's (Highbridge) Ltd**. And the "Gateway of Highbridge" this firm is able to trace its history back to 1875 when its founder bought the shop that had been bought 12 years earlier. Road users could see its imposing shop frontage as it was situated on the Cornhill, at the junction of Church and Market Streets.

The firm was an ironmonger and manufacturing diary engineers, continuing as such until the late 1930's; also a ship chandler for vessels that used the wharf area nearby.

For several years an illustrated catalogue showed the large selection of diary equipment, for example, cheese vats and moulds, diary bowls, milk churns and pails. Food troughs and other farming equipment were manufactured in workshops in Church Street. Many items were made 'in-house', some at the rear of the premises and there was a special building called the "Gunpowder House" where shotgun cartridges were produced, this building was near the old river bed. Around the 1930's Tyler's turned their attention to the construction and building industries when the milk industry became more centralised and made their own Equipment. Tyler's were a forerunner for the D.I.Y. enthusiast, selling paints; wallpaper and sundry goods needed by those who wished to decorate their own homes. During a period from 1949 to 1954 the company attended local Agricultural Shows with a display of their own equipment, electric power tools, Calor Gas supplies, fishing tackle and gardening requisites. In 1967,

although still trading as John Tyler, ownership had changed to John Bland (Cardiff) and in 1974 it changed to Perkins and Seaward. The big change came later in the year when Tylers finally disappeared from the Cornhill and moved to the premises vacated by Willsher & quick near the Coopers Arms. The move proved to be beneficial, but more changes were to come M.A.C. followed by United Builders Merchants and in 1987 ownership passed to Norcross who finally became Jewsons. The final move was to Tyler End. Isleport Business Park. Highbridge

(Information supplied by Arthur Burridge)

William H.Tyler

There must be few men who work in an office immediately below the room in which they were born three-quarters of a century ago. These were one of the many distinctions of Mr. William H. Tyler, Managing Director of Messes John Tyler (Highbridge) Ltd. On the Cornhill (junction of Market and Church Streets)

The business of which he was head was founded in 1870 and purchased from the founders by Mr. John Tyler in 1875. He added a house to the premises for his own occupation and in it his son, William was born. The house became part of the business premises and one its reception rooms serves as the Director's office. William was educated at Dr. Morgan's school at Bridgwater and was proud of several of his school reports, which were found among his father's papers; justly proud because they are excellent and place him first in his form.

At Christmas 1897 he entered his father's business, starting at the bottom of the ladder because his first job was to clean up the cellar. One of the signs of the times was, that on that very day two tons of horseshoe nails arrived and the Junior had to carry the 20lb. boxes from the horse drawn lorry to the store at the rear of the premises. He also had vivid memories of the 40 gallon barrels of paraffin oil, 15 to 20 which were delivered every week, because it was his duty to get these heavy loads down the slope to the back of the stores. One of the boasts of the firm was its daily delivery service, which was maintained practically all the time it has been Tyler's. When gas came to Highbridge it was John Tyler who put up one-third of the money and it was his propaganda, which made Highbridge gas conscious; his son regretted Tyler's no longer supplied the gas appliances for the area.

Outside Tyler's shop was the Jubilee Clock, which was erected in 1897, and it was just about that time William became Captain of the Fire Brigade. In 1898 he joined the volunteers in which he remained active until they were disbanded on the formation of the Territorial Army.

He remembers that in those days the normal working week was 73 hours and that on "high days" and "holidays" the shop remained open until 11 p.m.

In 1901 he joined the 'Mid-Devon Stores' and remained with Mr. H.J. Cordwent for twelve months; to gain further experience he joined Messrs. T. & S. Frost in a newly established builders merchants business in Exeter. After twelve months service with this organisation John Tyler received a telegram from his Father.........."Come home at once; disastrous fire".

He returned to Highbridge and for seven years served as an assistant;when his Father retired in 1909, he and his brother, as partners carried on the business using the name of "John Tyler & Sons". Not satisfied with running a successful business in Highbridge the Tyler brothers together with Mr. Daunton purchased the business of F.P. Prentice at 42, Regent Street, Clifton, in Bristol and thus took over a business that had been in existence for almost 100 years. For three years Mr. Tyler retained his interest in both businesses and tried to divide his time between Bristol and Highbridge, in 1914 he bought out his brother's share of the Bristol business and sold to his brother, his share of the Highbridge business.

1914 was a full year for Mr. Tyler, not only did he have the upheaval of his business life but he married and on the declaration of war joined the 4th Gloucestershire Regiment as a private putting on his uniform for the first time on Christmas Day. He quickly became a sergeant and two weeks after enlisting he was sent to guard the commissioned and went overseas with the 14th Worcesters. Early in 1918 after having recovered from the wounds he had received in France he was transferred to the Tank Corp, promoted to Captain, and made responsible for the training of a number of French-Canadian troops.

Demobilisation came early in 1919 and he returned to the management of the Bristol business that, in the war years, his partner Mr. Daunton had supervised. During the next ten years Mr. Tyler showed his pioneering spirit by purchasing large houses in the Clifton area of Bristol and converting them into flats.

At the early age of 45 he retired and went to live in Paignton but soon took up part -time work for Gilpin & Whitehouse, until 1934 when his brother died, he returned to the Highbridge business, in which he was joined by his nephew, Mr. J.F. Cary.

In the early part of the last war when Mr.Cary joined the forces, Mr.William Tyler returned to the house in which he was born. He was active in the business and was often found in the office or the shop. His ability to give detailed answers to the many questions submitted to him by his staff showed that he had good grasp of the business with which he had been connected, more or less continuously, for 61 years.

(Information from account by his nephew Mr John F.Cary.)

Fred Orchard's Chemist The first shop on the left of this picture is at present (2004) Bird's Furniture. Previous to this the shop had been a chemist for nearly 100 years.

First records of the property show that Mr Carpenter of Burnham opened a branch Pharmacy here in 1898, he later sold the business to Mr Fred Orchard in 1899.
Mr Ivor Channon started work for Fred Orchard in 1918

This is, (Circa 1935), what an array of medicines, nothing pre-packed and ready in those days; all dispensed on the premises. It is believed that the man on the left became a bomber pilot during the last war.

In 1956 Fred Orchard retired and the business became a limited company with Ivor Channon as Managing Director, with John Channon joining the business. The Channon family eventually bought the business from the Orchard family in1981 and continued to serve the town for a further 15 years until the final closure in 1996 after 98 years.

(Information and photograph supplied by John Channon)

Post Office 1984, not the original frontage. By 1861 the Post Office had been established in the town.

Around 1902 Henry James Channon was Postmaster, when letters posted by 10.00 am were delivered on the same day in Cardiff, Exeter, Plymouth and many other large towns.

Lewis's Shoe Shop, which was established by Mr.Joseph Lewis in about 1880, he became a member of the Urban Council during the war years became Chairman in1917/18 and was a Councillor for 23 years. For many years he was associated with the Highbridge Gas Co. together with Mr. J.Tyler and Mr. R. Knight.

(Photo supplied by Mrs V Crawford-nee Lewis)

R.Knight's the Grocers Shop decorated for the Coronation of King George VI.

Mary Chalker remembers the shops in Market Street, the Co-op and Knight's, both Grocers, were pre-supermarket type shops.

In Knight's everything was weighed and not pre-packed, they had a bacon slicer; it made a whooshing noise as it sliced the bacon or ham. Hocks of bacon hung from above and the smell Ooh! It was great; you can't describe it—no refrigeration in those days.

Knights would deliver you purchases on a bike that had a huge basket on the front; the lad would trundle around the town making deliveries.

Butchers Shops have always been present in the street, Hatchers was where F.Bishop now is. A real 'old character' was Mr Hatcher, he wore a straw boater and

(Photo supplied by John Channon)

there was always a cheery greeting when you passed his shop, the grill on the doorway was always open letting fresh air into the shop at all times. A few doors away was another butcher, Mr.Sparkes he also had his door open because in those days they did not have refrigerators, all the meat was hung in the shop, sides of beef, pork etc, all on view.

Market Street looking towards The Town Clock (Circa 1960's)

The large building on the right with its door facing forward, was Lloyds Bank, it is now the Head Office of the National Blind Children's Charity.

The Bridgwater Industrial Co-operative Society Ltd established their first premises between 1861 and 1875 in Church Street. Later their main shop was opened in Market Street opposite where the Town Green now is; it was one of the largest in the town and its sales covered a wide area; the deliveries being made by a cart or carriage that were drawn by horses stabled at the rear of the shop. On a bitterly cold morning and icy road conditions when deliveries were made to the Mark area it was sometimes necessary to wrap sacking around the horses hooves in order to obtain grip when it went up and over the Walrow railway bridge. A handcart made deliveries around Highbridge; this would include milk, bread and cakes that had been brought up from the Bridgwater Depot earlier that day.

It was a two-storey building, with groceries on the ground floor and furniture, clothing and household goods upstairs. During its time in the town additional services became available, including insurance, mortgage and for funerals. One fascination for children was the "cash railway", when paying for a purchase the assistant would place your money in a container and it was whisked overhead to the Cashiers Department. Your purchase was recorded and your change and receipt were placed back in the container that then returned it to you at the counter.

Over the years trading habits changed and the upstairs department closed in 1966, in March 1969 the grocery department became self-service; upstairs was converted into flats but in 1994 this branch of the Co-op finally closed. The Society also made coal deliveries from the Norris Coal yard at the wharf (now Jubilee Gardens); there was also, for a short period, a Butcher/Grocery store in Church Street (now Rob Fish Bar/Quick Sign Premises).

(Information supplied by Bob Rogers, Brian Hawkins and Reg. Pike.)

The views show Market Street in the year 2003 where very little has changed recently.

A chemist shop has been where Lloyds are, for many years, next door there was once the print works for Highbridges' 1st Newspaper in 1894, the Highbridge Echo, this ceased publication in 1905 being incorporated into the Bridgwater Herald.

Market Street

Trades and shops available at the end of 1940's and 1950's (a selection)

John Tylers (Ironmongers)	Wensley (Ladies H/Dresser)	Sealey (Tobacconist)
Hatcher (Butcher)	Una Bailey (Ladies H/Dresser)	Post Office
Shickles (Shoe Shop)	Knights (Grocer)	Fred Orchard (Chemist)
Sheppard & Sparkes (Electrical Goods)	Sparkes (Butcher)	Fisher (Newsagent)
	Co-op (Retail)	Sparkes (Dentist)
Dudderidge (G/Grocer)	Rossiter (Jeweller)	Willis (Cycle Shop)
Moggs (G/.Outfitter)	Bamsey (Decorator)	Twigg (Ironmonger)
Vickery (Mens H/Dresser)	Parsons (Chemist)	

Market Street

Trades and Shops available in 2004(a selection)

William Hill (Bookmaker)	Charlies (Ladies H/Dresser)	Presentations (Trophies/Engraving)
Bishop (Butcher)	Hair & Co (Ladies H/Dresser)	Birds (Furniture)
Pets Paradise (Pet Foods)	Waddell (TV Electrical Retail)	Smarts (News Agents)
Blue Belles (Bridal Wear)	Highbridge D.I.Y.	Maisey's (Baker)
Casey's (Solicitor)	Lloyds (chemist)	Yeungs Fish Bar (Fish and Chips)
Kwik Save (Super Market)	Dentist	Bengal Spice (Indian Takeaway)

The **Highbridge Express** was established in 1920,but it was in 1864 that a Mr. Patey first launched his own newspaper "The Burnham Star and Highbridge Express". Over the years many changes were made; titles changed and its format was enlarged from a single sheet to a four-page publication. The ownership also changed several times, and it changed from a tabloid to broadsheet and was then incorporated into the "Bridgwater Mercury"

The "Highbridge Express" as such came into existence during the 20th century, one of its many rivals, one being the "Local News" introduced by a Mr. Perkins of Church Street in 1906. This small four-page publication, printed in Highbridge, carried an article concerning the replacement of the Clock at Cornhill, entitled "Round the Clock at Highbridge", suggesting it was the centre of activities.

The publication did not last for many years and upon its death in 1920; Mr. Patey started the "Highbridge Express". The "Burnham Gazette" and "Highbridge Express" mirrored the activities of both towns and surrounding districts, it celebrated 100 years (1864 to 1964), and a Special Supplement was published. A comment at the time stated, "What the future holds in store no can for see"; little were they to know that both newspapers would effectively disappear. The Highbridge Express was incorporated into the Burnham Gazette in 1947.

The "Highbridge Independent" established in 1922 was incorporated into the Bridgwater Mercury in 1933.

An important addition to the way of life in Highbridge is the very popular Sunday Market; this is situated on the Cattle Market site and comprises a wide variety of traders. No matter what you may require, you will probably get it from the market. Meat, vegetables, fruit, flowers, D.I.Y., computer accessories, carpets, clothing, footwear, home entertainment, and -you name it –they have it!

A view of the Sunday Market, this is just a small portion of a Market that fills the Cattle Market area.

In 1915 this was the view from the Walrow Bridge when looking into Highbridge.

The Coopers Arms is on the left and the 'Old' Town Hall can be seen in the centre. The building just the other side of the pond still exists in 2004.

We are about to cross the Railway Bridge and enter Walrow past the site of the original station of the S.C.R. and Walrow Terrace, where Frank Foley was born.

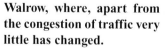

Walrow, where, apart from the congestion of traffic very little has changed.

(Photo supplied by Chris Brown)

We have reached the end of our stroll and are to leave Highbridge on the B3139 heading east.

On this 1909 comedy postcard the caption read "Did you hear we are leaving Highbridge"

BUT

Perhaps? They could be returning, now that the Regeneration has started.

We have come to the end of our look into the past of:

Highbridge
a Somerset Market Town,
and its People

A lot has happened since the Somerset Central Railway came to the town 150 years ago in 1854, much has changed and some has disappeared forever. Highbridge will, however, carry on; it is the next generation that has to ensure its life continues and that the Regeneration Programme is completed. We are sure this will enhance the town and improve the well being of its inhabitants, providing them with a proud and energetic community.

LIST OF SUBSCRIBERS

Presentations

Highbridge St. John's V.C. School
Highbridge Beechfield Infants School
King Alfred School
Highbridge Library
Burnham-on-Sea Library
Somerset Local Studies Library

H. Carver – George Reed Galleries (nee Stradling)
M.E. Akers – Highbridge
Geof & Sheila Amesbury -Burnham-on-Sea
Terence William Peter Arnold -Kennilworth
In Loving Memory of Mr. & Mrs. Les. Baker – Highbridge
Mr. Ralph & Jean Baker – Late of Huntspill Road, Highbridge
Carol Barnes (nee Parsons) West Huntspill
Neil & Doreen Barrett – Highbridge
Mr. & Mrs. W. Beale – Lympsham
Jim Bennett
Phil Bertenshaw – Weston
Mr. & Mrs. D. Besley – Watchfield – Highbridge
Gwen Besley
Alan Bezzant
Maurice Bishop – Dunster
Roger Bishop – Looe, Cornwall
Andrew Bishop – Burnham-on-Sea
Betty Bishop – Highbridge
Phil Blake – Highbridge
Mrs. Pamela Boucher
John & Paula Bowden – Highbridge
Mrs. S.R. Broadstock, – Clyce Road, Highbridge
Margaret Brown – Bridgwater
David Brown – Burnham-on-Sea
Gerald Buncombe – Burnham-on-Sea
Marjorie Buncombe
Pat Burge – Highbridge
Katy & Matty Burgess – Newbury
In Memory of Debbie Burke – Highbridge
Arthur Burridge – Highbridge
Mrs. Rosemary Burrow
Ken & Fay Burston
Mr. Roy Came – Severn Grove, Burnham

In Memory of Arthur Came
Marjorie Came – Abingdon
Sue Cannock – Heathwood
Donna Cardell (nee Welch) Cumbria
Edward & Gloria Carp (nee Smith) – Ashcott
Mr. & Mrs. S. Carpenter – Lock Keepers Cottage, Highbridge
Bob & Pearl Caulton (nee Baker) Burnham-on-Sea
Dave & Jo, – Worston Road, Highbridge
John Channon – Highbridge
Shane Chapman – Burnham-on-Sea
Paula Cherry – Highbridge
Mrs. Violet Chick – Highbridge
Alan & Sara Chick – Burnham-on-Sea
Tim Christian – East Huntspill
Robin Christian (Shrivenham – Wilts)
Colin J. Cicone – East Huntspill
Peter Cockburn – Ex. Huntspill
Mr. & Mrs. C.H. Conelley – Pawlett
Alex Cook & Will Cook – Wedmore
Mr. Roger L.F. Cook – Brunels Way, Highbridge
Mrs. Janet Cook – Highbridge
Jenny & Alan Cook – Brent Knoll
Jack Cook – (Worle)
Ellis Francis Cook – Berrow
Sandra Cooke (nee Meader) – Norfolk
K.J. Coombes – Edithmead
J. & N. Coombes – Burnham-on-Sea
Evelyn Coombes – Late of Highbridge
Mr. & Mrs. D. Cooper – Burnham-on-Sea
Mr. & Mrs. Ralph Cornish – West Huntspill
Mrs. G. Court (nee Mossman) – Fivehead
Mary & Reg. Cox – Highbridge
H. Sydney Cox – Highbridge
George & Valerie Crawford (nee Lewis) Highbridge
Ken & Enid Creamer – Spaxton, Bridgwater
In Memory of Edward Thomas Creswick
Mrs. Vera Crisp – London
Mike & Liz Critchlow – Australia
Mr. Royston J. Cummins – West Huntspill
John Davey – West Huntspill
Les Davey – Highbridge
Pete Davey – Wensley House, East Huntspill

Angela & Trevor Davies – Highbridge
Christine Davies – Burnham-on-Sea
Owen Davies – Burnham-on-Sea
Kenneth Denman – Highbridge
David S.R. Derham – Worle, Weston-super-Mare
Peter C.J. Derham – West Huntspill
Christopher Derham – Weybridge
Paul Derham – Guildford
Julian R. Derham – Weston-super-Mare
Trevor Dinham – Highbridge
Alice Kathleen Dodd (nee Jubin)Bridgwater
Robert John Dodd – Bristol
Anthony Raymond Dodd – Bridgwater
Mary Draper (nee Hooper) Highbridge
Michael Clifford Dubin – Bristol
Ian Dunbavan – Godmanchester -
    Cambridgeshire
Joyce Dunbavan – Highbridge
Graham Dunbavan – West Huntspill
Ruth Dyer – Highbridge
Peter & Eileen Dyer – Highbridge
Dorothy & Ken Dyer – Late of Highbridge
Mr. Michael A. Dyer – Weston-super-Mare
Michael Elkerton – East Huntspill
F.M. & P.M. Faulks
John & Jen Faulks – Westbury, Wilts
Clive & Clare Faulks – Highbridge
Keith & Christina Faulks – Northmore Green
Dave & Sue Faulks – Chilton Polden
Alice Faulks – Highbridge
In Memory of Margery Fielding
In Memory of Colin Fielding
Mrs. Joan Fisher – Plymouth
Bill Fisher – Highbridge
In Memory of Ruby Maud Flack
In Memory of Peter Foster
Fred & Sheila Foster – Bridgwater
Andrew Foster – Bridgwater
Jack Foster – Highbridge
Wilf Foster – Exeter
Louis & Evian Fox – Bridgwater
Audrey French (nee Baker) Burnham-on-Sea
"Frith House" Steart Drive, Burnham-on-Sea
Terry & Esme Fry – Burnham-on-Sea
Mrs. B.M. Green
Mr. William Griffin – East Brent
Elizabeth Grousson -Paris
Keith & Christine Haggett – Highbridge

Rosemary & Paul Haggett – Cambridge
Gail B. Hale (nee Foster) Virginia U.S.A.
John Hale – Brent Knoll
Andrew John Hale – Brent Knoll
Mark Hadrian Hale – Rumney, Cardiff
Robin Halstead – Burnham-on-Sea
Mr. Gerald D.G. Ham -Brunels Way, Highbridge
Miss Amanda L. Ham – London
Mrs. E. Ham – West Huntspill
Bill, Frances & Deborah Hancock – Edithmead
D.G. & H.E. Hand – Pawlett
Howard Hand – Burnham on Sea
Winston & Jean Hand – East Huntspill
Chris Handley – Fareham
Chris Hardwidge – Highbridge
Mrs. P.M. Harvey "Midway" Edithmead
Jack & Jean Hatcher
Mrs. Rosemary Hawkins – Highbridge
Richard & Jennifer Heal – Bow Farm,
    Highbridge
Sue & Godfrey Hebdon
Nicky Henning – Mark
Robert Hester – West Huntspill – Somerset
Denis Hewings
Peter & Brenda Higman – Mark
A.J. Hill, – Brent Knoll
John Hill – Highbridge
In Memory of Mrs. Freda Hoey (nee Woodberry)
In Memory of Jim Hooper "A Highbridge Lad"
Mr. R. Hooper, East Huntspill
Mr. R. Hooper – Highbridge
Mr. P. Hooper – Burnham-on-Sea
The Late Gordon Hoskin of London House
    Motors
Mrs. K.M. House
Alfie & Bradley House to Nanny Joan
Don & Liz Hunt – Bovey Tracey, Devon
Tony Hunt – Harrogate, Yorks
Kerri Hunter (nee Welch) – Cumbria
Susan & Nicholas Hurford – West Huntspill
Liz Hurley, Burnham-on-Sea
Kathleen Incledon – Highbridge
Janty & Andy -Old St Johns School, Highbridge
Carol Johnson in Loving Memory
John Jones – St. Lukes, Highbridge
Percival Henry Wilfred Jubin – in Memory
Douglas Kenneth Charles Jubin – Bridgwater
Clifford William James Jubin in Memory

Derek J. Kidner – East Huntspill
The King Alfred School
Brad & Zoe King – Dorset
Mr. & Mrs. A.S. Kirk – Clyce Road, Highbridge
Dr. Kirk J.M. – Illonois U.S.A.
Mr. & Mrs. Kirk R.J. Market Street, Highbridge
Fred W.H. Lack – Newport, Gwent
Mary & Ralph Ladd – Highbridge
Charles Langdon – West Huntspill
Michael R. Lawrence – Isleport
Millicent M. Lawrence – Mark
Mrs. Enid Lawson daughter of J.M. Hitchen
    M.I.C.E.,M.I.M.E.
Phillip Lewis – Woolavington
George Lewis – Uphill, Weston-super-Mare
June & Lawrence Lillycrop – Highbridge
Mr. & Mrs. J.M. Lindsey
Thomas H. Lipyeart – Highbridge
Mr. & Mrs. A. Lismore
Rev'd Robin P. Lodge, Vicar of Highbridge
Alan G. Lovell – Burnham-on-Sea
Pam & Phil Lyes – Highbridge
Anthony R. Lynham – Highbridge Burnham
Mr. Eric & Joan Lynham "Poplars" The Clyce
Barry Maisey, Maisey's Bakery – Highbridge
Ruby & Jack Major – West Huntspill
Rex Major & Family – Pawlett
Carole Marooney – Highbridge
Mr. & Mrs. B.A. Martin – Highbridge
Deanna Maslen (nee Came) Abingdon
Bob & Pat Masterman – Burnham-on-Sea
Lottie Matthews (formerly of Highbridge)
Gordon & Barbara May – Highbridge
John Maybery
Kirsty, Fiona & Alex McLaren "Bourn House"
    Biddisham
Maureen McLaren – Clyce Road Highbridge
Cris & Sylvia Meaden (nee Swift)Burnham-on-
    Sea
John & Brenda Meader – Highbridge
Colin Meader – Watchet
In Memory of Sis & Ben Mears
Mrs. D. Mear, Burnham-on-Sea
Chris & Marion Metcalfe – Highbridge
Tony Metcalfe & Dr. Allison Fulford –
    Highbridge
"Millards" of Highbridge
Norman G. Millward

Mitch & Norma (formerley of the "Railway
    Hotel" Highbridge)
Mrs. Phylis Mitchell – Kent
Collin Moore – Highbridge
Moore's Fish & Chip Shop
Leanne & Shawnie Moreton – Australia
In Memory of Bill Morris of Havage Close
Mr. & Mrs. J.H. Mossman – Burnham-on-Sea
Mr. Tony Mossman – Faversham, Kent
Mrs. Pat Newman – Tewkesbury
In Memory of Carol Ann Newbon
Stephen John Newbon
Kevin John Newbon
Andrew John Newbon
Mr. & Mrs. J Oakley – Walton, Street
Vour Orchard – Highbridge
Mr. & Mrs. F. Owen – Highbridge
Barbara Palin – Highbridge
Mrs. M. Joyce Parsons – Burnham-on-Sea
Len & Margaret Paul – Highbridge
Eileen & Jim Picton – Highbridge
Jodie, Sam & Jenna Picton – Highbridge
Ryan Picton – Highbridge
Joshua Picton – Highbridge
Lois Picton – Highbridge
Mrs. Patricia Pope (nee Inder) Highbridge
John & Vi Popham – Highbridge
Mr. Roger Pople – Burnham-on-Sea
Brenda & Roy Porter – Uphill
Ruth & Graham Powell – Highbridge
Mr. Ron Prout – Burnham-on-Sea
Pearl Rawles (nee Jubin) Berrow
Liam Philip Reddish – Burnham-on-Sea
Mr. Paul Reddish – Frome
Mr. & Mrs. R. & D. Reddish – Highbridge
Sam & Philip Reddish – Burnham-on-Sea
Reginald James Reed – Banwell
Mo Retford – Woolavington
Stephen Retford – Milton Keynes
Michael Retford – Chesterfield
Geraldine Richards – Burnham-on-Sea
Mr. & Mrs. S.J. Richards – Highbridge
Ken & Pat Ricketts
Andy & Tracy Ridgway – Burnham
John & Ann Rogers – Burnham-on-Sea
Bob Rogers – Burnham-on-Sea
Brian & Joan Rowden – Burnham-on-Sea
Valerie & Richard Rummery – Australia

Mrs. J. Salter – Highbridge
B. & D. Salvidge – Highbridge
Steve Sampson – Burnham-on-Sea
Paula Sandell (nee Rawles)
Amy & Nick Sandiford – Australia
In Memory of Richard (Dick) Sansom –
    Highbridge
Terry Sansom
Kate Severs – Scarborough
Ceritia Sharples (nee Foster) Weston-super-Mare
The Shattock Family – Highbridge
W. Sheils - West Huntspill
Sandra & Steve Sherriff – Highbridge
Pat & Colin Simpson – Burnham-on-Sea
Mr. Mervyn F. Sims – Pawlett
Sisters of St. Jeanne Antides – Ealing
Joe Skinner – East Huntspill
Jane & Stan Smith – Burnham-on-Sea
Michael Smith – Burnham-on-Sea
Tony Smith – Burnham-on-Sea
John Smith – Highbridge
Joan & Mike Smith – Highbridge
John Soloman – Highbridge
Eddie & Myra Spice – Highbridge
Nick Spice – London
Mrs. M. Stoyle – Plymouth
Terry & Margaret Street – Burnham-on-Sea
Joseph & Izaak Strong – Highbridge
Mrs. Angela Sugg (nee Inder)Banwell
Terry Temlett – Worle, Weston-super-Mare
Margaret Tidball – Weston-super-Mare
Trefoil Guild – Burnham-on-Sea
Geraldine M. Trythall

Mr. & Mrs. R. Turner – Burnham -on-Sea
Mr. & Mrs. R. Tye
Gabriele & Rolfe Ulrich -Fritzlar
Sqn. Ldr. Paul Upham – Berrow
Chris M. Varley – East Huntspill
Gaynor Walker – Church Street, Highbridge
Sue & Morris Wall – Watchfield
Margaret Wall – Clyce Road, Highbridge
Alan Warren – Solihull
Jasmine Welch – Cumbria
Lisa & Simon Wharton
Moira White – Clyce Road, Highbridge
Jean & Cecil Whitehouse
Steve & Julie Willoughby – Maisey's Bakery,
    Highbridge
In Memory of Peter Wilson
Mrs. C. Woodberry – Burnham-on-Sea
Stan & Thora Woodberry
C.F. Wright – Highbridge
Geoff & Marian Wright – Highbridge
Pam & Ken Wright – Highbridge
Wendy Wynn(nee Harding)Late of Huntspill
    Road, Highbridge
Alan & Stephanie Wynn (nee Wensley) Burnham
Fred & Nip Wynn (nee Meader) Burnham-on-
    Sea
Terry Yard – Spain
Sandra Young – Grimsby
Marina Young – Highbridge
Mike Young – Burnham-on-Sea

... and many anonymous subscribers